Excavating in Egypt

SOL JUSTITIAE

LAW

Robert B. L. Murphy

1 The citadel at Qasr Ibrim.

Excavating in Egypt

The Egypt Exploration Society 1882-1982

Edited by T.G.H. James

The University of Chicago Press

The University of Chicago Press, Chicago 60637

British Museum Publications Ltd., London WC1B 3QQ

Paperback edition 1984

Printed in England.

93 92 91 90 89 88 87 86 85 84   2 3 4 5 6

Library of Congress Cataloging in Publication Data
Main entry under title:
Excavating in Egypt.
    Includes bibliographical references and index.
    Contents: The early years/Margaret S.
Drower—The delta/A. J. Spencer—Thebes/W. V.
Davies—[etc.]
    1. Egypt—Antiquities—Addresses, essays,
lectures. 2. Excavations (Archaeology)—Egypt—
Addresses, essays, lectures. 3. Egypt Exploration
Society—Addresses, essays, lectures.
I. James, T. G. H. (Thomas Garnet Henry)
DT56.9 .E96   932   81–21947
ISBN 0–226–39191–4 (cloth)   AACR2
ISBN 0–226–39192–2 (paper)

Contents

Foreword T.G.H. James   *page* 6

1   **The Early Years** Margaret S. Drower   9

2   **The Delta** A.J. Spencer   37

3   **Thebes** W.V. Davies   51

4   **Abydos** B.J. Kemp   71

5   **El-Amarna** Cyril Aldred   89

6   **Saqqara** Geoffrey T. Martin   107

7   **Nubia** H.S. Smith   123

8   **The Archaeological Survey**   141
    T.G.H. James

9   **The Graeco-Roman Branch**   161
    Sir Eric Turner

Postscript T.G.H. James   179

Map showing sites explored by the Egypt   182
Exploration Society 1882–1982

Notes on Sources   184

Participating Institutions   186

Index   189

Foreword

The Egypt Exploration Society, the centenary of whose foundation is celebrated by the exhibition mounted in the British Museum during 1982, and by this volume, possesses a record of achievement in archaeological field-work and publication of outstanding importance in the history of Egyptology. It was founded as the Egypt Exploration Fund in 1882 by a small group of far-seeing scholars and interested amateurs brought together by a concern for the ever-increasing destruction of monuments in Egypt and for the lack of properly organised excavations. It changed its name from Fund to Society in 1919.

For the greater part of its hundred years its work in Egypt has been financed wholly from funds provided by its members, some of whom, like Sir Robert Mond, have borne the costs of complete excavations. Many museums and universities in Great Britain and abroad, institutional members of the Society, have, in return for their substantial support, benefited from the distribution of antiquities from excavations received through the generous policies of the Egyptian Antiquities Service. Since the Second World War the Society has received most of its funds for field-work from the British Government through the British Academy. Nevertheless, the support it continues to receive from private members and institutional members enables it to undertake an unusually large programme of field activities in most seasons.

From the earliest years the American Branch was particularly active in raising funds for the Society's field-work. The Branch was formally disbanded in 1946, but the Society retains a very large number of members, including many institutions, in the United States. Some measure of transatlantic support over the years can be gained from the lists at the end of this volume detailing the museums and libraries which have contributed to and benefited from the Society's work in Egypt and the Sudan. This support from America was quite crucial in the lean years between the wars, and it has more recently helped in a major way, in the form of funds from the Smithsonian Institution's Foreign Currency Program, to sustain Professor Caminos's epigraphic work at Gebel es-Silsila and the excavations at Qasr Ibrim.

The chapters of this book give some account of the foundation of the Egypt Exploration Society and of the work of the Society's expeditions in Egypt and the Sudan. Concentrating on the major sites and principal areas of activity, the successive essays reveal the exceptionally wide-ranging scope of the investigations and of the contribution they have made to the development of Egyptological studies during the past hundred years. It is a story with many heroes and a small army of supporting characters. The former are suitably commemorated in the accounts of their achievements in the field and in their publications; the latter are mostly unsung, but should not wholly be overlooked in the celebration of the centenary. Something is said in the first chapter of the support given to its expeditions by the Society's devoted Secretaries. There are also the successive members of the Society's Committees who have over the years guided the Society's affairs and planned its campaigns; the ordinary members who have stepped in to help whenever the need has arisen; the representatives of diplomatic missions who have eased the way for the Society's field-workers in difficult times; the commercial firms who have helped in many practical ways; the multitude of Egyptian officials who have provided support in the mounting and running of expeditions; and especially the Egyptian workmen, skilled and unskilled, who have laboured on the sites, sometimes helping the inexperienced excavator more than he realised, and always providing a form of technical continuity without which the excavator would have been sadly disadvantaged. To name one person or organisation in particular might seem invidious, but as an example of continuous support it may be proper to mention the travel firm of Thomas Cook and Son. Throughout the century of the Society's existence it has helped in many practical ways. In his early campaigns in the Delta and elsewhere Naville was loaned a houseboat by Cook's without charge; for many years Cook's office in Cairo served as the Society's Egyptian headquarters; its office remains the best address for contacting the Society's workmen in the field.

Many of the finest discoveries made in the course of the Society's excavations are to be found in the British Museum, and have been brought together with others from elsewhere in Great Britain for the Centenary Exhibition. The Fitzwilliam Museum, Cambridge, the Petrie Museum in University College London, the Bolton Museum and Art Gallery, and the British Library have all made generous loans. To the governing bodies of all these institutions especial thanks are due. The Egypt Exploration Society has itself loaned portraits, illustrative material, and papyri from the Oxyrhynchus archive and elsewhere. On behalf of the Society I can say thank you to the British Museum for organising this exhibition, and particularly to Dr. A. J. Spencer for choosing the objects for display and for preparing all the graphic material; also to Miss Margaret Hall and the members of her design team for mounting the exhibition so splendidly. Further, I can, on behalf of the British Museum, thank the Society for one hundred years of generous benefactions which have immeasurably enhanced the value of the Museum's Egyptian collections. The evidence of these benefactions remains to be seen in the Museum's permanent exhibitions and will continue to testify to the remarkable results achieved by the Society's excavators long after the centenary exhibition has been dismantled.

T. G. H. JAMES

2 Amelia Edwards.

1 The Early Years

M A R G A R E T S. D R O W E R

On the first day of April 1882 an announcement appeared in the pages of several leading daily newspapers and in the *Academy* and the *Athenaeum*, influential weekly papers with a bent towards literature and the arts. 'We have great pleasure', the statement ran, 'in announcing that the long-desired Society for the Promotion of Excavation in the Delta of the Nile has at last been constituted under very favourable auspices.' The new society, readers were assured, had the approval of many distinguished persons: the Archbishop of Canterbury, several bishops, the Chief Rabbi, Lord Carnarvon, the President of the Society of Antiquaries, and a considerable number of well-known personalities, including Robert Browning, Sir Henry Layard, the excavator of Nineveh, and Professor Huxley were named among the sponsors. 'It is proposed', said the *Academy*, 'to raise a fund for the purpose of conducting excavations in the Delta, which up to this time has been very rarely visited by travellers, and where but one site (Zoan, Tanis) has been explored by archaeologists. Yet here must undoubtedly lie concealed the documents of a lost period of Biblical history – documents which we may confidently hope will furnish the key to a whole series of perplexing problems.'

It was hoped, the article went on, that records of the four centuries of the Hebrew sojourn in Egypt might be found on a mound identified as the capital of the Land of Goshen and in the ruins of the cities of the Oppression, Pithom and Ramesses. Exploration at Naucratis, could the site of that Greek emporium be identified, would lend valuable illumination to an obscure period of Greek art. Moreover, the Delta was rich in mounds of famous cities such as San and Xois – 'this last being the capital of an early dynasty (the xivth) which is as yet wholly without written history'. If sufficient money could be raised, both Goshen and Naucratis could be simultaneously explored; otherwise Goshen would have preference.

The formation of this society was the outcome of a long series of informal discussions and negotiations over more than two years, and a copious interchange of letters between the two persons now named as Joint Honorary Secretaries: Reginald Stuart Poole, the numismatist, and the real begetter of the idea, the novelist and journalist Amelia Blandford Edwards.

Poole came from a distinguished family of Orientalists. His mother's brother, Edward Lane, the author of the celebrated *Account of the Manners and Customs of the Modern Egyptians* and translator of the *Arabian Nights*, had made his home in Cairo, and thither in 1842 his newly-widowed sister brought Stuart and his brother Edward to live. The two boys were partly educated by their uncle, Edward becoming an Arabist while Stuart studied Oriental coins and ancient Egyptian antiquities and taught himself hieroglyphs. The elder of Edward's sons, Stanley Lane-Poole, in his turn became an Orientalist and historian; Miss Edwards, reviewing his popular account of Egypt in 1881, said: 'Egypt belongs, by right of literary descent, to the Lanes and the Pooles.'

In 1852, by the age of twenty, R. S. Poole had already written a book on the chronology of ancient Egypt and contributed articles to learned journals on numismatics; he was in that year appointed to the Department of Antiquities at the British Museum where he found himself a junior colleague of the distinguished Egyptologist Samuel Birch. When in 1866 the Department was split, Birch became Keeper of Oriental Antiquities while Poole was assigned a post in the newly-created Department of Coins and Medals and given a residence in the Museum. For the next twenty-three years he applied himself with patience and devotion to arranging the coin collection and editing the Museum's great catalogue of coins, four of whose volumes he wrote himself; but his more general interest in the ancient world remained, and he lectured and reviewed books on classical and Egyptological subjects, on biblical history and on ancient art, as well as on numismatics.

Very different in temperament, though alike in her enthusiasm for ancient Egypt, was Miss Amelia Edwards, one of the foremost popular novelists of the day and the author of several travel books. In the winter of 1873-4, with several friends, she had visited Egypt in a leisurely fashion and loved every minute of it. They had hired a *dahabiyeh*, one of those houseboats furnished with sails and a crew of servants and sailors, that made trips up the Nile more comfortably and leisurely than Cook's steamers. They visited Philae, passed through the cataract, and reached the great temples of Ramesses II at Abu Simbel, where they moored for six weeks, while Miss Edwards carried out a little excavation of her own, clearing a hitherto unrecorded sanctuary which for some time afterwards bore her name. On her return to England she wrote a description of her voyage under the title *A Thousand Miles up the Nile*, which on its publication in 1876 became an immediate bestseller. In order to write this delightful and informative book she read extensively and consulted Dr. Birch and other experts including Poole on matters of historical and archaeological detail; by 1878 she was writing reviews and articles on Egyptological subjects for weekly journals such as the *Academy*, and corresponding with *savants* abroad, particularly with M. Gaston Maspero, a young professor at the École des Hautes Études and the Collège de France in Paris; she acquired a limited knowledge of hieroglyphs and was particularly interested in the subject of Egyptian religion.

During her travels in Egypt she had everywhere been troubled by the neglect suffered by the ancient monuments and the vandalism to which they were constantly subjected, under a regime which had neither the interest nor the resources to remedy the situation. 'I am told', she wrote of the newly-discovered chapel at Abu Simbel, 'that the wall paintings which we had the happiness of admiring in all their beauty and freshness, are already much injured. Such is the fate of every Egyptian monument, great or small. The tourist carves it over with names and dates, and in some instances with caricatures. The student of Egyptology, by taking wet paper "squeezes" sponges away every vestige of the original colour. The "Collector" buys and carries off everything of value that he can get, and the Arab steals it for him. The work of destruction, meanwhile, goes on apace. There is no one to prevent it; there is no one to discourage it. Every day more inscriptions are mutilated – more tombs are rifled – more paintings and sculptures are defaced. The Louvre contains a full-length portrait of Seti I, cut bodily from the walls of his sepulchre in the Valley of the Tombs of the Kings. The Museums of Berlin, of Turin, of Florence are rich in spoils which tell their lamentable tale. When science leads the way, is it wonderful that ignorance should follow?'

One figure had dominated the archaeological scene in Egypt for the previous thirty years, that of Mariette Pasha, the Frenchman whose discovery of the Serapeum at Saqqara, near the ancient city of Memphis, had been the start of a remarkable career of excavation. Appointed by Said Pasha, the Khedive of Egypt, as Director of Excavations in 1858, he was later entrusted with the task of forming a national museum in Bulaq, in which the antiquities which had hitherto been carried off to enrich the museums of Europe and the private collections of wealthy dilettantes might be preserved in the country of their origin. The first building allotted to him, a deserted mosque and some adjoining sheds, though unsuitable for the purpose, was large enough for the storage and display of statues and treasures, and Mariette set about filling it with antiquities gathered from his own excavations of temples and tombs throughout the length and breadth of Egypt.

By modern standards Mariette's methods were crude and his treatment of his workmen harsh. The Khedive put conscript labour at his disposal and his foremen drove the village gangs with the *kurbash*, the whip employed in the corvée; dynamite was employed to remove obstacles, and later buildings ruthlessly removed to reveal the earlier monuments beneath. The temples of Edfu and Dendera, and part of Karnak, were cleared; *mastaba* tombs in Maidum and Saqqara were cleared out by the dozen. No adequate record was made of most of his discoveries, and little attempt was made to conserve for posterity what had been exposed. Forbidding anyone but himself to excavate, he undertook far more than he could effectively control. But although he could not prevent the activities of tomb robbers and illicit diggers, he at least halted the depredations of dealers whose sole aim was to acquire objects for the European market, and the export of antiquities was banned by law.

In 1879 the political and economic troubles of Egypt moved towards a crisis. The Khedive Ismail, after a short but disastrous reign, was declared bankrupt and removed from office by the Sultan of Turkey; a state of emergency was declared, and Egypt was placed under the dual control of the French and the English, with the aim of rescuing the country from the parlous condition to which decades of mismanagement had brought it. The two Commissioners, Sir Evelyn Baring and M. de Blignières, had a formidable task; though their role was to be consultative rather than administrative, they were placed in control of the Ministries of Finance and of Public Works respectively, and within the latter the new Antiquities Department remained strongly under French influence.

Miss Edwards hoped, however, that in this new situation it might be possible to approach Mariette, to ascertain whether a body of subscribers in England, actuated by scientific interest and not by greed of gain, might receive the new Khedive's sanction to sponsor an excavation, preferably in the Delta. What reply she received to her

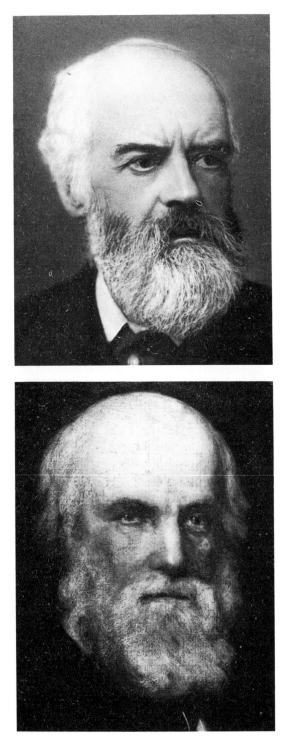

3 Reginald Stuart Poole, Keeper of Coins and Medals in the British Museum, 1870–93.

4 Samuel Birch, Keeper of Oriental Antiquities in the British Museum, 1860–85.

letter is not known, but it cannot have been altogether unfavourable, for in January 1880 she wrote to a number of Egyptologists whom she thought might support her scheme. If enough money could be raised, they might be able themselves to send out an expedition whose sole aim would be to rescue and to elucidate the ancient remains. Mariette's monopoly would be broken, for they would now be in a position to appeal to the authorities for permission to participate in the discovery of Egypt's past.

England, once leading the field, at that time possessed very few Egyptologists. Goodwin had died two years previously; the foremost living Egyptologist, Samuel Birch, was an old man near the age of retirement, and Peter Le Page Renouf, who had held the Chair of Ancient History in the Catholic University in Dublin, was now, at the age of fifty, a Government Inspector of Schools devoting his spare time to the study of the hieroglyphic language. Ernest Wallis Budge was still a student of Assyriology at Cambridge. Miss Edwards wrote also to several clergymen and others, like Ernest de Bunsen, whose interest was in biblical studies. She had even persuaded the editor of the *Morning Post* to throw open its columns to correspondence on Egyptian subjects. 'Hitherto', she said, 'Egyptologists who take advantage of the opportunity now hospitably placed at their disposal will find in the *Morning Post* such a medium of communication with the public as Assyrian and Greek archaeologists command in the *Daily Telegraph* and *The Times*.' To others she wrote of the need for stressing in the daily press the need for excavation and the desirability of opening a fund for the purpose.

Several enthusiastic replies were received: Professor A. H. Sayce, the Assyriologist, who spent much of his time in Egypt, wrote enthusiastically from Oxford; Poole recruited his friend Charles Newton, Yates Professor of Classical Archaeology at University College London and Keeper of Greek and Roman Antiquities at the British Museum, who had been the discoverer of the Mausoleum at Halicarnassus. Among the warmest supporters of the idea was Sir Erasmus Wilson, the eminent surgeon, who had recently retired from the Chair of Dermatology at the Royal College of Surgeons, and in the previous year had been elected President of the College. Among the many benefits bestowed on mankind by his teaching were the encouragement of sea-bathing and of the use of the Turkish bath (his name appeared, in the company of the singer Adelina Patti and the actress Mrs. Langtry, on an advertisement for Pear's soap). Skilful investment on the Stock Exchange had made him a rich man, and he employed his fortune in a number of charitable and public-spirited enterprises, the most notable of which had been to defray the cost of transporting the obelisk known as Cleopatra's Needle from Alexandria to England and erecting it on the Thames Embankment – an operation which had cost him something in the region of £10,000. His enthusiasm for Egypt, born of a sightseeing visit some years earlier, inspired him to begin writing a popular history of ancient Egypt; whilst in bed with bronchitis he read Miss Edwards's book, 'that elegant and interesting work', and was emboldened to write to the publishers requesting the author's address.

Thus began a friendship which was both happy and fruitful for them both: she helped him with his history, and he declared himself ready and anxious to contribute financially to any scheme whereby scientific exploration, whether survey or excavation, might be undertaken by a British team in Egypt. The honour of England, he declared, was involved, as it had been in his 'obelisk-snatching'. 'France and Germany', he wrote, 'have always had active and zealous labourers in the field, and the scientific character of England demands that she also should be worthily represented. It were vain, perhaps, to hope that an Archaeological Commission, like the Egyptian Commission of France, Germany and Italy, will ever be dispatched by the Government of this country to report upon and explore the treasures of the Nile Valley; but it is earnestly to be desired that private enterprise should do something towards vindicating our rational aim to a place among the scholars and Archaeologists of Europe'.

One obstacle stood in their way: Dr. Birch, who as the *doyen* among Egyptologists and Keeper of Oriental Antiquities in the British Museum was the most obvious choice as Chairman, declined to take any part in the new scheme or give it any support. Miss Edwards and Poole both tried to persuade him to change his mind, but he remained adamant; he had no use, he said, for what he called 'emotional archaeology' – excavation should have as its sole aim the production of museum objects; and these seemed unlikely, under the antiquities laws at the time in force, to be obtainable. On 11 June 1880, therefore, it was in the Coins and Medals Department at the British Museum that the first meeting was convened by Poole, after consultation with Miss Edwards who was unable to come up from her home in Westbury-on-Trym, near Bristol. At this first, nuclear, discussion there were present the Swiss Egyptologist M. Edouard Naville, Mr. James Cotton, the editor of the *Academy*, the Hon. Villiers Stuart, an Irish M.P. who had travelled frequently in Egypt and earlier done some excavating on his own account, and Newton. Five days later Miss Edwards herself was present when a larger meeting was held in the Council Room of University College London; Sir Erasmus Wilson, Villiers Stuart and Sayce were there, and probably others as well; it was decided to write once more to Mariette.

But Mariette Pasha was seriously ill, and no decisions could be taken. Miss Edwards and her friends bided their time. When in January 1881 Mariette died, nobody was surprised at the appointment of Maspero, who had recently been made head of the new French Institute in Cairo, to be Mariette's successor as Director of Antiquities and head of the Bulaq Museum. This was encouraging news, for Maspero was liked and trusted in England; but throughout 1881 the political situation in Egypt was critical: a near-rebellion among the officers of the Egyptian army led by Arabi Pasha brought a tightening of Anglo-French control. Maspero, while in principle favourable to the idea of an English mission, advised Poole that the time was not yet ripe. In the winter, however, when M. Naville, who was on very friendly terms with Maspero, went out to Egypt, he was asked to sound the new Director on a possible excavation. They spent some time together on Maspero's *dahabiyeh* in Luxor, and together carried out a small excavation at the pyramid of El Kula. Naville was able to report to London that Maspero had no objection to excavation by the new English society and would give them every facility in his power. Elated with this favourable reply, Poole and Miss Edwards called a meeting of those most interested on 27 March 1882, in Poole's room at the British Museum, and the formal resolution was drawn up which brought the Egypt Exploration Fund into being (at first the name Delta Exploration Fund was chosen, but Poole pointed out that this was too limiting: they might well be allowed to dig elsewhere in Egypt in future). At this meeting Poole and Miss Edwards were elected joint Honorary Secretaries, and Sir Erasmus Wilson, who promised a donation to start the Fund, was named as Treasurer.

Among members of the first Committee were Poole's Assistant, Barclay Head; Constantine Ionides, a wealthy patron of art whose collection of paintings and drawings was later bequeathed to the Victoria and Albert Museum; Professor Percy Gardner and Professor Sayce from Cambridge and Oxford respectively; Charles Newton and his deputy in the Department of Greek and Roman Antiquities, A. S. Murray; M. A. Terrien de la Couperie, an expert on Chinese, who was later to occupy the Chair of Comparative Philology at University College London; and Villiers Stuart. Sayce and Villiers Stuart were appointed the Fund's 'agents' in Egypt. An official announcement was circulated to the Press, and Miss Edwards again wrote to her wealthy friends asking now for donations towards the projected work.

Not all was plain sailing, however. It had become clear that 'emotional archaeology' was not enough: the search for history alone was not going to attract many sub-scribers. The Louvre was filled with fine objects from Egypt: why should not England enjoy a similar benefit from excavations financed by the British public? Misled by Sayce who in a letter from Egypt had assured them that Maspero had no objection to allowing some of the finds to be taken by the excavators, the hopes of the newly formed Committee rose high. But Maspero soon disabused them of their illusions: he was, he said, unable to promise any such concession since the law of Egypt forbade the removal of any antiquities whatever; the best they might perhaps hope for was that some small antiquity might be granted them by the Khedive 'en don gracieux' – as a gracious gift. The first leaflet sent round that spring accordingly stated: 'A Society has been formed for the purpose of cooperating with Professor Maspero, Director of Museums and Excavations in Egypt, in his work of exploration. The Society under-takes to conduct excavations especially on sites of Biblical and classical interest, without infringing the Egyptian law, by which objects found are claimed for the Boolak Museum. M. Maspero, on his part, agrees to the publication of the results by the Society.'

Who then was to conduct the excavations? This question also bristled with difficulties. Among those to whom Miss Edwards had written on 27 February was her old friend Heinrich Schliemann. Hotfoot from the plains of Troy came his answer: he was certain that she would not be able to raise the funds she hoped for in England, 'for those who take a warm interest in your success have not got the means to assist you, whereas those who have got them think it an absurdity to dig up the *rotten* remains of the past. But I shall no doubt be able to finish the Troad until August [sic], and, how would it be if you, Mrs. Schliemann and I dig up Naukratis next winter? If you could persuade Mrs. S., who has remained in Athens, I am quite ready to undertake this or Goshen'. This unexpected suggestion was put to Maspero, whose reaction was immediate: on no account, he said, would he sanction the employment of the quarrelsome and tactless M. Schliemann. Instead, he suggested that the Fund should send out a young man (preferably an Englishman) who might work under Maspero's instruction and eventually take over the conduct of the work and the credit for it. But if such a person could not be found, he would consider favourably any real scholar proposed by the Committee.

In May, soon after the receipt of this encouraging news, Poole delivered a course of three lectures to an audience gathered in the drawing-room of the Vicarage of St. Mary Abbots in Kensington. He told them that plans were well advanced and that the proposal had the support and encouragement of the new Director. He pointed out that since the initiation of the scientific exploration of Egypt by Napoleon Bonaparte, with the exception of Col. Vyse's architectural survey of the Pyramids, England had taken no part in the discovery of Egypt's past. It was expected that the project now under discussion – the exploration of an area where, it was hoped, light might be thrown on the vexed question, much under discussion at the time, of the route of the Exodus – would involve only a moderate expenditure; no more, he pointed out, than the cost of keeping a pack of foxhounds.

In the summer of 1882 Edouard Naville, on a visit to London, was asked by the Committee if he would undertake the first season's excavations, supposing that enough money could be raised: the public response had so far been limited. Nothing could be planned, however, for Egypt was again in a turmoil; this time the army was in open revolt, Europeans had fled from Cairo, Alexandria had been burnt and the British Consulate razed, Arabi Pasha was besieging the city. The British army sent to quell the revolt marched through the Wadi Tumilat (the very 'Land of Goshen' where Naville was proposing to excavate) and at the Battle of Tell el-Kebir, on 13 September, Sir Garnet Wolseley's forces routed the rebels. Cairo was occupied by the British army the next day, the Khedive returned, and on 7 November Lord Dufferin arrived in Cairo to take control of the demoralised country. Maspero, who had stayed on as long as he could in order to protect his precious antiquities against possible looting, had been forced to leave for France in the late summer, but as soon as he could he was back at his post, relieved to find that the Museum was untouched.

At last the time was ripe. Sir Erasmus Wilson placed £500 at the disposal of the Fund at once, and promised a subsequent £100 if it should be needed. This was a princely sum in those days and Naville made his plans. In January 1883, when the Nile had subsided enough to make excavation in the Delta possible, he set out; he was cordially received in Cairo by Maspero, who was himself anxious to see responsible work done in Egypt which might stem the flow of illegal treasure-hunting and increase the Museum's collection. He was as good as his word, and at the end of Naville's season at Tell el-Maskhuta (see p. 37) the Fund learned that two of the best sculptures found, a granite falcon and the kneeling figure of a scribe, both with inscriptions of importance to Naville's identification of the site with Pithom, were to be presented by the Khedive to Sir Erasmus Wilson. Both these antiquities subsequently arrived and were at once presented by Sir Erasmus to the British Museum. Since that time the Museum has been the main beneficiary of any distribution of antiquities brought back by the Society. The Egyptian Government, pressed by Maspero to modify its regulations, agreed in the following year that any antiquities not required by the Bulaq Museum might be exported by the finders, provided that everything was first submitted to the authorities for inspection.

The success of the first season's excavation, with its biblical interest, was widely publicised and Naville was highly praised, though not all scholars accepted his

5 The granite triad at Pithom (Tell el-Maskhuta), first site of work of the Society.

identification of Pithom, the store city of the Exodus. The debate continued in the pages of journals like the *Academy*. At the first Annual General Meeting of the Fund, held in the Lecture Hall of the Royal Institution on 3 July 1883, Naville gave a lecture on the results of his work, and members who had subscribed £1 or more were promised his memoir as soon as it appeared. The interest aroused, and the announcement that the next target was to be Zoan, the great city of San, brought in a number of donations from new supporters. Sir Erasmus Wilson, who was now elected President of the Fund, contributed £1,000, and Mr. W. Fowler had promised £50 for Tanis, if nineteen others would give the same amount. M. Naville had himself been to Tanis, and had high hopes of recovering some splendid monuments from the place.

When it came to making plans for the winter, however, M. Naville wrote that he was unable to go out to Egypt owing to pressure of work; he was in the last stages of his great book on the funerary papyri. 'Send me a young Englishman', Maspero had said, 'and I will train him.' Egyptologists at that time could be counted on the fingers of one hand, but there was a young man who, while no hieroglyphic scholar, possessed experience of archaeological work in Egypt, had produced during that summer a book on his work at the Pyramids which had been highly praised by the reviewers, and was ready and anxious to go back to Egypt. This was William Matthew Flinders Petrie. His connection with the British Museum, and with Poole himself, went back to the days when, as a boy in his teens, he had collected coins for the Museum when he found them in antique shops. He had several publications to his credit and was known in archaeological circles as a careful observer and a meticulous recorder.

Maspero, who already knew Petrie and thought highly of his work, was willing to accept him on terms which he could not have offered to Naville. Petrie was to work for the Fund, but under Maspero's direction. All that he found was to belong by right to the Museum at Bulaq, but under the new terms he might take home duplicates that the Museum had no need of. At last, it seemed, it might be possible to produce what the subscribers wanted: small and large pieces for their local museum collections. Petrie, setting out in November 1883, stopped for a few hours in Paris to visit Maspero there, and the terms of his 'engagement' were agreed. He would be acting as Maspero's agent, but in fact he would be given a free hand at Tanis. In addition, he was given permission to purchase objects on behalf of the Museum. For Maspero, a man with considerable experience in archaeological matters, realised that with the advent of Petrie important new aspects of Egyptian antiquity were to be studied for the first time: the Fund had acquired an 'explorer' very different from Naville.

In many ways the two men were diametrically opposed in character and talents. Naville was an Egyptologist of the old school, a man steeped in the study of the hieroglyphs, one of the most distinguished figures in the world of Oriental scholarship at the time. He was currently engaged in a monumental work of scholarship, a variorum edition of the *Book of the Dead*. His interest in field-work was simple: excavation he regarded as a method of bringing to light inscribed monuments which would furnish new texts for his interpretation. The larger the monument, the longer and more important the text was likely to be. He hoped, therefore, to unearth temples and colossal statues: he dug by piece-work, rewarding his gangs of excavators by the amount of earth they shifted – so many cubic metres a day. Broken potsherds and small objects of little intrinsic value he disregarded, since to record them would be a waste of digging time. The removal of earth debris was sometimes farmed out to engineers and contractors; it is fair to say that had the bulldozer been invented Naville would have welcomed its use.

Petrie, on the other hand, realised what no other digger in Egypt had guessed – that much of the true history of Egyptian civilisation was to be read in the trifling things, the potsherds and the bricks, the beads and flints and small domestic objects whose broken fragments filled the debris of every settlement site and every cemetery. He was anxious to preserve every man-made object found, and to be shown even the trifles that the finder deemed to be rubbish. He had therefore instituted a system of rewards: he paid every digger the market value of what he found, lest he conceal the object in the folds of his clothing and hand it over later to a native dealer – one of those jackals who habitually haunted the fringes of archaeological excavations.

Maspero was entirely converted to this point of view. Petrie guaranteed to show everything he acquired, by purchase or by excavation, to the Museum officials at the end of his 'dig'; Maspero agreed to refund to the excavator the reward which he had been paid on each object if the Museum wished to retain it; the rest Petrie could take home to England. When this arrangement was first explained by letter to the Committee, they were full of alarm, particularly since Petrie's scheme involved also the purchase of objects not found in the digging but brought by the local villagers as the fruit of their own illicit explorations. But seeing that the authorities at Bulaq approved, they consented to the arrangement and the large quantity of material brought home, though it included many packing-cases full of broken pottery and stone fragments for Petrie to study, produced also many small objects such as beads, small vessels, wooden implements and little glazed mummy-shaped figurines which could be presented to museums in England and elsewhere as a tangible return for the donations of the Fund's supporters.

Petrie was under no illusions about the difficulties confronting him in excavating at Tanis. Naville had visited the site in 1882 and pronounced it 'affreux'. In 1884 cholera was raging in Cairo; the whole district of Bulaq, in the centre of the city, was forcibly evacuated and the houses burnt by the police. The political situation was still unstable, and the Egyptians of the Delta region felt suspicion and distrust of foreigners. Corruption, a legacy from the old days of Khedivial misrule, was still rife and nothing could be done without *bakshish*. Inefficiency and muddle wasted precious days in the passage of boats and the transport of materials down the Nile to the site. The confused state of the currency too caused endless difficulties: coins of almost every European country were in use alongside the piastre, and the calculations of fractional values that resulted were a source of endless arguments and delays. At the end of the season, in the intense heat of midsummer, Petrie made and packed his own boxes, then reported to Maspero in Cairo, and came home well pleased with the generosity of the 'division'. On his return he set about arranging and cataloguing his finds for public exhibition; they were on show at the rooms of the Royal Archaeological Institute, at Oxford Mansion in Oxford Circus, and attracted a considerable number of visitors, some of whom were interested enough to become subscribers to the Fund with an annual contribution of £1 (later raised to £2), or to donate a larger sum. Henceforward the exhibition in London became an almost annual feature of the Society's activities.

The finances of the Fund appeared to be assured: Sir Erasmus Wilson, the gentle Maecenas who had made possible what had seemed an unattainable dream, had provided the slipway down which the Fund's explorations could be launched. But his health gave rise to anxiety; he was forced to give up teaching and retire to his house at Hastings, where he became increasingly frail. At the news of his death, in August 1884, Miss Edwards was stricken with grief for the loss of a dear friend, but also with bitter disappointment: he had intended, she assured Stuart Poole, to alter his will so as to endow the Fund generously and leave them free of financial worries; in the event he had left them nothing. Henceforward the money was to come in in pounds rather than in hundreds of pounds, and the recruitment of subscribers was to become a constant source of anxiety and of unremitting effort.

During these early years a number of members gave public lectures on ancient Egyptian topics, in which they mentioned the activities of the Fund and spread enthusiasm for its work. The Rev. H. G. Tomkins, a founder member of the Committee, in October 1883 addressed the Church Congress at Reading on 'Recent Advances in Biblical Criticism and in Historical Discovery on their relation to the Christian faith'. Miss Margaret Harkness, the Fund's first paid Secretary, and Miss Helen Beloe, who as Lady Tirard served on the Committee for many years subsequently, in the years 1884–6 gave a series of 'Lectures to Ladies' at the British Museum, to which admission was by ticket: half the proceeds went to the Egypt Exploration Fund. Before the days of the cinema, such lectures enjoyed wide popularity.

An active member of the Fund wrote in 1885 to Miss Edwards from Clapton that he was giving talks with his 'lime-light lantern' in the Free Library at Bethnal Green on the topic of Egyptian research in its relationship with the Bible. 'The audience', he said, 'continue to increase and the interest in the subject, in this East of London, among both the well-educated and the less fortunate people, would I am sure please you very much.' Last time he had talked for two hours, and his audience had 'listened with intense interest and in perfect silence and attention'. Mr. Poole himself was a tireless lecturer and travelled long distances by rail for this purpose, and Miss Edwards, a popular and effective speaker, was several times invited to tour the northern cities in 1887 and in the following years.

Admission to the first Annual General Meetings, at which excavators reported on their discoveries, appears to have been limited to an audience of subscribers only; they were usually held in the auditorium of the Royal Institution. But the proceedings were fully reported in the weekly journals such as the *Academy* and the *Athenaeum*, and more briefly in *The Times* and the *Morning Post*, and this publicity drew new contributions and fresh subscribers. The Fund was fortunate to find in Mr. James Cotton, himself a member of the Committee and later to be its Honorary Secretary, an editor eager to publish interim bulletins on the progress of excavation – a sort of 'dispatches from the Front' which the 'explorers' sent back from camp through Poole or Miss Edwards. This valuable source of publicity dried up when Cotton resigned his

6 (*Top*) Objects from the cellar of house 35 at Tanis.

7 (*Bottom*) Petrie's boat at Minyet el-Qamh in the Delta, 1883.

editorship of the *Academy*, and the paper changed its character, becoming almost entirely literary in outlook and content. Archaeological reports were still sometimes to be found in other daily and weekly papers, and the *Illustrated London News* reported the annual exhibitions at length.

During the summer of 1884 Petrie received a letter from a young man, Francis Llewellyn Griffith, who had been studying Egyptology and learning the hieroglyphic language for some time on his own. He was anxious to know if there were any chance for him to visit Egypt and there pursue the subject in which he was passionately interested; he was, he said, unfortunately without resources of any kind. Petrie saw here an opportunity to train a disciple in his own ideas and methods. He consulted Miss Edwards, who with characteristic energy cast around among her friends for sponsors; a special fund was set up to provide a studentship to the value of £250 a year, to which Griffith, the only candidate, was appointed for an initial period of three years. A condition of the award was that the student should spend the winter and spring in Egypt assisting one or other of the explorers; the rest of the year was to be spent studying in Europe and helping to write up the results of the campaign. The scheme worked well; as will be seen, Griffith played an important part in the work at Naucratis and was later instrumental in founding the Archaeological Survey and editing many of its publications. He later married Miss Edwards's friend and companion, Kate Bradbury, and lived to become England's most distinguished Egyptologist, and the first occupant of the Chair of Egyptology in Oxford. To Petrie he was a godsend, for though he often complained of his pupil's slowness and lack of practical aptitude, he could 'follow a wall' – as Naville emphatically could not – and understood and appreciated Petrie's insistence on the scientific value of small objects and the importance of the study of pottery. Though he later turned increasingly to philology, and engaged less in field excavation, Griffith's early training with Petrie remained of great value in the counsels of the Fund.

At the second Annual General Meeting, in October 1884, Miss Edwards was able to announce that the Fund already had 171 American donors and subscribers, of whom 'three are heads of colleges, twenty-seven, dignitaries of the church, nineteen, distinguished University professors, and thirty-two, members of Congress'. The American Branch, as it became, owed its inception and subsequent rapid expansion largely to the energy and enthusiasm of its Treasurer, the Rev. William C. Winslow of Boston, who was to work tirelessly on behalf of the Fund for many years; in 1887 he was made a Vice-President. Most of the early subscribers in the United States were New Englanders, and the first museum to benefit materially from the Fund's discoveries was naturally enough the Boston Museum of Fine Arts. After the British Museum, the largest and best collection of antiquities was shipped there every year. The first American Vice-President was the poet and author Russell Lowell, who during the years when he was Ambassador at the Court of St. James had made many English friends, among them both Miss Edwards and Sir Erasmus Wilson. Many Americans were attracted to the enterprise because of its biblical aspect; early in 1885 an anonymous donation of $25 was sent 'In Memoriam C. G. G.'. 'You all know', said Poole in his address at the General Meeting of that year, 'what that touching tribute conveys. Khartoum had fallen: England has lost her hero "sans peur et sans reproche" –

and behold, an unknown hand is stretched forth from the far side of the Atlantic with a gift to his memory – a gift in furtherance of a work which its Biblical relations would have supremely interested Charles George Gordon.' In lighter vein the poet Whittier wrote to Winslow:

> I am glad to have my attention called to the excavation of Zoan. The enterprise commends itself to every reader of the Bible, and every student of the history and monumental wonders of Egypt. I would like to have a hand in it. I hesitate a little about disturbing the repose of some ancient mummy, who perchance,
>> Hobnobbed with Pharaoh glass to glass
>> or dropped a halfpenny into Homer's hat
>> or doffed his own to let Queen Dido pass
> but curiosity gets the better of sentiment, and I follow the example of Dr. Holmes [Oliver Wendell Holmes] by enclosing an order on Lieut. Governor Ames for one of his best shovels.

The American Branch grew swiftly and was very much encouraged when in 1889 Miss Edwards was invited to visit the United States on a lecture tour lasting five months. Mr. Winslow and her publicity manager planned for her an exacting programme of meetings and talks during which she visited colleges and clubs in some sixteen different states and lectured 115 times. Always she talked about the new discoveries and everywhere she was fêted, while subscribers flocked to the Fund.

From the outset the Society was not without its opponents. The most persistent and violent criticisms came from an American engineer by the name of Cope White-house, who had first visited Egypt in 1879 and had thenceforward made the geography of the Faiyum region the subject of some startling theories of his own. Naville and the Fund, he maintained, were wrong: Zoan and the 'store cities' of the Book of Exodus were to be found near Memphis at the mouth of the Faiyum, which was the true Land of Goshen. His views, publicised in articles in the American Press and in privately printed pamphlets, did not unduly worry Naville and Petrie, though Miss Edwards and Stuart Poole were upset when the *Athenaeum*, a rival literary weekly to the *Academy*, published anonymously a scathing review of Naville's *Pithom* which they attributed to his pen. 'When the subject of Pithom', the review stated, 'was brought up before the Congress of Orientalists at Leiden in 1883, it was received as a joke, no one for a moment believing in it. It is not possible that scholars from all parts of the world should hold without good reason that Pithom has not been discovered. Any Society or Fund which succeeds in making excavations in Egypt will do good and serviceable work; but it is essential that its committee should be composed of Egypt-ologists and men who understand Egyptology, and not like that of the Egypt Explor-ation Fund, where Egyptologists are conspicuous by their absence, and where the members appear to be elected for distinction in any other science rather than Egypt-ology.'

Miss Edwards was denied by the Editor of the *Athenaeum* any opportunity of answering this attack; but Naville counselled a dignified silence, even when 'Copious' (as they nicknamed him) continued to thunder his polemics against them. He even went so far as to accuse Naville and his assistant Jaillon of forging inscriptions. His statements usually betrayed to scholars the curious limitations of his knowledge, but they must sometimes have puzzled the Fund's subscribers, and they evidently gave Dr. Winslow some sleepless nights.

Poole and Naville suspected, in the review quoted above, another hostile influence in the persons of Birch and Budge, called by Miss Edwards 'the B's'. The Oriental Department of the British Museum, as the chief beneficiary of the treasures brought home by the Fund's excavators (the Museum had in those days small funds only for the acquisition of new exhibits) might have been expected to support the work of the Fund even if they did not actively participate. Dr. Birch, however, remained adamant; the old man would have nothing to do with the Fund. He expressed the view, at meetings of the Society for the Promotion of Biblical Studies of which he was President, that Naville was wrong in his reconstruction of the route of the Exodus, and he resisted all efforts by Miss Edwards and Poole to win him over – 'a portcullis to block a pyramid' was Poole's description of his obstinacy.

Wallis Budge, Birch's assistant in the Department from 1883, adopted a similar attitude towards the Society, and so, after the death of Dr. Birch at the end of 1885, did his successor, Peter Le Page Renouf, himself a philologist with little interest in, or understanding of, archaeology. He was invited soon after his appointment to be a member of the Committee of the Fund, but he refused. Wallis Budge, who was the Keeper from 1893 to 1924, remained aloof, and the first representative of the Department to develop a cordial relationship with the Fund was H. R. H. Hall, who as Assistant to Budge, was seconded from the Museum to work with Naville at Deir el-Bahri from 1903 onwards, and was later for a time Honorary Secretary of the Egypt Exploration Society (as it had then become) and editor of its *Journal*. For more than half a century now there has been close co-operation between the Society and the Egyptologists of the British Museum, and the Society has greatly benefited from the generosity of the Trustees.

From the beginning Poole and Miss Edwards acted as Joint Honorary Secretaries of the Fund and for the first year or two they were left to do practically all the work. He, in London, kept the accounts, dealt with official correspondence, and enlisted new subscribers from his circle of acquaintance and among those of the eminent whom he thought might be likely donors. She, in Bristol, wrote articles for the papers on the work of the Fund and the discoveries of its 'explorers'; she wrote copiously to her friends and to the influential and wealthy, asking them to contribute to the Fund, either as regular subscribers, committed to an annual sum, or as donors of larger amounts. Printed pamphlets were sent to prospective contributors outlining the aims of the Fund, but she preferred the personal approach and wrote, in her vigorous sloping Victorian hand, endless letters explaining the urgency of the need to rescue the past. In those days before the telephone, and without typewriters, Miss Edwards and Poole corresponded daily by letter, sometimes sending several briefly scrawled notes by different posts in a single day. His was the diplomatic and cautious counsel, hers the ready pen. He sometimes found himself obliged to curb her enthusiasm and in his letters repeatedly implores her to 'do nothing rash', to consult him before rushing into print, and to ask him before writing off on her own account, as she had done to Schliemann. By reading the drafts of her articles he was sometimes able to put her right on matters of Egyptological fact. He complained that she was unbusiness-like, she neglected to send in regularly lists of her new members, and she was apt to leave large cheques uncashed.

Like all public-spirited people who run voluntary societies, Miss Edwards and Poole were overworked and under-qualified: spare-time amateurs who had undertaken more than they could reasonably have been expected to do. Poole's letters constantly bemoan his exhaustion, and commiserate with Amelia on hers: 'Like you, I am stupefied with tiredness', she wrote once. Petrie often received conflicting instructions from the two Secretaries. Nor were their requests always well considered. When he was at Nebeira (Naucratis) in 1885, Miss Edwards, anxious to provide the maximum encouragement for her subscribers, wrote asking him, when he went to San, to procure and send home 1,000 bricks made without straw from the site of Naville's store city, Pithom. (Poole in a separate letter asked for 'twenty to forty'.) Petrie, while expressing himself willing to comply with her request should she insist, felt bound to point out the huge cost of such an enterprise, since the bricks were so large and heavy that only two of them could go to a box, and it would take him and his assistant, Griffith, a week's work to pack them. He further pointed out that M. Naville himself disliked the idea of associating himself with 'a trade in relics', and would not claim that any particular brick had been made by an ancient Israelite, since ancient Egyptian bricks, on any site, were frequently made without straw.

Poole, attempting to carry out the business of the Fund after a long day's work in the Museum, was sometimes at his desk until two in the morning. He was not a man who knew how to delegate responsibility, and Flinders Petrie's letters make frequent complaints that matters have not been attended to, that proofs have been delayed, that this or that blunder has been made. Petrie was a man who hated muddle and abominated waste; in the administration of the Fund he found both. He had always prided himself on his frugality: to save money for the work in hand he lived on iron rations, eating Arab bread and ship's biscuits; he walked many kilometres a day rather than hire a donkey; and in the fierce heat of summer he made his own boxes for the transport of antiquities, to save the expense of a carpenter. He complained of the Committee's prodigality: they made no effort to obtain competitive estimates for printing the memoirs but had 'negligently wasted' more than £100 by accepting the original figure suggested by the printer.

M. Jaillon, the contractor engaged by Naville to shift blocks at Bubastis (and in fact, in spite of Petrie's shocked protest, to take charge of excavation work in Naville's absence in Cairo), was being paid three times the usual rate for such work. A reasonable complaint, too, was the treatment of his precious finds from Naucratis and Tanis, which he and Griffith had carefully sorted and labelled and laid out on tables in Oxford Mansion for distribution. These he had found on his return the following summer, still undistributed and in a state of chaos. Poole had omitted to tell him that the breakages and confusion were partly the result of an unfortunate accident during the winter: a workman had fallen through the skylight on to the table, 'and so much shattered the Oxford collection that it had not been worth sending. Fortunately the man was not killed, but he produced a sad confusion among the Naucratis and San pottery'.

Matters came to a head in the late summer of 1886: Poole announced his intention of resigning from the position of Honorary Secretary on the plea of overwork. Petrie and Miss Edwards, who were exchanging very frank letters and appear to have been much in sympathy, hoped that the time had come to make changes in the Executive: the very size of the Committee and the eminence of some of its members had proved an obstacle to efficiency. Meetings were rare and almost all the Society's business was being conducted by a small sub-committee of six, most being members of the Coins and Medals Department in the British Museum, with Newton as their Chairman. At their frequent meetings in the dining-room of Mr. Poole's official residence they were making major decisions of policy and authorising major expenditure, writing communiqués to the Press and engaging staff for exploration.

Petrie appears to have been the first to point out the unconstitutional nature of some of these decisions; time and again he had written to Poole in protest, pointing out that Miss Edwards, as Joint Honorary Secretary, ought to be a party to all such deliberations. In fact, her absence from London meant that she was seldom consulted on matters of policy, a matter about which she felt keenly and not a little hurt. 'I think I might have been taken into the Council', she wrote to Poole, 'especially as, if I am not mistaken, my account for 1885–6 is larger than even Winslow's or yours . . . I do not see the use of my giving up everything, earnings, time, health and home duties – if I do not have the least confidence reposed in me by the Committee, and am only told of things after they are done.' She had some cause for complaint, for she had had to give up her creative writing altogether and, unlike Poole and the others who were salaried public servants, was in some financial straits as the result of her devotion to the Fund. The award to her of a State pension of £250 a year in 1891 was a belated acknowledgement of her services.

Petrie drew up a set of proposed new rules and had them printed. They provided for quarterly meetings of the Committee, and a monthly statement of petty expenses and business transacted on the Secretary's authority, to be circulated to all Committee members for their approval and signed ratification, any item not ratified to be held for discussion at the next quarterly meeting. But these proposals were never circulated by Newton. At a meeting on 6 October the Executive decided to dissolve themselves on a plea of overwork. In their report to the Committee on 12 October 1886, at which their resignation was tendered ('which they do the more readily since some members of the General Committee regard their activity as unnecessary'), they made the suggestion 'that the General Committee should meet not less than once a fortnight in future'. Their resignation was accepted; but the abolition of the Executive – which appears to have been Miss Edwards's suggestion in the hope of broadening the basis of policy decisions – in effect made little difference to the running of the Fund. Few Committee members were able to attend these frequent meetings, and though Poole for a time relinquished his secretarial post he remained an active participant in all their deliberations. Miss Edwards took over sole responsibility for editing the memoirs and seeing them through the press.

Petrie saw no alternative but to resign, though Miss Edwards begged him to remain and to try and reform the management from within. Henceforward he excavated on his own, with the aid of private funds provided by benefactors and by

8 (*Right*) Schist sarcophagus of Psamtik at Nabesha (British Museum, EA no. 1047).

9 (*Below*) View of the fortified camp at Daphnae.

his own initiative. It is clear from his letters to Miss Edwards (with whom he continued to be on terms of great friendliness) that he regretted this step and hoped one day to be able to work for the Fund; he had no personal animosity against Poole, but found it impossible to work under his direction. Ten years later, after Poole's death in February 1895, he again worked for the Fund, and for ten years, from 1896 to 1905, his excavations were financed and published by it; but when the Fund's finances were low, at a time when American subscriptions had fallen off and only one expedition a year was possible, it became a choice between Naville, working at Deir el-Bahri, and Petrie who has plans to dig at Tell el-Yahudiya in the eastern Delta. The Fund felt unable to let Naville go, and so Petrie finally resigned, never to return. It was understandable that loyalty to their first 'explorer', who was now over sixty, should have inspired their choice, but with hindsight and in the judgement of later archaeologists the Fund's loss was disastrous.

In a lecture given by Griffith at the Half-Centenary meeting of the Society in October 1932, in which he summarised the Society's archaeological record, his opening words were these: 'On reviewing the work of the Egypt Exploration Fund or Society during the fifty years of its activity, one may on the whole congratulate it warmly, in spite of its unfortunate conservatism and half-hearted support of the new methods of work during the first three quarters of its existence.' He went on to contrast the methods and abilities of the two men under whom he had learned his trade: Petrie, intensely practical,

> taught in the home and the workshop, endowed with senses and intellect which registered all his surroundings almost before he had seen them, was the all-sufficient hero of my early days in archaeology. It seemed to me at that time that nothing was beyond his powers unless to accept and obey the rulings of others. When suddenly called upon, he could conjure up the plan of a buried city, reproduce the time-tables of distant railway stations, or design to a nicety a perfectly balanced book cradle for Lepsius' colossal *Denkmäler*. If there had been any purpose in producing rabbits out of his hat, I am certain that he could and would have performed that and many other tricks on request . . . But in spite of his energy and power, he never wasted an ounce of them. He lived simply for archaeology, though occasionally, on revelations of incompetence and mistrust in the governing powers, he threatened to abandon archaeology for chemistry or some other career of research. To such a man every potsherd and every brick was pregnant with archaeological significance; to live and explore with him for months together . . . was an education of supreme value. But it certainly spoiled one for cordial co-operation with anyone less gifted in the philosophy and treatment of material things, and I must confess with shame that too often I met the naïve observations of the scholarly Monsieur Naville with unconcealed impatience . . . The attitude of my chiefs to their work was radically different. The aristocratic Naville was willing to spend time on raising historical questions by copying and interpreting inscriptions, but to him the less said about the base work of digging the better, and as to collecting observations on pottery and the like, it might be fitting for the mere scientist, but it was no work for a man trained in the humanities. Hence when, with the assistance of an architect, he had excavated and planned the site of the temple of Pithom, it was no surprise that practically nothing

was to be seen on the plan except an enclosure without an entrance . . . But such were the methods of the old school, which has only become extinct in the last few years, making way for the splendid new school of scholarly scientific and enthusiastic excavators which now prevails in every country of the world . . .

Many of the 'new school' who subsequently worked for the Fund, men such as Howard Carter, Bernard Grenfell, Somers Clarke, Garstang, Ayrton, Wainwright, Currelly and Brunton, had all of them worked with Petrie and learned from him; Frankfort had been his student at University College London, and the skilled Egyptian excavators from Lisht and from Quft, trained by him, were employed – as their descendants are still – by every archaeologist working in the soil of Egypt.

One matter gave members of the Fund grave concern, though they felt that, as a Society, it was wiser not to incur the displeasure of the Egyptian Government. Travellers returning from Egypt, and those whose duties permitted them to travel round the country, reported a continuing deterioration in the condition of the monuments and antiquities. The officials of the new administration, it seemed to many, cared little for Egypt's past; they were too busy trying to solve her present difficulties. The country's revenue, largely derived from the taxation of an impoverished peasantry, did not allow for any but the smallest expenditure on conservation of the monuments. The British occupation of Egypt indeed seemed to have increased the vandalism already suffered by tombs and temples: increased prosperity in some areas, resulting from a new-found security against extortion, gave birth to many new building enterprises in the Nile Valley, and in the province of Asyut walls of ancient bas-relief were being broken up and sent to the limekilns or embedded in embankment walls; the attention of the city governor was called to these depredations, but he did nothing to stop the plunder.

In August 1888 a number of interested and influential people met in the Fulham studio of the convener, Edward Poynter R.A., a painter of great reputation who was later to become President of the Royal Academy. Among those at the meeting were the Director of the National Gallery, Sir Frederick Burton, who took the chair, the painter Alma Tadema, and the Egyptologists Wallis Budge and Flinders Petrie. At this meeting a Committee for the Preservation of the Monuments of Ancient Egypt was formed, with Poynter himself and Henry Wallis as Joint Honorary Secretaries. The Committee's prospectus was drafted and revised as more influential people joined; in November of the same year the name 'Committee' was altered to 'Society', and the aims were defined as 'the preservation of the splendid and interesting remains of the land of the Pharaohs, by aiding the Egyptian Government, as far as the means and influence of the Society will admit, to maintain them and save them from further ruin, to protect them from the depredations of the Arabs, and from injury done by tourists and others, by means of doors or enclosures, and by the appointment of responsible guardians and inspectors; and, where possible, by walls calculated to resist and neutralize the encroachments of the Nile'. The President of the Royal Academy, Sir Frederick Leighton, was now among the members of the Committee, as also were Sir Henry Layard, the Assyriologist, Renouf, from the British Museum, and Sir Charles Newton; Poole joined for a time but later withdrew his name, though he continued to advise Poynter. A. H. Sayce and Miss Edwards were enrolled as members of the Society, and so were the artists Holman-Hunt, Burne-Jones and G. F. Watts.

It was decided to tackle the Egyptian Government directly: the Foreign Office in London was approached and the Foreign Secretary, Lord Salisbury, undertook to forward the Society's proposals to the administration in Cairo. The first objective, it was decided, must be to raise funds whereby necessary work of conservation and protection of the monuments might eventually be financed; the second, to secure the appointment of an Inspector sent out from England to report on the measures needed and to superintend the work of repair and consolidation. Ideally, he was envisaged as an officer of the Royal Engineers with a penchant for archaeology and a knowledge of the hieroglyphs. It was suggested that this paragon, could he be found, ought to be paid for by the money raised in Egypt by a Government levy on tourists visiting, now in their hundreds, the monuments of the valley of the Nile.

The Committee's agitation had some immediate effect: on the instructions of the Ministry of Public Works a French engineer, Grand Bey, drew up a report on the 'Actual Condition of Egypt's Temples and Monuments', and at a meeting of the Bulaq Museum Committee on 22 January 1889 the Sirdar, Sir Francis Grenfell, proposed that orders should be given for the repair of those temples in most urgent need, and for doors to be fitted to the Tombs of the Kings. The basic cost of this work, £700, should be provided by the charge for admittance to the Museum, a tax of £1 a head on all tourists, and the sale of antiquities at the Museum. He offered military labour for the repair and maintenance of the temples of Kom Ombo and Philae.

Much encouraged, the Committee in London prepared and circulated an appeal for funds. Sir Colin Scott-Moncrieff, writing to welcome this move, suggested that the S.P.M.A.E. should amalgamate with the E.E.F.; 'one advantage of this', he wrote, 'would be that the expenditure could all be put under M. Naville'. The idea was not well received by Poole and his colleagues, who pointed out that the objects and interests of the two societies, though closely linked, were different. But the Committee of the E.E.F. did not oppose a proposal of the S.P.M.A.E. to borrow the services of Count D'Hulst, Naville's assistant, during the winter of 1889 to cut through the mounds of medieval Fustat, the site of ancient Cairo; they even offered to pay part of his expenses. Perhaps fortunately (for his experience of archaeology with Naville did not include the finesse of digging stratigraphically) the scheme does not seem to have materialised.

The following February the antiquary and traveller the Rev. Greville Chester reported from Egypt that the damage daily done to the monuments was a matter of increasing concern: the well-known relief of the colossus at El-Bersha had been partly hacked out within the last four months and the paintings in the tombs at Beni Hasan badly defaced. Other instances of recent damage were reported to the two societies. By March over £500 had been raised by the S.P.M.A.E. and the Prince of Wales had consented to become its patron, and Lord Wharncliffe its President. As Miss Edwards wrote to Poynter in June, 'Nothing – absolutely nothing – but the appointment of salaried guardians can avail to prevent these acts of vandalism'. She

10 (*Top*) Granite shrine of Ramesses II at Tanis.

11 (*Bottom*) Clearing the temple of Queen Hatshepsut with the Decauville railway in use.

was happy to be able to tell him of the special fund which had been set up by the E.E.F. for the purpose of making a thorough record of the ancient monuments (the genesis of the Archaeological Survey at this time is described below, p.141 ff.).

The S.P.M.A.E. next turned its attention to an attempt to stop the Egyptian Government from moving the contents of the Bulaq Museum to a derelict Khedivial palace out in Giza; not only was it far from Cairo and relatively inaccessible to tourists, but the building itself, they submitted, was totally unsuitable and a grave fire hazard. The move to the new site, however, went ahead, and Sir Evelyn Baring was adamant that protest was useless, since the Egyptian Government could not afford to build a new museum. He also made it clear that he would be opposed to any attempt to press the Government to accept an English Inspector, since the Antiquities Department was entirely in the hands of the French and would certainly not tolerate such a move. The idea was finally dropped in favour of a scheme to safeguard the Great Temple of Karnak 'from further decay and dilapidation'; for this purpose the sum of £500 was sent out by the S.P.M.A.E.

By 1895 a pump-house was completed, and further drainge works were paid for by the Society in 1896; the surplus remaining from the fund, some £40, was voted to assist the Egypt Exploration Fund in their scheme to protect the temple of Hatshepsut at Deir el-Bahri. Both the S.P.M.A.E. and the E.E.F. were deeply concerned at the proposal to drown the temples of Nubia by building a dam at Aswan (Poynter was almost equally disturbed by a proposal to build the dam in imitation of a temple pylon – an architectural design which he felt to be entirely inappropriate). Both Societies gave public expression in the Press to their disquiet, and sent protests to the authorities in Egypt through the usual channels. They could not stop the dam, but at least they could register the protest of scholars against the destruction of the monuments and urge that a proper record be made before it was too late.

One step for the improvement of the running of the Fund was achieved by Petrie before he left in 1886; this was to secure for the administration an office and the part-time services of a clerk. The Royal Archaeological Institute (of whose Committee Petrie was a member) was willing to lease a room in their premises at Oxford Mansion for the Fund's permanent use, and their part-time clerk, Hellier Gosselin, consented to devote one day a week to the Fund's business for the modest salary of £30 a year. Now all letters from the office were duplicated and kept in a neat ledger in a copperplate hand. At the Annual General Meeting in December a new set of rules was read out, and the objects of the Fund were for the first time properly defined. They were:

> 1. To organise excavation in Egypt, with a view to further elucidation of the History and Arts of Ancient Egypt, and to the illustration of the Old Testament narrative, insofar as it has to do with Egypt and the Egyptians; also to explore sites connected with early Greek history, or with the Antiquities of the Coptic Church, in their connection with Egypt.
>
> 2. To publish, periodically, description of the sites explored and excavated and of the antiquities brought to light.
>
> 3. To ensure the preservation of such antiquities by presenting them to the Museums and similar public institutions.

In the following year the Fund was incorporated as a Society under the Companies Act, through the services of a legal member of the Committee, Mr. T. H. Baylis, Q.C. Miss Edwards, now sole Honorary Secretary, engaged Miss Emily Paterson, a private secretary, to help her with correspondence.

In this year, 1887, it was decided to write to Sir John Fowler – a civil engineer who had not only achieved distinction in England by designing part of the Metropolitan Railway and building the Forth Bridge, but had for many years been chief engineering consultant to the Khedive – asking him to fill the vacant office of President of the Society; his knowledge of Egypt and its political leaders was to stand the Fund in good stead until his death in 1898. Later Presidents included Sir John Evans, the Earl of Cromer, Field Marshal Lord Grenfell and Sir John Maxwell.

Naville continued to work for the Fund, and when Petrie left, he saw an opportunity to reverse the policy agreed by the Committee, to give *bakshish* (a tip) for small objects found. A memorandum on the 'Purchase System' was therefore drafted for a Committee meeting in January 1888, requesting explorers to be instructed 'that wages and not gifts be the usual method of remunerating excavators; exceptions to be reported by Explorers with their reasons'. The motion was immediately and vigorously opposed in a counter-memorandum sent by Miss Edwards, who was unable to attend the meeting. She pointed out that small objects even if of no particular historical or archaeological interest were of the greatest value to the Fund. 'Mr. Petrie', she pointed out, 'brought away many hundreds of worthless ushebtis (figurines) and many lbs. weight of ordinary mummy beads from Tell Nebesheh in 1886. The authorities at Boulak would simply have flung these objects into the Nile, but they have probably done more to popularise the Fund and interest our subscribers than all the more important objects put together'. 'Our subscribers', she went on, 'are the *General Public* and they need to be stimulated by Popular means. Our great provincial towns have local museums, and I find wherever there is a local museum, there is an eager desire on the part of the authorities and townsfolk to obtain objects for their museum. My recent tour in the North has brought all this part of the working of the Fund very closely under my notice. I have repeatedly been promised subscriptions and donations, if a contribution of objects were likely to follow.' The motion was defeated, but in Naville's subsequent reports small artefacts are seldom mentioned or adequately described.

It had in fact been Petrie's boxes of antiquities that had brought the Fund into bad odour with the Egyptian authorities for a time. Maspero resigned, to everyone's regret, in 1886 owing to the ill-health of his wife, and named as his successor as head of the Antiquities Service Eugène Grébaut, a young Egyptologist who had been a pupil of his. At first the excavators of the Fund were glad that it was he and not the unpopular Brugsch, Maspero's deputy in the Museum, who had been given the appointment, but it soon became clear that difficulties lay ahead. Grébaut showed himself hostile to all but the French, and a rumour spread round Cairo that Petrie had that spring removed from Egypt many crates of antiquities without authorisation. This accusation, a serious matter for the Fund, was strenuously denied by Petrie; Miss Edwards wrote herself to Maspero in Paris, who confirmed that the rumour was false: the boxes had been cleared. he said, and he was aware of their contents, none of which were wanted by the Museum. In fact, they contained some 500,000 sherds of pottery from which Petrie hoped to compile a 'corpus' or repertory of pot shapes – a novel idea at the time. Grébaut accepted the explanation, but from that time relations between the Fund and the French authorities in the Museum had to be carefully handled; the old liberality of Maspero had gone, and new regulations restricted the export of antiquities.

Lists of objects from the early excavations distributed by the Fund show how greatly local museums did in fact profit from its activities. The British Museum was always the greatest beneficiary, followed by the Museum of Fine Arts, Boston, and later other museums in the United States, in acknowledgement of the generous contributions made by the American Branch to the finances of the Fund. Then came the provincial collections of the north of England, Liverpool, Sheffield, Bolton, York and Edinburgh; Naville's Geneva had its share, and University College London, where both Poole and Newton occupied chairs, as also did Hayter Lewis, the Donaldson Professor of Architecture and designer of the north and south wings of the College, who was for many years a member of the Committee of the Fund. One public school, Charterhouse, was listed as a recipient in these early days. Later other schools and institutions were added, and the sorting, allocation and distribution of antiquities on their arrival in England was no small task. Usually it was done after the close of the summer exhibition, but in the case of very large statues or blocks it was found that a great deal of money could be saved by redirecting them on the docks at the quayside to their destination in the U.S.A., or elsewhere abroad, as soon as they arrived from Egypt.

In the spring of 1887 Miss Edwards went up to Liverpool for this purpose, and it was at Millwall Docks in London, in October 1891, meeting the antiquities from Ehnasya, that she caught the lung infection that was to be the cause of her death. She should never have been allowed to go. Her strenuous tour in the United States, in the course of which she broke her arm, had greatly exhausted her, and she never properly regained her health. Her death on 15 April 1892 marked the end of an era. In the obituary notice which Poole wrote for the *Academy* he said, 'While enduring the hardest labour, Miss Edwards did not fear to add to its weight, and while carrying out a daring project, she was able to adopt a wholly new enterprise. A rare faith was hers in her work and in each new labourer who came to her aid. In loyalty to her memory and to the cause she loved, let her example stir us who remain to carry on her cherished work in her own spirit!'

After Miss Edwards's death, her secretary Miss Paterson took over the work in London, and became the General Secretary of the Fund, while the office was moved to larger premises at 35 Great Russell Street, convenient for the British Museum. In 1919, the year of Miss Paterson's retirement, the Fund's premises were moved once more to 13 Tavistock Square. At the same time there was a general reorganisation of its activities after a period of comparative inactivity during the First World War, and its name was changed to the Egypt Exploration Society. Miss Paterson's successor was Miss Mary Jonas, and she guided the affairs of the Society until 1939, when her duties were taken over by Miss Winifred Keeves.

The Society's move to Hinde Street north of Oxford Street in 1933, to rooms in

12 Professor
Naville
directing
excavations at
Bubastis.

the building owned by the Palestine Exploration Fund, when the lease of the Tavistock Square office expired, gave it larger and better premises. In 1968, however, it was decided to purchase freehold premises and so remove the constant anxiety of rising rents. The present headquarters of the Egypt Exploration Society in Doughty Mews, east of Russell Square, has since become a thriving centre for visiting Egyptologists, for students, and for excavators writing up the results of their explorations, as well as for members who read and attend classes there. Through the generous gifts and bequests of members a very useful working library has been built up. It continues to grow by purchase and gift, and a binding fund, initiated by Miss Mary Crawford, Secretary of the Society from 1963 to 1979, helps to maintain the many valuable volumes it contains. Membership of the Society now numbers well over 2,200 and includes specialists and enthusiasts from all over the world. Miss Amelia Edwards would be well pleased.

2 The Delta

A. J. SPENCER

The early excavations of the Egypt Exploration Fund in Lower Egypt constitute one of the most important explorations ever carried out in the Delta region. The decision to work in the Delta was not motivated by a desire to give priority to town sites in urgent need of excavation; such ideas did not apply in 1882, the choice of the Delta being influenced instead by political considerations and a wish to recover evidence for biblical history. The interest in biblical matters among the members and supporters of the Fund is shown by the very first excavation memoir, entitled *The Store-City of Pithom and the Route of the Exodus* (1885). The identification of the town of Pithom in the eastern Delta was precisely the kind of result which could be expected to attract interest in the early days, since here was the discovery of a city mentioned in the Bible as having been constructed by the Hebrews, an apparent confirmation of biblical accuracy. So deep was the concern with biblical history that when Naville cleared a number of brick chambers in the temple area at Tell el-Maskhuta, these were immediately identified with the store magazines upon which the Hebrews were supposed to have laboured, although they were really no more than the foundations of temple buildings. In any case, Naville's identification of Tell el-Maskhuta with Pithom was by no means the certainty that he claimed.

An interest in ancient Egyptian culture for its own sake developed gradually among the supporters of the Fund, being aided to a great extent by the appointment of Flinders Petrie as one of the Fund's field excavators. In the 1880s Petrie was an archaeologist well ahead of his time, with a wide range of interests and a clear recognition that the recovery of the maximum amount of information on ancient life depended on the study of all kinds of material. He first worked for the Fund in 1883 at Tanis, another biblical site, and achieved impressive results, both in the recording of the inscribed monuments which lay on the site and in the excavation of new areas. Particularly interesting groups of antiquities were recovered from the clearance of houses belonging to the first and second centuries AD, including important remains of carbonised papyri.

It is probably true to say that at that time Petrie was the only excavator in Egypt who had the ability to save such fragile material. Fortunately for archaeology the houses had been thoroughly burnt at some period, ensuring a rich hunting-ground for objects, since people do not take time to remove their possessions from a building on fire. Although the houses had been looted before being destroyed, only the items of intrinsic value had been removed; much of interest was left behind. The richest house was number 35, belonging to a man named Asha-ikhet, a portrait statue of whom was discovered in the cellar. Owing to a misreading of the owner's name at

13 (*Top*) A colossal red granite head of Ramesses II at Tanis.
14 (*Bottom*) The brick 'store-chambers' at Tell el-Maskhuta.

the time of the finding of this statue it is described in the excavation report under the name Bakakhuiu. Small figures of divinities were found in great numbers, including among others Ptah-Sokar, Horus, Nefertem, Montu, Bastet and Isis, together with a terracotta figure of Venus. Bronze vessels were also found, and a few tools of iron, whilst of other materials there were stone mortars, glass vessel fragments and pottery vases. Nearly all the objects from this house were presented as a group to the British Museum. The excavations of 1883 were not restricted to Tanis, and Petrie carried out small test diggings at nearby *tells*, among which were Benha (Tell Atrib) and Tell Sueilin.

Although the scale of the excavations prevented Petrie from supervising all parts of the work constantly, he introduced far more effective control than had been the rule on earlier excavations in Egypt. The Fund was the first foreign institution to take up regular excavating in Egypt, and the methods of operation had to be devised as the work proceeded. It is fortunate that Petrie was employed at this time, since a person of his ingenuity was well-fitted to the invention of new techniques, which were to be copied by his successors both in the later work of the Fund and in that of other organisations. Petrie was not the kind of excavator who simply stood around on the site and waited for the workmen to tell him of any discoveries. He put far more physical hard work into the progress of the dig than most archaeologists before or since. As an all-to-rare exception among Egyptologists, he was a man of great practical ability, which proved to be a great asset for the running of an excavation, where technical problems over equipment or organisation occur at frequent intervals. He was quite prepared to construct the roof for his dig house, or to make all the crates for packing antiquities, or to get down in the midst of the work in order to turn over granite blocks with a crowbar. The respect he earned from his workers was probably largely due to the fact that he was the only European they had seen who was not afraid of getting dirty.

The diversity of Petrie's abilities enabled him to run large-scale excavations single-handed for much of the time. He was his own photographer, accountant, site supervisor, surveyor, epigrapher and archaeologist – a variety of roles now usually shared by a whole group of specialists, who, as individuals, are all too frequently unable to deal with anything outside their own narrow field. Much of Petrie's success was due to exceptional adaptability, and adaptability is vital on a dig. To work in such a manner required great energy and drive, and Petrie certainly possessed both. The hours of work at Tanis were from 5.30 until 11.30 am, and 2.30 until 6.30 pm, but the recording of the objects would keep Petrie busy until 10 or 11 o'clock at night; in addition, he did all his own cooking. Walks of fifty kilometres or more to visit ancient sites presented no obstacle to him at all, despite the fact that he was often ill owing to the poor conditions in which he lived on his excavation.

Among the tumbled granite blocks of the temple of Tanis he discovered the remains of a colossal statue of Ramesses II, originally over 25 m high, but cut up for building stone in the Twenty-second Dynasty. This statue, when complete, was surely the largest figure ever set up by the Egyptians, its original location probably having been Qantir.

The second season of excavation by Petrie for the Fund was carried out not at

Tanis but at Naucratis on the opposite side of the Delta. Petrie's continued participation in the work of the Fund was due to the strong support of Amelia Edwards, although other members of the Committee viewed the young archaeologist with less favour. An assistant who joined Petrie at the latter's request was Francis Llewellyn Griffith, who was to become a truly great Egyptologist in later days.

Naucratis was Petrie's own discovery; he had tracked down the site by following up reports on the provenance of an archaic Greek figure which he had purchased at Giza. The statuette was reported to come from a site called Nebeira, close to the town of Damanhur in the Delta. Petrie went there in 1883 and eventually came to a place which was covered with fragments of archaic Greek pottery. On returning to the area in 1884, he and Griffith stayed in an old house in the vicinity of the *tell*, and noticed two blocks of stone lying near the entrance, one of which proved to bear an inscription on the underside giving the name of the city of Naucratis – the first evidence of the identity of the site. This was the city established early in the Twenty-sixth Dynasty as a garrison for the Greek mercenaries employed by Psammetichus I, later developed under Amasis as the sole trading centre for the Greeks in Egypt. The culture of the town had been almost entirely Greek, although a few Egyptian traditions, such as the making of scarabs, had been adopted with vigour. The settlers brought with them their own divinities, and the remains of temples dedicated to Apollo, Aphrodite, Hera and the Dioskouroi were found.

Despite the damage done to the mounds by *sebakh*-diggers, it was possible to reconstruct the plans of the individual temple enclosures, and also of some of the domestic areas. A fortified camp was discovered, consisting of a high tower-like building on a podium of brickwork, surrounded by an outer wall. Within the podium were separate compartments, some of which had probably been domed over and used as cellars. The fact that the entrance to the structure was situated at a high level above the ground was a clear indication of the defensive nature of the building. From the sites of the Greek temples came masses of fragments of decorated pottery, many with archaic Greek inscriptions, as well as votive figurines and architectural elements.

At the southern end of the town lay the great *temenos* of the Hellenion, the main sanctuary and administrative centre, mentioned by Herodotus. An Egyptian temple was also built at Naucratis, and later reconstructed by Ptolemy II, whose foundation deposits were found under the corners. These deposits, containing model tools, vessels, tablets of various materials and glazed plaques, were the first to be discovered in Egypt. The work at Naucratis was continued for a second season in 1885–6 by Ernest Gardner, whilst Petrie and Griffith returned to the eastern Delta, to explore further the sites in the neighbourhood of Tanis. Gardner recovered more material from the town, and also succeeded in finding the cemetery, in which the Greek settlers had been buried in coffins of wood, terracotta or stone. From the burials came a variety of everyday objects, including bronze mirrors, bangles and rings, toilet vases and alabastra.

After leaving Naucratis, Petrie and Griffith settled at Tell Nabesha, also known as Tell Farun, and prepared to begin excavations in January 1886. Their dig headquarters consisted of two rooms, which they shared with rats and ants. The site consisted of

15 (*Top*) Excavating the cellar of a Roman house at Tanis, number 35 of Petrie.

16 (*Bottom*) The shrine in the temple of Wadjet at Nabesha.

low mounds, among which lay the scanty remains of two temples, one of which had been the main temple of the city, whilst the other was a smaller structure situated at right angles to the axis of the enclosure. The latter building yielded foundation deposits of Amasis, consisting of pottery vessels and small plaques of various materials, some inscribed with the name of the king. Like the majority of temples in the Delta, the buildings had been extensively destroyed, but the inscriptions and stone fragments recovered from the ruins showed that these had been sanctuaries of some importance, whose history extended back to at least the Twelfth Dynasty. The temples were dedicated to Wadjet, and a large statue of the goddess stood in the granite shrine which formed the sanctuary of the main building. Nabesha was found to be the site of the town called Imet, capital of the Nineteenth nome of Lower Egypt. Among the ruins of the temple were found statues and blocks bearing the names of Sesostris III, Ramesses II, Merenptah, Sethos II, Sethnakhte and Ramesses III, with numerous references to Wadjet, lady of Imet. The lower half of a fine statue of Sesostris III was also discovered, made of hard yellow quartzite.

Excavations were also carried out in the cemetery of Nabesha, in which were found tombs of the Ramesside age and later. Of special importance was the discovery that some of the Nineteenth Dynasty tombs were constructed of red burnt bricks, which previously had been considered to belong solely to the Roman Period. Pottery coffins were found, of a style which later proved to be quite common in the Delta. The tombs were all underground structures reached by shaft entrances, but the denudation of the ground had left many of them much closer to the surface than was originally the case. Some of the tombs contained pottery and forked spear butts of non-Egyptian type, and Petrie suggested that they were Cypriote, dating them to the Twenty-sixth Dynasty (about 600 BC).

Although Petrie was correct in claiming that the objects were of foreign origin, his dating was incorrect. Subsequently found to be widespread in Western Asia and to belong to the period 1300–1100 BC, they are of interest in showing the influence of foreign ideas upon this part of Egypt, close to the Asiatic frontier. The Saite tombs were larger and more solidly constructed than those of earlier times, and they contained *shabti*-figures and amulets typical of the age. Some were equipped with massive anthropoid coffins of stone, one of which, belonging to a certain Psamtik, son of Patjenfy, was later transported to the British Museum. A number of small objects and coins, mostly of the Ptolemaic Period, were obtained from limited clearances among the houses of the ancient town.

All the later stages of the excavations at Nabesha were carried out by Griffith, whilst Petrie went on to the site of Tell Dafana (Defenneh), the ancient Daphnae. There he made the important discovery of the fortified camp, established by Psammetichus I for his Carian and Ionian mercenaries, and mentioned by Herodotus. The identification was confirmed by the finding of Greek pottery around the fort and of foundation deposits of Psammetichus I under the corners. The fort was very similar to the one at Naucratis, standing on a high substructure of brickwork, with domed internal compartments. From the ruins of this building came a whole range of objects: Greek decorated pottery, jar-seals bearing the names of kings of the Twenty-sixth Dynasty, faience vases, amulets, beads, iron tools and weapons and remains of vessels in silver or bronze. Also there were many weights of metal or stone, providing useful evidence on ancient metrology. Petrie, who had a special interest in such matters, devoted a complete chapter of his report to the study of these weights.

Griffith, after finishing at Nabesha, had moved on to another site at Gumaiyima, where a large temple enclosure awaited investigation. Beneath the temple platform he found another set of foundation deposits, containing plaques and model tools, but unfortunately no inscription to date the building. From the general layout and the architectural features, the temple appeared to belong to the Ptolemaic Period. Large numbers of figures of deities were discovered, made of bronze or plaster, but a more important find was the evidence for glass-working in the enclosure. A number of subsidiary buildings in the *temenos* contained moulds, uncut canes of mosaic glass and other manufacturing elements, providing valuable evidence on the glass industry of Ptolemaic Egypt.

Many of the mosaic slices were of the highest quality; one particular example, bearing a figure of the goddess Nekhbet in four colours on a blue ground was only 4 mm square. A large quantity of inlays were in the form of individual hieroglyphic signs, used for making inlaid inscriptions upon wooden temple furniture. One such piece of furniture was actually found by Griffith: a wooden naos with inlays of glass, but unfortunately only the loose inlays have survived. The mosaics were formed by laying thin rods of different-coloured glass together to form the required pattern, fusing them into one unit, and then drawing the cane out in order to reduce the thickness. Very many of these pieces are now in the Egyptian collections of the British Museum.

Some of Griffith's work in the Delta took the form of exploration rather than excavation, and his reports included useful comments on a number of sites which he visited and briefly examined. In an archaeologically neglected area like the Delta these small scraps of information are still of value.

At the time of Petrie's and Griffith's excavations at Naucratis, Edouard Naville had also been working for the Fund, at a site called Saft el-Hinna, where he found the remains of a granite shrine of Nectanebo I of the Thirtieth Dynasty, some pieces of which were already in the Cairo Museum, or Bulaq Museum, as it then was. The publication, *The Shrine of Saft el Henneh and the Land of Goshen* (1887), is essentially devoted to a description of this monument, with copies of its inscriptions and scenes. The naos, or rather the remaining parts of it, since some fragments are missing, is covered with religious texts and scenes of great interest, revealing underlying beliefs from the earliest times. A whole range of divinities is shown, not only the well-known members of the Egyptian pantheon, but also rare deities and composite gods, some in unusual forms.

The god Soped, to whom the shrine was dedicated, is shown in a number of different manifestations, many of them indicating his character as a protector of the frontier of Egypt against outsiders. In common with many religious scenes of this late age, nearly all the figures are accompanied by label texts giving their names – a great help to the study of iconography. One strange deity, with a body made up of part man and part bird, crowned by four ram's heads, has the marvellous caption, 'four faces upon one neck'. Around the lower part of the monument ran three horizontal lines of large hieroglyphs, containing the dedication text of Nectanebo I. Naville paid brief visits to Khataana and Qantir, where he bought a few antiquities from local people, and then he attempted excavations at Tell el-Rataba in the Wadi Tumilat. These excavations were not carried very far and were not very productive, although a fine bronze *khepesh*-scimitar was recovered and sent to the British Museum.

In the early winter of 1887 Naville and Griffith moved to Tell el-Yahudiya and Tukh el-Qaramus for a short season of excavations. The former site proved rather unrewarding, with the result that attention was soon diverted to the nearby necropolis, in which graves of the Late New Kingdom and of the Roman Period were recorded. Many of the burials were contained in pottery coffins with roughly modelled face masks, such as had previously been found by Petrie at Nabesha. The graves took the form of tumuli covering single or multiple burials, the coffins enclosed in rough gabled structures of brick. Funerary goods were found both inside and outside the brickwork consisting mostly of pottery, but also including a few bronze vessels and arrowheads. Most of the coffins had been painted in imitation of cartonnage body-cases, and some bore debased representations of Egyptian gods and faulty hieroglyphic inscriptions.

At Tukh el-Qaramus the excavations were concentrated on what proved to be a large temple enclosure, although the stone buildings which had stood with it had been completely destroyed, leaving only their foundations. Trenches cut by Naville and Griffith revealed several foundation deposits, some of which were located on the axis of the building instead of at the corners in the more usual manner. One deposit contained a green glazed composition plaque bearing the cartouche of Philip Arrhidaeus, thereby providing a firm date for the latest rebuilding of the temple.

The memoir on these explorations, the seventh in the series produced by the Fund, contained a number of valuable observations on various sites in the Delta, both Naville and Griffith having spent some time travelling around making notes on scattered inscriptions and standing ruins. Naville investigated Bilbeis and Sebennytos, but was more impressed by the ruins of the temple of Isis at Behbeit el-Hagar, where he would have liked the Fund to have taken up excavations. He also visited a small *tell* at Abusir, the ancient Busiris, centre of the Osiris cult in the Delta. Griffith, meanwhile, was tramping over the mounds of Tarrana (Terenuthis), Heliopolis, Damanhur and Qantara, before setting out on a trip to Sinai in order to study the archaeological relics of El-Arish. This excursion provided him with a stock of descriptive anecdotes with which to fill the introductory section of his report.

Indeed, both Griffith and Petrie were skilled at including fascinating comments on the lighter side of their explorations in Egypt. One looks in vain for such light relief in more modern excavation reports; it is almost as though excavators are afraid of putting in any casual anecdotes in case they might be accused of frivolity or lack of scholarship. And yet a few relaxed paragraphs of description in an introduction to a memoir would do much to attract ordinary members of the public to support the Egypt Exploration Society, whilst in no way devaluing the scholarly content of the report.

This is Petrie's description of his camp at Dafana, an isolated spot well away from

17 Work in the cemeteries at Tell el-Yahudiya.

any centre of habitation:

> I never spent two months more smoothly than while heading our desert camp. Yet the people had not much to content them; they came without any shelter, and nothing but what they wore; they had dry bread to eat, and brackish water to drink; and they worked for sixpence a day, most of them for but five days of the week, as they had to walk twenty-five to forty miles to fetch their food. Some of them, indeed, never left the place, but had a donkey-load of provisions brought over once a week. Their shelter they made up, partly by digging a hole in the sand mounds, partly by booths of thin tamarisk bushes; some were content with a lair hardly more than a dog's hole, while some made an approach to distinct chambers in their construction. With all this, a merry party they were; excepting one or two older men, there was scarcely a lad over twenty or a girl over fifteen in the whole lot. Each night a blazing row of camp fires flickered their yellow flames up into the starlight, all along the line of booths which skirted the canal banks; mounds of sand tufted over with dark tamarisk bushes backed the line, while the distant ruins of the *kasr* showed dimly on one side, and the gleam of the sluggish canal on the other. Parties would go out into the half darkness, and form a circle to hold a *zikr* of the howling derwishes, for we had one holy man among us who led such devotions; and the grim sawing howl would go up by the hour together. Perhaps some girls would sing on in their wild Arab unison on another side, or a group of boys enjoy a hearty game. Such was our feast of tabernacles, where we had at last got clear of the official curse of the mammon of unrighteousness.

The next major undertaking of the Egypt Exploration Fund was the excavation of the site of Bubastis, again carried out under the direction of Naville. The difference in approach between the two excavators working for the Fund – Petrie and Naville – is clear from their publications: Petrie's volumes contain details of large stone monuments and smaller objects; Naville's reports contain the large stone monuments to the exclusion of practically all else. Nowhere is this difference more apparent than in the comparison of the volume *Tanis* II, *Nebesheh and Defenneh* with *Bubastis*. Unfortunately, Petrie left the Fund to work independently – a great loss to the Fund, although probably few of the Committee realised the fact until later – making many important discoveries on his own account. That the Fund had to ask him to excavate on their behalf once again in later years was a significant measure of his ability and success.

A remarkable feature of the work at Bubastis was the recovery of material from early periods, usually inaccessible in the Delta owing to the high level of the subsoil water. We do not know whether the granite blocks inscribed with the names of Cheops and Chephren came originally from a temple at Bubastis or had been quarried in later times from the mortuary buildings around the Giza pyramids. The inscriptions of Pepi I, however, have been shown by later discoveries to have belonged to monuments of this king at Bubastis. The major part of Naville's excavations at the site consisted of an investigation of the temple of the cat-goddess Bastet, the ruins of which still remained as impressive mounds of fallen granite. All the visible blocks were turned over and searched for inscriptions, whilst clearances were made to reveal other stones and statues which lay more deeply buried. It is a sad fact that of most Delta temples only the parts built of granite remain, all the softer stones having been quarried away for other purposes.

Naville's efforts were rewarded by the discovery of various monuments, which between them bore the names of twenty-five different rulers, from the Fourth Dynasty to the Ptolemaic Period. A number of statues of great interest were brought to light, including the lower half of a figure inscribed with the name of King Seuserenre Khyan, of the Fifteenth or Hyksos Dynasty. Another relic of the same age was a granite block bearing an inscription of King Apophis. Many of the inscriptions had been usurped in later times, as in the case of a colossal statue of Ammenemes III of the Twelfth Dynasty in grey granite, the base of which bore a text of Osorkon II of the Twenty-second Dynasty. This statue was one of a pair set up in the temple, but unfortunately neither figure was complete when found; one head was sent to Cairo and the other, together with the fragments of the throne and legs, came to the British Museum. The head of the latter statue is a masterpiece of Egyptian sculpture, which on style alone cannot belong to anyone other than Ammenemes III; like its counterpart in Cairo it had originally been fitted with inlaid eyes.

Among the later monuments discovered were a number of fine Ramesside statues and very many inscribed blocks of Osorkon II, who was responsible for major additions and renovations to the temple of Bubastis. The inscriptions of this king were so numerous that they were made the subject of a separate memoir, *The Festival Hall of Osorkon II in the Great Temple of Bubastis* (1892). The scenes and texts upon this building were found to be of great interest, since they related to the *Sed*-festival of the king and provided valuable information about the different stages of the ritual. Although the original monument had been reduced to scattered blocks, it was possible to establish the location of many of the joins between the stones and to reconstruct large sections of the reliefs on paper. We see the king carried in procession or seated upon his throne, in addition to participating in the various ceremonies. With him are shown his wife, the Queen Karoma, and several daughters. A great number of priests, officials and other persons are shown making ritual gestures or standing in attendance, many of them bearing archaic titles whose significance is not fully understood, and which may even have been largely obscure to the contemporaries of Osorkon II. Among the pieces of this monument in the British Museum is a large slab of red granite bearing a fine relief of Osorkon and Queen Karoma.

Another aspect of the excavations at Bubastis was the investigation of the cemetery of cats, sacred animals of Bastet. They were buried in pits, and, on the evidence of nearby ashes and charcoal, Naville assumed that they had been cremated. This seems very unlikely, the whole idea of cremation being abhorrent to the Egyptians, since it involved the destruction of the body and consequential termination of the afterlife. Mixed among the animal remains were bronze figures of cats, of the goddess Bastet and of other deities such as Nefertem, in exactly the same manner as bronze figures were deposited in other animal cemeteries excavated more recently by the Society at Saqqara.

After the concentrated effort made on the excavations of the temple of Bubastis,

47

18 A colossal granite head from a statue of Ammenemes III, found at Bubastis (British Museum, EA no. 1063).

Naville returned in 1892 to another season of more diverse exploration, visiting a selection of *tells* in the Delta, as he and Griffith had done in 1887. The results of this survey were combined with a report on work at Ehnasiya (Ahnas) el-Medineh, near the Faiyum, and published in the memoir on that site. The Delta sites surveyed were Mendes, Tell Baqliya and Tell el-Muqdam. Of Mendes Naville gives a brief description, with some details of the great naos of Amasis in the temple. Tell Baqliya was a town mound already in the process of disappearing for good, to judge from the comments made by Naville about the gradual levelling of the site, but he managed to copy and publish a few inscribed monuments which were lying in the village close by. The results of exploration at Tell el-Muqdam (Leontopolis) were more substantial, particularly because of the discovery of two quartzite statues of Sesostris III, unfortunately lacking their upper portions. The remains of each statue consist of the throne, with inscriptions at the sides, and the legs of the figure, both statues being extremely similar to a statue-base of the same king found by Griffith at Nabesha. All three of these monuments are now in the British Museum, and despite their greatly damaged condition they are still extremely interesting pieces of sculpture.

The activities of the Egypt Exploration Fund in the Delta conclude with work at Buto, a site first identified by Petrie in 1886, tested in 1904, and to which the Society returned for more serious excavations sixty years later. The 1904 survey was carried out by Petrie and Currelly, but did not constitute much more than a brief visit. Difficulties were heightened by the fact that the Petries' stores had been sent to Alexandria by mistake, leaving them camped at Buto without any equipment for an archaeological expedition. Nevertheless, a few worthwhile observations on the site were collected and published as a short chapter in the excavation memoir on Ihnasiya. The high level of the subsoil water was noted – a feature which was to give problems in the later work on the site – and the significant visible remains were described. The top levels of the mounds were covered with houses of the Roman Period, a cemetery of the same age lay a short distance to the north, and the temple was situated in the hollow in the midst of the town.

The temple site was one of the main areas of work in the recent excavations at Buto, carried out by the Society under the direction of Dr. M. V. Seton-Williams. These excavations confirmed many of Petrie's observations on the site, particularly his opinion that the temple had been intentionally destroyed in antiquity. The excavations revealed only scant traces of a once-fine building, enclosed within walls of brick and limestone, the latter faced with quartzite slabs held by copper tenons. From the evidence of plaster fragments bearing the name of Amasis, it is presumed that the temple was rebuilt by him, especially in view of the fact that he was responsible for the reconstruction of several other temples in the Delta. Some fragments of statues that had once stood in the temple were recovered from the ruins, most of the figures having been deliberately smashed at the time of the destruction of the building. Excavations in another part of the site revealed many kilns for the manufacture of pottery, a major industry at Buto in the Ptolemaic Period. Other finds included public baths of Roman date, and, rather surprisingly, an archaic cylinder seal, which must have been turned up from deeper levels during ancient disturbance of the mound.

With the end of the 1968–9 season, the Society's excavations at Buto were suspended, and they have not yet been resumed. The Nile Delta and, for that matter, all ancient town sites in the cultivated valley of the Nile are the priority sites for excavation now; unlike desert cemeteries, they will not survive the combined effects of water seepage, salt action and man-made destruction for very much longer. The Egypt Exploration Society, having been first to initiate a regular programme of excavation in the Delta 100 years ago, is now once again shifting its attention from the desert back to towns in the cultivation. One of the Society's field expeditions has recently begun working on the site of Memphis, capital of Egypt for much of its history. The importance of this site is paramount, and it is sincerely to be hoped that the expedition will be able to recover something more of the history of Memphis before the encroachment of agriculture and of modern buildings renders the ancient levels inaccessible.

3 Thebes

W. V. DAVIES

> The tourists who annually swarm into Thebes seldom depart from the ancient
> city of Amon without visiting the magnificent natural amphitheatre of Deir el
> Bahari, where the hills of the Libyan range present their most imposing aspect.
> Leaving the plain by a narrow gorge, whose walls of naked rock are honeycombed
> with tombs, the traveller emerges into a wide open space bounded at its further
> end by a semi-circular wall of cliffs. These cliffs of white limestone, which time
> and the sun have coloured rosy yellow, form an absolutely vertical barrier. They
> are accessible only from the north by a steep and difficult path leading to the
> summit of the ridge that divides Deir el Bahari from the wild and desolate Valley
> of the Tombs of the Kings. Built against these cliffs, and even as it were rooted into
> their sides by subterranean chambers, is the temple of which Mariette said that 'it
> is an exception and an accident in the architectural life of Egypt'.

Thus did Edouard Naville, in suitably evocative terms, open his introductory
account of the Egypt Exploration Fund excavations in the great mortuary temple of
Queen Hatshepsut of the Eighteenth Dynasty (about 1490 BC) at Deir el-Bahri on the
west bank of the Nile at Thebes. The year of writing was 1894, when already two
seasons of excavation had been completed under his direction. The remains of the
building had, by then, been largely exposed, and for the first time it had become
possible to view its overall plan and to appreciate the design of what was, as Mariette
had already been able to observe, a unique monument – an Egyptian temple built in a
series of ascending terraces, connected centrally by ramps and embellished with
colonnaded halls. It was, by general consent, an exceptionally fine building, embody-
ing in its structure a sensitive blend of the artificial and the natural. Especially remarkable was the effect, when viewed from a distance, of the colonnades, their pillars in
'proto-Doric' style, evoking for many 'Grecian architecture and the beauty of a
Greek temple' – the ultimate accolade in an age when ancient Greek art was the
unquestioned touchstone of perfection. The temple made a great impact on the
public imagination, drawing visitors in increasingly large numbers, as it continues
to do today. Naville was surely right in calling it 'the finest advertisement the Fund
ever had'. For him, additionally, the work was a personal triumph, for his ambition
to clear the temple had been realised in the face of the most bitter campaign of
vilification directed against him by his old enemy, the Fund's other chief excavator,
Flinders Petrie.

There can be no doubt that Deir el-Bahri was a site after Naville's own heart.
The 'deblayer of great temples' had long coveted the queen's edifice as 'one of the
best places in Egypt', likely to produce the kind of pickings which would suit his own

tastes as well as sustain the interest of the Fund's subscribers: 'It is a temple . . . the walls of which are covered with the most interesting inscriptions. Perhaps in clearing it we may come across a chamber filled with mummies . . . coffins . . . not small objects, and if we had any, they would be most useful to distribute.' This was precisely the kind of unscientific attitude towards excavating that so infuriated Petrie, who particularly deplored Naville's disregard of minor objects: '. . . as a general result experience shows that from 50 to 100 cases of small antiquities are found in a season's work, on almost any good site. Such a mass of material from my own annual work is now preserved in various public museums and private collections. But so far as I am aware, not a tenth of this yield has reached England from the Fund work, and of what little has come there is hardly any published record or illustration. It cannot be imagined that every site of M. Naville's work has been so uniformly barren of material . . .'

Petrie was appalled to hear of the Fund's plan to send Naville to a site as demanding as he knew Deir el-Bahri was likely to be. In communications to the Committee and other learned bodies, he was uncompromising in his criticisms of Naville and his prospective assistant, Count D'Hulst: 'Let me state exactly what is needed for D. el Bahri. (1) Accurate plans. (2) Good knowledge of Egyptian architecture . . . (3) Recording every distinctive piece as found. (4) Close knowledge of local prices . . . (5) Accurate artistic copying of all the sculptures . . . (6) Accurate facsimile copying of any graffiti found . . . (7) A backbone of workmen from a distance *already trained* to careful work . . . (8) A testing of the ground close by, so as to settle where the stuff can be thrown without having to be all moved again . . . Not one of these requirements will be fulfilled by Messrs. Naville and D'Hulst. The two Newberry's and Carter might do it. And if the Fund like to waste money by letting N. and H. be there as a compliment they may; only those gentlemen must not have any real power over the work.'

Petrie's solution was to direct Naville to Karnak where 'he may find things in statuary, etc . . . and he can exercise all his talents in the inscriptions. Above all he can do a minimum of *harm*: which ought to be a first consideration to anyone with a conscience on the subject'. Naville himself was unmoved by these attacks and bore the insults with some dignity: 'I thought at first of answering; but I am so adverse to begin a discussion which would have no end and which would soon take a personal character with such a man as Petrie, that I thought I should do better to disregard his attack. It is not the first time that Petrie expresses his contempt for my work; I know he never did it so openly as this time; but I can do without his approval.' He left for Egypt, as planned, in the first week of January 1893, and on arrival quickly set about acquiring the requisite concession. In his absence, however, the Committee's resolve weakened, so much so that at their next meeting, held on 1 February, it was decided to telegraph Naville: 'Telegraph what site agreed. Committee prefers Karnak. Suspend action till committee replies.' Naville received this the next day at Aswan, where, as it happens, he had just succeeded in clinching the *permis* for Deir el-Bahri with de Morgan, the Director-General of the Antiquities Service. He was utterly exasperated. In his letter of reply written the following day on the steamer between Aswan and Luxor he offered his resignation: '. . . if my work is of so little value, not

19 The site of Deir el-Bahri in 1892, before the excavations.

to say none, as Mr. Petrie thinks it, I shall not impose myself any longer on the society, and it is far better that I should go.'

Of course Naville did not go and indeed had no intention of going. Ignoring the instructions, he returned to Thebes, quickly set up camp in a house in the village of Qurna, and began excavations at Deir el-Bahri on 7 February, thus presenting the Fund with a *fait accompli*. Although steps were subsequently taken to remove Naville, the action was never carried through, largely because it was thought it might jeopardise the Fund's good relations with de Morgan. Naville had 'won', having held his ground in every sense, but Petrie's criticisms were not without some lasting effect. The quality of Naville's team was improved as a consequence (the notorious D'Hulst was dispensed with), and his work more closely scrutinised than would otherwise have been the case.

Deir el-Bahri was by no means a virgin site before Naville's intrusion. The ruins of the queen's temple had been visited by travellers since the first half of the eighteenth century, and by the middle of the nineteenth the site was already celebrated as a rich source of mummies, coffins and other 'anticas', for which the local inhabitants were used to dig freely to sell to tourists. The first scientific exploration was that of the French expedition of 1798, who published a detailed description and plan of the site as it stood then. It was subsequently explored to a greater or lesser extent by such *savants* as Champollion, Wilkinson, Lepsius, Mariette and Maspero. To Lepsius goes the credit for ascertaining, from the inscriptional evidence, the identity of the original founder of the temple (despite the fact that her name and figure had been systematically mutilated by the vengeful Tuthmosis III); but the greatest physical impression on the site was made by Mariette, who excavated there on three separate occasions, in 1858, 1862, and 1866.

The first of these was the most significant, for it was then that he had laid bare a large section of the south end of the temple, including the Hathor-shrine and the part of the middle colonnade bearing the famous reliefs showing the queen's expedition to the land of Punt. The two subsequent campaigns were carried out chiefly in order to form collections of coffins and mummies, the one for the Museum of Bulaq, the other for the Paris Universal Exhibition of 1867, and it was a similar aim that motivated later exploration by the Antiquities Service, culminating in 1891 with the discovery, to the north of the temple's lower court, of a cache containing 153 mummies belonging to priests of the god Amun. For all this activity (and to some extent because of it) over two-thirds of the temple remained to be revealed when Naville began work in the February of 1893, and this area was covered by enormous mounds of rubbish and debris, ancient and modern.

A fair idea of what sections of the temple had already been exposed and of the nature of the task facing Naville is shown by a photograph taken in 1892, a few months before work commenced. In the centre beneath the cliffs (the west end of the temple) can be seen the south and middle sections of the upper platform with its granite entrance portal leading into what once may have been a hypostyle hall. Just visible in the rear wall of the platform, directly in line with the portal, is the entrance to the temple's rock-cut sanctuary, a series of three communicating chambers, the innermost a Ptolemaic addition. Prominent in this area are the mud-brick remains of

20 Professor Naville supervising the excavations.

the Coptic monastery from which the site Deir el-Bahri, 'Monastery of the North', takes its name. The tall building on the left is the monastery tower, and behind it, mainly hidden from view, is the church, for which the Copts had utilised Hatshepsut's 'Southern Hall of Offerings'. These 'impertinent Christian additions' were to receive short shrift when the work of clearance and restoration began in earnest. Below and to the south of the upper platform can be seen the ruined entrance-hall and doorway to the subterranean shrine dedicated to the goddess Hathor, and to the north of this the Punt-section of the middle colonnade. Running down eastwards, to end eventually at the south-east angle of the lower colonnade, is the retaining wall of the middle platform, and emerging from the debris in the foreground is the top of the lower colonnade itself. The mounds which can be seen covering the temple's north end were over 12 m high in parts. It was to one of these mounds, in the north-west section of the upper platform, that exploration was first directed 'in order to ascertain the plan and extent of the temple on that side'. In this first season Naville was accompanied by John Newberry as architect and Howard Carter, whose task it was to make facsimile copies of the scenes and inscriptions on the temple walls.

Naville's good relations with the Antiquities Service paid off handsomely right at the outset, when he was allowed to borrow, from work in progress at the Temple of Luxor, a number of Decauville cars and some 460 m of tramway lines, equipment which greatly facilitated the removal and disposal of rubbish. The tracks were laid along a flattened surface leading from the excavation to the extremity of the northern mounds, at which point the cars shot their contents. The rubbish was then loaded into another set of cars and taken to a shoot some 245 m away. The tramways were lowered and altered in position as necessary. Over 200 men were employed, some to hack at the mound, others to carry the rubbish and service the cars. The final dumping-point was an ancient quarry, which had originally served to provide shale for the embankment of the temple avenue. Naville deplored Mariette's carelessness in dumping indiscriminately and congratulated himself on finding a spot where there was 'no risk of covering either building or tombs'. He had an unfortunate habit of giving such hostages to fortune. Years later, in this same quarry, the American archaeologist, Herbert Winlock, was to discover the 'secret' tomb of Senenmut, the architect of Hatshepsut's temple.

With the Decauville cars in full swing and Naville making little effort at detailed recording, the work of clearance went forward at a tremendous rate. By the end of this first, abbreviated, season of five weeks, all the chambers of the north-west section – 'the Northern Hall of Offerings', the Altar Court and Vestibule, and the 'Chapel of Tuthmosis I' – had been exposed, and it had been conclusively proved that Mariette's conjectural restoration of this side of the temple, as published in his plan, was incorrect. The Altar Court, with its great white altar *in situ*, was a quite unexpected feature, as was the so-called Chapel of Tuthmosis I with its splendidly preserved portraits of the king, his wife Ahmes, and his mother Senseneb. The altar was a magnificent and (at the time) unique example of its kind. Dedicated by Hatshepsut to the sun-god, Re-Harakhty, it consisted of a large rectangular platform, of fine white limestone, 4.9 m wide, 4 m long and 1.5 m high, decorated at the top with a torus moulding and cavetto cornice and approached on the west by a flight of ten shallow steps. Such altars had been known to exist in Egyptian temples, as they were represented in tomb-scenes at El-Amarna, but this was the first actual example to be uncovered.

As well as Pharaonic remains, more of the Coptic monastery was revealed, including, interestingly, the kitchen, its earthenware cooking-pot still in place. What 'left-overs', if any, it may have contained of the monks' last supper go unrecorded. Naville was not interested in such 'anthropological' matters, especially if it pertained to the detested Copts. More important to him was the fact that the kitchen walls had been partially built with stone blocks taken from elsewhere in the temple. Among them were fragments of the now-celebrated scene depicting the transport of obelisks by boat (from the lower colonnade). Apart from a number of Coptic ostraca, portable antiquities from this section of the temple were few, though one striking discovery was the panel and door-leaf from a large ebony shrine, which was finely carved with scenes showing the Kings Tuthmosis I and II offering to Amun. Now in the Cairo Museum, the shrine was considered by Naville to be the most important single antiquity discovered in the queen's temple. Splendidly drawn, it is one of the very few objects to be reproduced in the final publication.

The main work of the second season (1893/4), and by far the largest task to be undertaken in the entire temple, was the clearance of the northern half of the middle platform. Here the accumulations were greater and more complex than anywhere else. They covered an area which had been utilised as a cemetery from the Twenty-first Dynasty down to the Roman Period and was riddled with graves and mummy-pits, many, of different dates, intruding into one another. Most had been plundered, and the refuse from these diggings was thoroughly mixed up with material from the Coptic occupation levels and from the rubbish dumped by Mariette thirty years before. In short, the site was a stratigraphist's nightmare, which would have sorely tested the retrieving abilities of the most scientific operator. Naville was undaunted. Without hesitation he directed his men in medias res and solved the matter by removing it wholesale. A photograph taken in January 1894 shows the clearance in progress with the great man himself 'supervising' rather precariously from the top of a fast-disappearing mound. It was his proud boast that during the five months or so of this season over 60,000 cu. m of material covering an area of 6,410 sq m were removed – a remarkable feat of earth-moving given that the bulldozer had not yet been invented. Out of this huge mass came few recorded objects, though, not surprisingly, at the end of the season there were plenty of mummies and coffins for distribution to subscribing museums, and one relatively untouched area near the northern colonnade is reported to have yielded a quantity of scarabs and beads together with storage jars and an interesting coffin (now in the Museum of Fine Arts, Boston) which had been used as a container for embalming material. As on the upper platform, however, the major fruits of the season consisted of the standing architectural features, all of which, with the exception of the northern colonnade, were decorated with finely carved scenes and inscriptions. Scarcely less interesting than the Punt-episode on the south was a 'propagandist' scene in the corresponding position in the north representing the divine birth of Hatshepsut and containing a fictitious account of her appointment and coronation under Tuthmosis I. Beyond this, in the corner of the terrace, balancing the Hathor-shrine on the other side, was a similarly subterranean shrine dedicated to the god Anubis, which opened on to a hypostyle hall, a jewel of its kind, in a near perfect state of preservation.

Back home, meanwhile, anxiety, fuelled by Petrie's supporters, persisted over Naville's competence as an excavator. As a result, the archaeologist D. G. Hogarth was dispatched to Deir el-Bahri in the middle of the second season ostensibly to assist in the general operation of the work but also tactfully to observe Naville's conduct of the excavation, on which he was then to report. Hogarth appears to have been instrumental in introducing several improvements, among them closer supervision of the actual digging and a more careful noting of the exact place and relative position of finds. It was also due to him that a second artist was subsequently sent out to assist the over-burdened Carter, in the event his elder brother, Verney Carter, of whom it was said 'he draws as well as his brother'. But despite his awareness of certain shortcomings, Hogarth's report was, in the end, favourable to Naville, vindicating him on the two issues over which there had been most argument, namely his practice of clearing material away without due care, and his method of payment to the workmen.

While agreeing with Petrie that 'every relic of antiquity however small has its value', Hogarth argued that the mounds at Deir el-Bahri were too turned over and confused in their content to be worth spending too much time over: 'When he [Hogarth] had first gone there he had thought it would be possible to discover a certain amount of the history of the temple from the study of the stratification of the mounds but he should never forget his disillusionment, for when they were about sixteen feet down they had come upon a small fragment of a German newspaper of the year 1875. This was by no means a singular experience, for they were continually coming upon remains of the latter part of the nineteenth century in parts of the temple thought to have been previously untouched.' He also concluded that Naville's method of paying each man a fixed wage with supplementary *bakshish* was the best system in the circumstances. Petrie advocated a system whereby the men were paid the market price for everything they might find, so making it in their own interest to hand over all they discovered. According to Hogarth, this method was impracticable at Deir el-Bahri because 'we live here in close proximity to huge stores of small antiquities, with which, as soon as we were known to be buying, our work would be "salted" profusely'. Moreover, he had the proof, for when shortly after his arrival the payment-for-objects system had been introduced, for a brief experimental period, there had been an immediate 'increase in the finds and decrease in the quality of the scarabs'.

An event which coincided with Hogarth's arrival and certainly contributed to the improvement in supervision was the completion of a new camp-house. Previously the staff had lived almost two kilometres away from the work. The new house was actually on the site, only a short distance away from the south colonnade of the lower platform, and was orientated in such a way that 'the windows of the living room commanded an uninterrupted view of the temple'. It was economically built, Naville getting his own back on the Copts by reusing bricks from their monastery, and the accommodation suitably austere, at least to Naville's mind, who warned in a

21 (*Top*) The altar of Re-Harakhty in the temple of Hatshepsut.

22 (*Bottom*) The two temples in 1907, with the Society's house on the left.

letter concerning the intended visit of the artist Miss Paget that 'she will have to rough it. She will have to accept many discomforts which frightened even gentlemen. Our house is as simple as possible. We do not indulge in any luxury . . . our house is not to be compared to those which Morgan built for himself and the museum officials. The beds are hard and the furniture elementary'. He added mischievously: 'If Miss Paget begins with Petrie I daresay our way of living will compare favourably with her first experience of an explorer's life.'

The third season (1894/5), the final season of excavation proper, saw the main body of the temple completely cleared. The walls of the lower colonnade were found to have suffered more than any others at the hands of the Copts, who had extensively pillaged the blocks for their own use. In consequence, much of the decoration was lost, either destroyed or scattered around the temple, incorporated, like the obelisk-scene, in various secondary buildings. In order, therefore, to retrieve as much as possible, the Coptic structures were systematically dismantled, and, as expected, the haul was considerable, yielding not only missing sections of the lower colonnade but also of the Punt-reliefs and other decorated areas.

While this search was going on, 'tidying up' operations took place in other parts of the temple, during the course of which several unexpected discoveries were made. Most notably, an intact tomb of the Saite Period belonging to three priests of Montu was found in the floor of the vestibule of the Hathor-shrine, entirely overlooked by Mariette, and to the south of the retaining wall of the middle platform was uncovered an undisturbed foundation deposit, containing over fifty model implements inscribed with Hatshepsut's name. It also emerged that certain rectangular brick constructions placed at the entrance to the 'Southern Hall of Offerings' on the upper platform, previously thought to have been beds for the monks, were in fact graves. When dismantled, they were found to contain multiple burials, two or three to each tomb, the bodies stacked on top of one another.

The completion of excavation was far from marking the end of the work. A huge backlog of recording and reparation remained to be got through and this was to occupy the Fund for four more costly seasons. During this period, under the supervision of Somers Clarke and Howard Carter, many hundreds of loose bricks and fragments were properly sorted with as many as possible reconstituted and rebuilt into the walls. To protect the decoration large sections of the temple were repaired and roofed over, and to prevent further falls from the cliffs the north and west retaining walls were rebuilt. The recording of the decoration proceeded slowly but surely. The method employed by Carter was that of making full-scale tracings against the wall, which were then reduced by means of a grid to a smaller scale, the reduction being carried out *in situ* as a constant check on accuracy. The finished drawings, which were produced in pencil or, more often, crayon, so as better to reproduce the subtle line of the original carving, were then collated again by Naville in front of the wall. By such painstaking means were the many thousands of metres of decorated wall surface gradually turned into a superb facsimile record, amounting to nearly 770 plates in the six splendid royal folio volumes of the final publication. This record of Hatshepsut's temple, the work of Carter and his assistants, Verney Carter, Percy Brown, Rosalind Paget, and Charles Sillem, over six long seasons in the field (1893–8), is acknowledged to be one of the greatest epigraphic contributions to the science of Egyptology and undoubtedly constitutes the Fund's major scholarly achievement at the site of Deir el-Bahri.

Well before the work at the queen's temple was brought to a conclusion, Naville had made plans to extend the excavation into the large expanse of terrain to its south. Already at the end of the season of 1897 he had made a sondage beyond the enclosure wall near the Hathor-shrine and discovered a number of tombs dating to the Eleventh Dynasty, from one of which came a curious wooden wheel. He was soon urging upon the Fund that it should apply for the concession to excavate the remainder of the site. The Committee agreed and, despite the fact that the area in question had been reserved for the Antiquities Service, Naville's application to de Morgan was successful. From want of funds, however, the work was deferred from year to year, until finally, in 1902, Naville forced the Committee's hand by threatening to give up his permit. The 'go-ahead' was then given for 1903, but even so it was understood that exploration was to be tentative and that if no immediate results were forthcoming the work would be discontinued. Again, the gods of Deir el-Bahri smiled upon Naville. Within a couple of weeks of the start of the work he had discovered the mortuary temple of King Nebhepetre Mentuhotpe, of the Eleventh Dynasty (about 2010 BC), founder of the Middle Kingdom, and the continuation of the project was assured. While the existence of another royal building on the spot had not been unsuspected – the excavations of Lord Dufferin in 1858/9 and the presence of loose architectural fragments and blocks had intimated as much – the size and nature of the construction that was eventually to emerge was totally unexpected.

In superficial appearance the area, before excavation, resembled that of the Hatshepsut temple before it was cleared, the entire site being covered by a great quantity of rubbish and debris. It was, however, far less churned over than the Hatshepsut area and the accumulation for much of its depth was entirely ancient, a fact which helps to explain why this excavation was to yield a far greater number of objects than the first. Another significant factor in this respect was the presence, as co-director, of H. R. H. Hall, a member of the staff of the British Museum. Being a 'museum man', Hall had a special interest in objects and with an eye to the future division of finds ensured that as large a quantity as possible of the antiquities uncovered were retained and recorded (with results clearly discernible in the 'object-count' of the final publication, when compared with that of the earlier Hatshepsut volumes). Others of the supervising team, which had a generally more competent look about it than those of earlier seasons, included E. R. Ayrton and C. T. Currelly, both of whom had previously worked with Petrie.

Work started on 5 November 1903 in the area, where Naville had previously left off, immediately to the south of the Hatshepsut temple. Progress was rapid. By December the north-east corner of the new temple together with the sandstone pillars inscribed with the king's name in the lower colonnade had been cleared. The men, we are told, were greatly inspired by the discovery and worked as never before: 'The *towaris* plied their *turyas* (hoes) with a will, the basket-boys flew, and the rubbish disappeared like magic.' So, unfortunately, did a section of the camphouse. An avalanche, caused by the dislodging of a large stone from the rubbish,

23 The passage to the burial-chamber of Mentuhotpe II in his mortuary temple.

undermined the foundations of the nearby building with the result that Naville's kitchen collapsed into a tomb-pit 'with cook, utensils, and stove'. Amusing as the incident now seems, at the time it was a very serious matter, which jeopardised the entire season's work. Madame Naville, who took a great pride in her cuisine, for which she was famous, was greatly put out by the loss of her kitchen. Showing a proper sense of priorities, she insisted that the excavation be discontinued immediately and that Naville return with her to Switzerland. There can be no doubt as to who 'wore the trousers' in the Naville household (a tradition of female dominance that persists to the present day in many Egyptological camp-houses). She could not be resisted and close-down was imminent when help came from an unlikely quarter, from one of Naville's 'arch-enemies' (Petrie was not the only one), Kurt Sethe of the University of Berlin, who was living nearby in the 'German' house. The two men had not been on speaking terms for some time because of a scholarly dispute carried on between them in print concerning events in the reign of Queen Hatshepsut. The story is well known of how Sethe, learning of the calamity, magnanimously invited the Navilles to stay with him – on condition that Hatshepsut's name was not mentioned. The invitation was accepted and for several weeks the two scholars enjoyed each other's company and conversation without a hint of acrimony. Alas, the reconciliation was short-lived. When their kitchen had been repaired, the Navilles returned to their camp-house, and at once the feud with Sethe was resumed.

The crisis of the kitchen overcome, the work proceeded without further interruption. By the end of the second season (1904/5) the area of the temple platform and the courts on the north, south and east had been cleared. All was in terrible ruin, for the temple had been systematically destroyed, after falling into disuse, in the Twenty-first Dynasty. Its plan, however, was plain and showed beyond doubt, what was probably the most generally important point to emerge from the excavation, that in its basic features – raised platform, central ramp, flanking colonnades – this Eleventh Dynasty temple (2010 BC) had provided the inspiration for the terraced design of its larger Eighteenth Dynasty neighbour (1490 BC). The platform itself was formed of natural rock artificially squared and levelled, and then lined with limestone blocks. It was approached by a ramp in the middle of its eastern side and this was flanked by colonnades on the lower level. At this same level, on the north and south of the platform, were open courts.

The most striking feature of the building, nowhere repeated in Hatshepsut's temple, was a *mastaba*-like structure, which occupied the central section of the platform and was believed by Naville to be a pedestal for a pyramid (a view now disputed). Made of a mass of rubble with an outer revetment of heavy flint boulders, and faced originally with fine limestone blocks, it measured 18.3 m square by 3 m high. Around it was a colonnade or ambulatory closed in by a wall, and between this and the outer edge of the platform another colonnade. As in the Hatshepsut temple, the halls and colonnades had once been decorated with painted reliefs, but only a single scene, a procession of boats in the lower colonnade, remained in place. The others had been reduced to fragments, many thousands in number, deliberately smashed when the temple was broken up. A variety of scenes could be recognised among them – hunting, warfare, boat-building, cattle-counting, as well as several portraits and figures of the king involved in various ceremonies. The building had served not only as a temple (to the gods Amun and Montu, and the dead king) but also as a place of burial. Within the west wall of the ambulatory were located six finely decorated chapels belonging to ladies of the king's harem, their shaft-tombs sunk in the rock behind them (two of them missed by Naville, to be found later by Winlock). Three other such tombs had been sunk in the northern upper colonnade.

The finds were spectacular in quantity and quality, and the British Museum, among others, owes some of its finest pieces to the work of these two seasons. An important body of sculpture included a painted limestone head of Mentuhotpe, a limestone Osiride figure of Amenophis I, a painted limestone statue of the vizier of Ramesses II, Paser, a beautiful alabaster head of a cow, and a number of black granite statues of Sesostris III, one of which is considered to be a masterpiece of Egyptian art. From the tomb of one of the royal ladies, named Kauit, came a magnificent limestone sarcophagus decorated in sunk relief with inscriptions and scenes from daily life. It was not monolithic but made of several sections which had been lowered separately and put together in the tomb. It was dismantled and removed in the same way and transported to the Cairo Museum, where it stands out even in that rich collection. Sadly in fragments was another sarcophagus, even more beautiful, belonging to the lady Kemsit, which came to the British Museum, as did a group of funerary objects of the same lady. In addition to the sculpture and tomb furniture, a huge quantity of small antiquities – *ex votos* of the devotees of Hathor – was recovered from the northern court, where it had been cast out as refuse from the Hathor-shrine of the Eighteenth Dynasty temple. The same area had been used many centuries later as a rubbish dump by the monks of the Coptic monastery, and among their 'throw-outs' were inscribed ostraca and a reused canopic jar bearing a fine little drawing of an angel.

In the midst of all these discoveries the exact location of the king's tomb remained for quite some time a mystery. Naville was convinced that the central building of the platform had served as the base for a pyramid and that this was none other than the 'pyramid-tomb' of Nebhepetre, which, as recorded in the famous Abbott Papyrus, had been inspected and found intact in the Twentieth Dynasty. When soundings in the centre and corners of the pedestal revealed nothing, he concluded that the burial-chamber was either at a great depth below or, more probably, sunk in the rock beneath the west end of the temple. This latter anticipation looked to be fully justified when, at the very end of the second season, in the centre of the west court was revealed the entrance to a wide sloping passage which disappeared beneath the rock in a westward direction. There was good reason to think that this was the entrance to the king's tomb, but Naville was properly cautious: 'Will it lead to a royal tomb . . . or will it end abruptly, unfinished, perhaps, at the foot of the cliffs?'

A little over a month's work at the beginning of the third season (1905/6) provided the answer. At the end of the passage, which turned out to be 152 m long, was a chamber lined with granite and occupied by a large alabaster shrine. Inevitably, with the entrance being in such a prominent place, the contents had suffered the same fate as the temple's superstructure. The floor of the chamber was covered by a thick carpet of debris containing fragments of all manner of tomb furniture – models of

24 (*Right*) The
Eighteenth Dynasty
Hathor-cow
shrine as found
(Cairo Museum,
no. 38574-5).

25 (*Below*) Removing
the figure of the
Hathor-cow, with
Ayrton supervising.

granaries and boats, servant statuettes, tools and weapons, shreds of linen, and the head of a canopic jar. Although no coffin as such was found, all the evidence pointed to this having been the burial-chamber of King Nebhepetre Mentuhotpe. But, curiously, Naville would have none of it. For him it was a 'subterranean sanctuary, the place where the *ka* of the King was worshipped'. The burial-chamber was somewhere else 'in the neighbourhood or some distance off'. If so, it remains undiscovered to this day.

Apart from the dromos and burial-chamber, the major discovery in the western end of the temple was the Hathor-shrine to the north of the west court (now known to be an adjunct of the then-undiscovered temple of Tuthmosis III). The unexpected revealing of the shrine is vividly recorded by the American artist Joseph Lindon Smith:

> I visited Naville, who was working at the temple of Deir-el-Bahari, and who, in the vicinity of his camp, was also doing a clearing job on a great hill of ancient debris. One morning I found him warning his head *reis* not to continue digging at this spot for fear that a loosened boulder would cause the whole mass to fall like an avalanche. I started away and a moment later heard the tremendous roar of Naville's expected avalanche. I turned and was enveloped in clouds of dust. As the dust settled, I saw Naville and the *reis*, both uninjured, gazing at an opening in this hill of rubbish. And on the exact spot where Naville had given the warning to cease digging was the opening into a shrine with a vaulted roof. At the entrance was a life-sized stone statue of the Goddess Hathor, represented as a cow, in perfect condition, standing on a stone platform and led by a man. Hathor wore the customary disk and tall horns, and at either side of the headdress were lotus blossoms extending from the neck to the feet. In later years, whenever I looked at this treasure in the Cairo Museum, I recalled Naville's expression of stunned amazement at his first sight of this enshrined Hathor cow.

The 'magnificent cow', as Naville called it, caused a great stir of excitement throughout the camp. A message was at once dispatched to Cairo, and soldiers were sent to guard it. It is reported that before they arrived 'Mr. Currelly kindly sat up all night with the cow to protect her from harm'.

The cow was a veritable *dea ex machina*. Only a few days before, Naville had received a telegraph which had plunged him and the team into despair. It informed him that owing to the Fund's parlous financial condition it would not be possible to continue the excavations in the following season, and requested him to leave the site in such a condition that work could be continued there at some future date, either by the Fund or by the Egyptian Government. However, the news of the holy cow, miraculously preserved in the midst of destruction, attracted a large number of visitors, amongst whom was a wealthy American, W. F. Laffan. So impressed was he by what he saw that on hearing of the prospective closure of the work he promptly offered to finance it to the tune of £1,000 (in those days a very large sum of money), on the sole condition that the *pro rata* share of the division represented by his donation should go to the Metropolitan Museum, New York. The offer was readily accepted by the Fund, and Naville was thus enabled to complete one more season (1906/7), during which he finished the clearance of the western end of the temple, consisting of the hypostyle hall and beyond it the small sanctuary cut in the rock, initially explored by Lord Dufferin nearly fifty years before. As it turned out, the finds of the season were largely architectural, the haul of antiquities being in no way comparable to that of earlier years, but in recognition of Laffan's act of generosity, the Fund allowed the limestone sarcophagus of the lady Henhenet, discovered in the second season, and provisionally earmarked for the British Museum, to go to New York.

Since the temple and its decoration were so badly destroyed, there was no possibility of large-scale restoration or recording of the kind carried out in the queen's temple (although a notable contribution in the circumstances was the work of reconstruction and coloured drawing, done by Madame Naville, of the royal shrines and sarcophagi). With the clearance finished, the site was handed back to the Antiquities Service in spring 1907. Of the fourth and last season Naville wrote: 'This has been the last campaign, and there will be no more at Deir el-Bahri, since we may now say that Deir el-Bahri is finished.' Time has told how mistaken he was in this conclusion. Deir el-Bahri had a great deal more to offer, as the explorations of the Metropolitan Museum (1911–31) and the German and Polish expeditions of more recent years have shown. Nevertheless, the Fund had every reason to feel at this juncture that they had given and got good value during their fourteen-year occupancy of the site and that the time was now opportune to move on. It had been the most ambitious and expensive programme of work they had ever attempted, driving them, with all their other obligations, to the point of insolvency on more than one occasion. But their commitment, and Naville's persistence, had been well rewarded, producing results of fundamental importance to knowledge of the art, the architecture, the history, and the religious and funerary practices of the ancient Egyptians. For these reasons, Naville's shortcomings as an excavator notwithstanding, the work at Deir el-Bahri will always rank as one of the Fund's pre-eminent achievements in the field.

In addition to the work at Deir el-Bahri, there were several smaller projects mainly of an epigraphic nature with which the Fund were involved at Thebes, the fruits of which were published in one or other of the Fund's series. The first of these was undertaken by Norman de Garis Davies, whose work for the Archaeological Survey is described in Chapter 8. Since 1907 Davies had been employed by the Metropolitan Museum of Art, New York, to collect from the Theban tombs a body of records 'which would serve as a ground for study and investigation and when given to the world through publications be a contribution to our knowledge of the art and life of ancient Egypt'. The first major objective of this project was the well-known painted tomb of Nakht at Qurna, which took several seasons to complete (1907–11). During this period Davies, who lived in a house among the tombs with his wife Nina, a talented artist in her own right, busied himself with work in as many other tombs as his official duties would allow. In his own words: 'Set in the midst of paintings threatened with disaster or calling loudly for speedy publication, I gradually found myself also with a certain amount of material on hand, the fruit of leisure hours.'

The result of these 'erratic enterprises', as Davies modestly termed them, was the complete recording of five tombs, four of the Eighteenth Dynasty and one of the Eleventh, all in a damaged and dilapidated state. Two among them may be specially mentioned, namely that of the vizier Dega, who had served under the very King Mentuhotpe whose temple had been the object of the Fund's last campaign at Deir el-Bahri, and that of Mentuherkhepshef of the reign of Tuthmosis III, which is remarkable for its unusual scenes of funerary ritual. Sections of the latter had been copied and published by the great French scholar Maspero some years before. Comparison of Davies's work with this earlier effort shows clearly the standard of excellence to which he had now brought the art of accurate epigraphy. Davies donated the material to the Fund's Archaeological Survey, an arrangement which suited both parties well. For Davies it ensured the means for the 'speedy publication' he had desired, while the Fund, who were hard-pressed at the time to find enough publications to fulfil their obligations, obtained another memoir 'ready-made', as it were, to deliver to their subscribers. It appeared under the title *Five Theban Tombs* in 1913.

The recording work of Norman and Nina Davies did not take place in isolation but was part of a large concerted effort, begun in the early 1900s, to conserve the Theban necropolis. Initiated by Howard Carter, after he had left the service of the Fund to become Inspector-General of Antiquities for Upper Egypt, the process had been carried on energetically by his successor, Arthur Weigall, who enjoyed the co-operation of Robert Mond and Alan Gardiner. By their efforts order gradually emerged out of what previously had been 'dust and ruin'. Scores of tombs which had lain open and neglected were cleared and identified, and measures were taken for their restoration and protection. By 1913 over 250 private tombs had been numbered and catalogued, enabling for the first time a considered view to be taken of the nature and state of the necropolis and a proper assessment to be made of the priorities for work. As a direct result Gardiner instituted a series of monographs on specially selected tombs, to be produced under the auspices of the Egypt Exploration Fund. He enlisted the aid of Nina and Norman Davies, who despite their heavy commitments were always ready to extend their recording activities.

Under the general title *The Theban Tomb Series*, five memoirs were ultimately produced between 1915 and 1933, containing a full record of nine tombs, one of the Twelfth Dynasty – the highly important tomb of Antefoker, the vizier of Sesostris I – and the remainder of the Eighteenth Dynasty, the most significant of these being the tombs of Amenemhet and Menkheperresoneb of the reign of Tuthmosis III and the tomb of Huy, the viceroy of Nubia in the reign of Tutankhamun. Nina Davies was responsible for most of the line-plates and for all of the several coloured copies, a technique of reproduction at which she excelled, Gardiner for the descriptive texts, the translations of the inscriptions and the general editorship, 'not to mention the cost of the whole enterprise', as he was at pains to point out. The choice of tombs was judicious and the final treatment masterly, a happy marriage of Egyptological knowledge and artistic skills.

The contribution of Gardiner to the preservation and recording of the private tombs at Thebes was immense, but it was equalled, if not surpassed, by that of another wealthy Englishman, Robert Mond, a member of the Committee of the Egypt Exploration Fund since 1906 and a future President of the Society (1928–38). The great success of Weigall's campaign to identify and protect the tombs was largely due to the 'enlightened liberality' of Mond, who made funds and personnel available

26 Reconstructed relief in the tomb of Ramose. Eighteenth Dynasty.

for the work, and financed the publication of the catalogue of the tombs prepared by Gardiner and Weigall. As well as unselfishly supporting the work of others, Mond worked his own concession – reopening, clearing and restoring a large number of tombs at Qurna. The most notable of these was that of Ramose, the vizier of Amenophis III and Amenophis IV, one of the most celebrated and handsomely decorated tombs on the west bank. Undertaken under the aegis of the University of Liverpool, the work on the tomb was directed for Mond by W. B. Emery and took three full seasons (1924–6) to complete, a large and complicated task, involving the restoration of fragmentary reliefs and the reconstruction of columns and other architectural features. For Mond the great expense entailed was more than justified: 'Only those who have seen the delicacy of the bas-reliefs . . . can realize the satisfaction I have derived from this task, a satisfaction which surpasses any which can be obtained by the personal possession of some of the world's master-pieces.'

Provision was made for the tomb to be published by Emery and T. E. Peet, but when this plan fell through, owing to the latter's premature death and the former's increasingly heavy commitments in other directions, the task devolved upon the ever-reliable Norman Davies, who was able to make use of preliminary matter prepared by Emery, including his excellent plans. In order to hasten the already-delayed project, Davies did not on this occasion adopt his favoured method of copying, which was to take full-scale tracings, but used a quicker technique, that of drawing from enlarged photographs, working, however, always in front of the original so as to ensure accuracy. His line-copies, which form the bulk of the record, were supplemented by a number of remarkable colour reproductions by Nina and a series of very fine photographs taken by Harry Burton of the Metropolitan Museum. The resultant volume, *The Tomb of Ramose*, which appeared in 1941, is the most sumptuous publication of a single tomb ever produced under the Society's name. It was a cruel blow of fate that Mond should die before its appearance, and thus be deprived of seeing what he would have undoubtedly regarded as the crowning glory of his Theban work. In memory of her husband, Lady Mond undertook the full financing of the publication, as she did also of a second volume, *Seven Tombs at Qurneh* (1948) by the same author, which records the more important of the other Theban tombs which had lain in Mond's concession. Published as 'Mond Excavations at Thebes', these splendid volumes form a fitting tribute to the vision and generosity of a man who regarded his wealth 'as a trust to be used in the advancement of knowledge' and was one of the greatest benefactors not only of the Egypt Exploration Society but of British Egyptology as a whole.

4 Abydos

B. J. KEMP

[March 1899.] On the eve of my departure from Abydos, I made a last visit to the necropolis of El-ʿAmrah: on the way, in the village of El-Khâdrah, after having passed the temple of Seti I, I met a small caravan, composed of two donkeys: on the first of these docile animals, a lady was mounted and near her walked, with naked feet in Turkish slippers, a man with unkempt beard, of very brown complexion, whom I took for a Greek *mercanti*; a servant rode the second donkey and followed the travelling couple. I attached no importance to this encounter, for I was far from suspecting that the travellers whom I had just met and whose tent I saw set up further on, opposite the site that I had explored that very year, were no other than M. and Mᵐᵉ Flinders Petrie. That evening, when I learnt that the two persons whom I had encountered in the morning and whom I had found lunching in the temple of Ramses II, at the time of my return from El-ʿAmrah, answered to this well-known name, I was at first surprised at not having recognised M. Petrie whom I had seen on two occasions, the first at Luxor, the second time in London – I believed him then to be occupied beside Dendereh – surprised also that he had not recognised me, and I wrote him a letter wherein I complained in a friendly way that he had not forewarned me and that he had thus deprived me of the pleasure that I would have had in inviting him to dinner and showing him my work. He replied to me that he had not been able to forewarn me because he was making an excursion to visit all the localities on the left bank where there were Egyptian tombs. I thought no more of this incident. Unforeseen circumstances hindered me in returning to Egypt and I was thinking in the month of March 1900 of requesting the extension of the duration of my concession, when I learnt by accident, from the reading of an article by M. Maspero and from a scholar who had himself returned from Egypt, that M. Petrie had worked all winter at Abydos, at Om el-Qaʾab, precisely at the place of my excavations of the three first campaigns.

Thus began the Society's fruitful and long-standing connection with Abydos. The writer of this picturesque description of Petrie's prospecting visit to the site in March 1899 was a French Coptic scholar and would-be archaeologist, Émile Amélineau (*Les nouvelles fouilles d'Abydos*, seconde campagne 1896–7 (Paris, 1902), p.II). Since he possessed the official permit for excavation at Abydos and had already put in three seasons there, his tone of hurt surprise is understandable. But however ethically dubious Petrie's move in taking over the concession may have been, subsequent generations seem unanimously to have endorsed it. In place of a verbose and unfocused antiquarianism Petrie brought to excavation a business-like approach which almost immediately put into the hands of scholars and the public concise and clearly illustrated accounts of a well-thought-out excavation programme. It set the tone for a decade and a half of British excavation at Abydos, begun by Petrie and continued by others.

The site had initially attracted interest because ancient sources, both Egyptian and classical, had made Abydos an important centre of the cult of Osiris, god of the dead. The high point for Amélineau in his work at Abydos had been the discovery of the actual 'tomb' of Osiris (subsequently seen to be the tomb of a First Dynasty king); whilst from the activities of nineteenth-century dealers, collectors, looters and the work gangs of Auguste Mariette, Abydos had been revealed as a rewarding source of good antiquities. It was a valuable concession to be allowed to work.

This first phase of the Society's work at Abydos – from Petrie's first season to the outbreak of the First World War – came to be spread over four separate areas, each of which revealed a different aspect of the unusual history and archaeology of the site. The ex-Amélineau concession, the Umm el-Qa'ab, was to be the most spectacular in terms of discovery. On a low desert rise, two kilometres from the edge of the cultivation, and backed by the picturesque cliffs and sand drifts of the Libyan desert plateau, the kings of the First Dynasty (and two of the Second) had been buried. When Petrie began, knowledge of this period, which is now placed at the end of the fourth and the beginning of the third millennia BC, was insubstantial.

The tombs had the form of brick chambers built in fairly shallow pits. Around several of them clustered groups of small burial-chambers for the bodies of members of the king's household. Centuries later one of the tombs had been reidentified by enthusiastic priests as the tomb of Osiris and reconstructed, and this finally brought in throngs of pilgrims who had left behind votive pots, giving to the site its distinctive sherd-covered appearance and its modern name: Umm el-Qa'ab, 'mother of pots'. This subsequent piety, together with robbery in ancient and probably medieval times, and the exercises of Amélineau, had left the site in a sad and confused condition. Petrie turned it into a vindication of the value of systematic collection and study of small fragments, even from the dumps of one's predecessors. His two rapidly published volumes provided a succinct account of the architecture of the tombs, revealed the stylistic essence of Early Dynastic material culture largely from fragmentary evidence, and gave to the names of kings from Manetho's first two dynasties a reign-by-reign identity in archaeological terms. Here, one could say, was the very tomb of King Djer, the second king of the First Dynasty; on this plate one could see the jewellery worn by him or by one of his court. And not only jewellery: stone vessel shapes, mud-brick sizes, scratched marks on pottery, anything of possible cultural value was included. The civilisation of Egypt's formative period lay revealed from work of a purely archaeological nature.

Archaeological sites are difficult to exhaust completely. The possibility remained that Petrie had not found all. Encouraged by this, one of the Society's later directors at Abydos, E. Naville, returned to the Umm el-Qa'ab in 1908. But widespread trenching produced remarkably little, except a boost to Petrie's reputation for thoroughness. The vision of an undiscovered tomb has remained chimerical. In 1977 an expedition of the German Archaeological Institute in Cairo made a fresh start there. But the expressed purpose this time was a more thorough study of the architecture.

27 Professor and Mrs. Flinders Petrie at Abydos in 1900.

The modern tourist to Abydos is generally taken to see just the temples of Kings Sethos I and Ramesses II of the Nineteenth Dynasty (about 1309–1224 BC). But these are only peripheral to the real heart of Abydos, which lies about one kilometre further along the edge of the fields to the north-east. This site of the ancient town is now one of picturesque ruin and confusion. Much of the accumulated layers of rubbish and houses which had come to form a substantial mound have long ago been quarried away and taken by local farmers to spread on their fields as a fertiliser; likewise the stonework has been plundered in times past for lime burning. Mariette had, in the nineteenth century, looked for the tomb of Osiris here; Amélineau had eschewed it. Petrie tackled it in two seasons, 1902 and 1903.

Any stratified town site of long occupation presents a daunting excavation prospect. When much of it has been long indurated by ground water, even the basic job of distinguishing and separating mud-brick walls from the surrounding earth becomes a major problem, as Petrie noted in his report. Petrie's procedure was to plan the structures as his workmen exposed them, and to measure frequent spot heights on both walls and on the locations of small finds. From this information a series of nine plans was prepared, showing features at more or less the same level, which were supposed to represent the condition of the site at succeeding periods. He also took frequent measurements of brick sizes, and attempted to tabulate how the sizes varied over time. It was not, however, part of his method to draw sections. Although his procedure reflected the fundamental relationship between age and depth, it also glossed over local but crucial irregularities: in particular, it ignored the effect of foundation trenches for walls, which tend to make the base of a wall level with adjacent artefacts of an earlier period. Nevertheless, the amount of data he recorded, some of it remaining unpublished in notebooks, provides a sufficient base for some reassessment and reinterpretation of his results.

He concentrated his work towards the low-lying centre of the site. This proved to be where the main temple to Osiris had stood, and before that the shrine to the predecessor of Osiris at Abydos, the funerary god Khenty-amentiu. To the normal problems of excavation were added some specific to this type of site. For the arch-aeology of temple sites tends to be complicated by the fact that when a major rebuild-ing or enlargement was decreed the builders were inclined to dig out deep foundations, cutting into earlier strata in order to place the new masonry as far as possible on fresh ground, often created by spreading sand in the cutting. At Abydos the topmost level seems to have belonged to a shrine or shrines of the New Kingdom and Late Period, smaller in scale than one might have expected. Beneath this Petrie distinguished elements from a Middle Kingdom temple, but it is likely that some of this was simply part of the New Kingdom foundations. These layers of stonework all rested on part of an imposing late Old Kingdom brick enclosure, consisting of a double wall with stone-lined portal, storerooms of various kinds, and the late Old Kingdom temple itself.

This was a brick building of a modesty which has since become familiar from other early sites. In and around it were found many votive objects and pieces of temple equipment, together with inscriptions concerned with the administration of the temple. The votive objects included a range of faience and ivory figurines which

28 (*Top*) Excavating the First Dynasty tomb of King Den.

29 (*Bottom*) Excavating in Cemetery F, 1909.

exemplify both craftsmanship in materials which tend not to occur in cemeteries, and a stratum of popular religious belief and practice separate from the realm of formal religious texts. A few of the pieces were outstanding historically and artistically, two in particular. One is an ivory statuette of a king in festival robe often ascribed to the Early Dynastic Period; the other is a seated statuette of King Khufu (Cheops), builder of the Great Pyramid, a masterpiece of miniature art only 7.3 cm high. Petrie recorded (*Abydos* II (1903), p.30): 'The head was broken from the body by the accident of digging, and was lost in the earth, where it was only recovered by three weeks of incessant sifting.'

Finding the late Old Kingdom temple was a major discovery, the significance of which can be better appreciated today. Petrie's report, despite remaining ambiguities, presents this crucial level of the site with a fair measure of detail and intelligibility.

Both in this area and, by means of trenches, in surrounding parts of the ancient town Petrie continued digging down to the underlying desert sand. The physical condition of the site prevented any serious record being made of the houses and other buildings of these lowest levels, so we have no plans to tell us how the first town of Abydos looked. But, as an important compensation, Petrie drew large numbers of pots and other artefacts, and noted their heights above basal sand. He thus provided an outline stratigraphy. If we extract from his plates of drawings the material from the very lowest levels, we have the evidence which should tell us when the town first reached a respectable size. This seems to have been during the transition from the end of the Predynastic Period to the early part of the First Dynasty. With the exception of limited and somewhat ambiguous information from Hierakonpolis, excavated only a few years before, this remains a unique published record in the realms of settlement archaeology in Egypt, a piece of pioneering work which sadly produced little follow-up.

For Abydos it is also a record which is going to be difficult to improve upon, as Petrie pointed out (*Abydos* II, p.1):

> Happily the very exceptionally low Nile of last summer gave us the best opportunity that we could ever hope to gain. When I went out in November, just after the inundation, the water in our pits was even lower than when I had left it in April, instead of being several feet higher as is usually the case. I was thus able to begin a season with better conditions than are generally obtained at the dry end of the season; and the water continued to recede as the year advanced. No better chance could be ever hoped for, and whatever was possible to be done without enormous pumping works was completely in our power. We made use of the chance by clearing as much of the site as we could deal with, down to below this exceptional water level, and no one will ever see more without such pumping as is never likely to be attempted.

Prophetic words. The constantly high water-table created by modern irrigation works has subsequently made the problem much worse than in Petrie's day. But there is still much to be done on the site. Petrie largely ignored the irregular strip of banked-up debris, the Kom es-Sultan, which is all that survives of the upper part of the ancient town mound. This has in recent years become one focus of attention for the Pennsylvania-Yale expedition to Abydos, which currently holds the concession for the town and temple area.

Mud and water were not the only hazards which Petrie faced. 'One stormy night a man carried off a statue of over a hundredweight from our courtyard. I tracked him and made drawings of his feet from various impressions, as the toes were peculiar. I got a local man to tell tales which led to identifying the thief. He was arrested; at the police court his feet exactly tallied to my outline.' Petrie, it should be noted, was friendly with Baden-Powell. 'Another time a man came in the dark and shot at close range at the first person who came out of our mess-hut, which was my wife. Happily she escaped.' (*Seventy years in Archaeology*, p.185.)

The desert lying behind the town, and extending south-eastwards almost to the temple of Ramesses II, is for the most part one huge cemetery. This is apparent to anyone who walks across its pitted and undulating surface from fragments of whitened human bone and shreds of mummy wrappings. Local conditions seem to encourage the winds which sweep the desert in spring and early summer to deposit sand rather than to use it to scour away any standing brickwork. As a result, the mud-brick chapels which were built above ancient tombs seem to have survived in unusually large numbers, as have the limestone memorial tablets placed within them.

The history of exploration within the cemetery is, however, a tragic one. During the nineteenth century, over extensive areas, the teams of looters and the gangs of Mariette's labourers working in the surface sand creamed off most of the inscriptions. The underground burial deposits which belonged with them were either looted as well, or were left for the early archaeological missions to find. Thus a unique opportunity for relating objects to details of the people who had originally owned them was lost. Certain areas on the fringes of the cemetery escaped, but on the whole these areas were worked by British expeditions not financed by the Society, and their published record is very poor. The greatly confused condition of the ground and the problem of coping with the amount of drift sand, often piled high by previous diggers, discouraged methodical clearance or detailed mapping. The Society's cemetery work at Abydos, which began with Petrie and continued for some years after his departure, thus appears somewhat fragmentary and disjointed. Certain areas are, indeed, difficult to locate on the ground at all.

The results of the cemetery work were published according to the priorities widely accepted in Egypt at that time and for a good while later. The principal procedure was to illustrate the material culture of the different periods by selecting well-preserved tomb groups, and distinctive and characteristic individual objects. In this way changes in pottery and beads and small statuary could be followed over the dynasties. Viewing a cemetery simply as an archaeological site to be methodically cleared with total recording and publication of finds in whatever conditions they were found is an alternative which has remained alien to archaeology in Egypt. The material found covered every period of Egyptian history, and, indeed, the cemetery is still used by a Coptic village. Over 5,000 years of burial have produced a dense mixture of material from different periods. The earliest graves found dated to the two main phases of the Predynastic Period, thus to before about 3200 BC, and here there was also a bonus in the form of settlement remains. These evidently belonged to a period before the town had been founded, when a small population lived in tiny scattered villages. The main village site was excavated with considerable care, and the publication included a preliminary classification of the flint industry. Beside it, and also on another part of the site, well-preserved grain-parching kilns were found, which added an interesting dimension to our limited knowledge of predynastic domestic economy.

This excavation was the work of T. E. Peet whose early archaeological training outside Egypt is apparent through much of the three volumes of excavation report for which he was partly or largely responsible. The first two volumes also bear witness to the fact that his more objective approach to archaeology had brought him into conflict with his co-director at Abydos, E. Naville, who had a picturesque alternative explanation to offer for the finds which Peet, along with many others, accepted as prehistoric. This division evidently ran very deep. Alan Gardiner explained in his obituary of Peet (*Journal of Egyptian Archaeology* 20 (1934), pp. 68–9): 'Peet came equipped with the experience and standards of classical archaeology, and the less rigorous methods to which he had to conform could not fail to gall him. Nor could he approve of the re-excavation of the early dynastic Royal Tombs at Umm el-Ga'âb, an undertaking which in fact proved singularly sterile. In course of time it was arranged that his work should be more or less independent of Naville's.' A dour, sceptical man, Peet stood in sharp contrast to Naville, a grand but ageing figure, deeply conservative in religion and politics, and used to a more heroic strategy of attack on sites of antiquity. The two lived at Abydos in separate dig houses, parted by a low hill.

Three further discoveries in the cemeteries deserve separate mention. One was a small version of the catacombs for mummified animals made famous through Emery's later discoveries at Saqqara. This one was for dogs, and lay adjacent to a large well cut through the desert gravels and within its own enclosure. The second concerned the context of the feature which dominates the northern part of the cemetery, a rectangular enclosure of mud brick, measuring 123 m by 64.50 m, and still reaching a height of 11 m in some places. Its modern name is Shunet ez-Zebib. Throughout almost the entire time that the cemeteries had been in use its bulky oblong shape spread itself across the centre of the cemetery plateau. In its silence, age – it dates to the end of the Second Dynasty, about 2700 BC – and impressive size it is now a ruin of considerable visual and imaginative impact. The Society's excavations provided the first evidence that it was not originally as isolated as it appears now, but that it was one of a group of related buildings of this early date. Petrie completed the clearance of the area in 1921–2 for the British School of Archaeology in Egypt. The joint results seem to show that each of the kings buried on the Umm el-Qa'ab was at the same time commemorated by a monumental enclosure, of which the Shunet ez-Zebib was the last and largest, and that to begin with the stretch of desert behind the town was an appendage of the royal cemetery.

Ancient texts make the cemetery the site of some of the religious processions which formed part of the re-enactment of the death and resurrection of Osiris. Another of the Society's discoveries was of a remarkable document concerned with the effect that this had on the proper use of the cemetery. It appears that the central valley

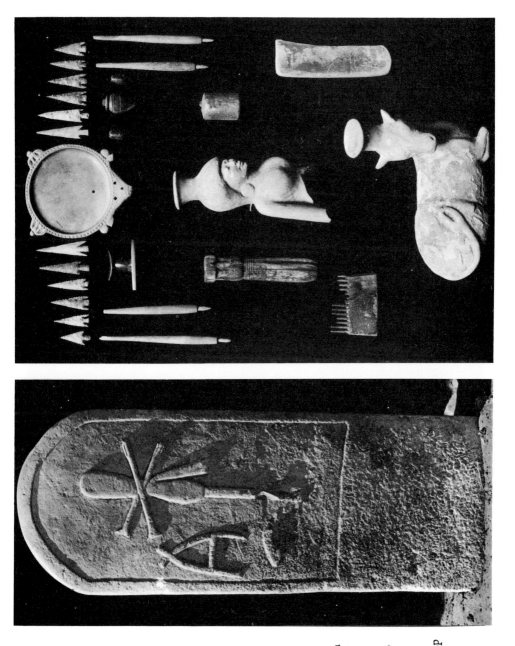

30 (*Right*) The stela
of Meretneith
from the First
Dynasty royal
cemetery (Cairo
Museum,
no. 34550).

31 (*Far right*) Group
of objects from
grave D.29.
Eighteenth
Dynasty.

which divides the cemetery into two parts had been set aside for the processional route, and that its sanctity required that it be kept free of burials. A decree was therefore enacted forbidding burial in this part, and laying heavy penalties on people who transgressed it. Copies of this pronouncement, on granite slabs, were erected at various points around the cemetery, and one of these, which had itself become the focus of offerings as a sacred object in its own right, was found in 1899–1900 by one of the Society's teams at a distant point in the North Cemetery, to the south-west of the Shunet ez-Zebib.

By 1913 the organised cemetery excavations of the Society were virtually at an end, although a few graves were dug during the 1920s. On looking at the area today it is hard to find a single part which has been left undug by someone in the past. The sand and confusion which hampered methodical work early in the century are still everywhere, and would represent a heavy expenditure for any renewal of the work. Nevertheless, excavation at selected points can still prove profitable. The Pennsylvania-Yale expedition, working where the cemetery begins to merge with the town site, a part where the Society's directors did not venture, has made a discovery in recent years which adds a further chapter to the archaeology of Abydos: an area of Middle Kingdom cenotaphs built evidently by men who wished to be commemorated at Abydos, but buried elsewhere, presumably near their home towns.

The wish to be represented at Abydos by a memorial of some kind was held by kings as well as by commoners. This led to the fourth area of the Society's early work, at Abydos South. The results remain as enigmatic as when they first appeared.

Behind the town and the cemeteries the desert continues to run back to a curving line of cliffs, which approach the edge of the valley and then turn to run parallel with it at a distance of about three kilometres from the ancient town site. Just beyond the turn, the site of Abydos South commences. The part that is the easiest to understand is the most distant. By the edge of the desert a small pyramid had been built, and on a line running back from it to the cliffs were three other structures: one of uncertain shape and purpose built on terraces at the foot of the cliff, a winding underground rock tomb, and a square brick chapel. This last was found to contain a handsome limestone stela, now in the Cairo Museum, bearing a decree issued by King Amosis, first king of the Eighteenth Dynasty (about 1570 BC) in favour of his grandmother, Queen Teti-sheri. Its purpose was to provide her with a chapel at Abydos in addition to a tomb at Thebes. This inscription, together with a certain amount of other local evidence, served to date the whole group of structures and to point to their purpose: they were to provide for King Amosis a memorial at Abydos in the form of a complete tomb-complex which would remain, however, only symbolic – a cenotaph to complement his tomb at western Thebes.

At the nearer end of the site a second alinement of buildings was discovered: by the edge of fields the foundations of a rectangular temple, and beneath the cliffs another underground tomb, but more elaborate than that of King Amosis. This was located within a large T-shaped enclosure, beside which were several large and empty *mastaba*-tombs. Most parts had been reduced anciently to their very foundations, and even their date is not quite clear, although it must almost certainly belong within the Middle Kingdom. Part of a statue of Sesostris III found at the temple provided the

32 (*Right*) The 'Shunet ez-Zebib', a building connected with the mortuary cult of King Peribsen. Second Dynasty.

33 (*Below*) Ptolemaic burial, as found in tomb E.422 (cartonnage in The Brooklyn Museum, no. 12.911.2).

only positive evidence.

These excavations involving arduous, large-scale clearances for which rewards were fairly limited were graphically described by Canon H. D. Rawnsley and N. Rawnsley, who had visited Abydos during the work (*The Resurrection of oldest Egypt* (1904), pp. 33–4):

> For on the sloping ground . . . huge tips of sand and rubbish run out towards the plain. In the heart of them is a great devil's punch-bowl, a hollow whose sides are slopes of treacherous sand, with a single winding path, up which long lines of native boys pass the palm-leaf baskets filled with rubbish. Deep, deep down in this hollow one sees the dark opening of a rock shaft leading to the tomb passage a quarter of a mile into the heart of the cliffs, where gangs of naked men toil and pant and sweat in the thick, hot air . . . Our friend admits that it is somewhat trying to work by candle light in a deep rock tomb. The ground temperature, to begin with, is 80 degrees Fahrenheit. You have to overturn gigantic paving stones and work the pick and crowbar in places that never admit of an upright posture, and the only ventilation is the almost imperceptible drift of hot air out along the roof and cool air in between the feet . . .

Two seasons of work (1901–2) were expended on the site, each time with only a single archaeologist involved, first A. E. P. Weigall and then C. T. Currelly, and it was never finished, as the published report explained (*Abydos* III (1904), p. 20): 'About a quarter of a mile to the south of the cemetery, excavations were made upon a sandy hollow which appeared to be another great tomb. A large pit, as big as that of the great tomb in the *hôsh* (enclosure), was emptied, but when brick construction was reached near the bottom, it was decided to leave the work until the next season, as it was evident that another great rock building was about to be disclosed which would perhaps require several months to clear.' But nothing further was ever done. The sanded-up hollow in the desert lies there still.

The Petrie tradition of quick and staccato publication saw reports of most of the Society's town and cemetery excavations in print by 1914. Two other major projects yet remained for the 1920s and 30s, however. Both involved a change of style and tempo, and centred on the most remarkable monument at Abydos: the temple of King Sethos I (about 1300 BC).

Sethos' temple stood within its own enclosure surrounded by an imposing mud-brick wall. Also within the enclosure were storerooms and, on the north-east side, elements still deeply buried beneath the modern village. The rear part was given over to a remarkable underground building discovered by Petrie in the winter of 1901–2, and dubbed by him the Osireion. As finally uncovered, it consists of a pit cut in the desert, into which was built a hall of massive blocks of limestone and sandstone, roofed with granite slabs supported on squat monolithic granite pillars. The centre of the hall had the form of an island, and was surrounded by a very deep channel kept filled with water from an underground conduit discovered later, in the 1940s, by the Egyptian Antiquities Department. Behind the hall lies a transverse chamber with pitched roof on which are carved religious scenes and texts. The whole complex is reached by a descending corridor likewise decorated with religious matter. Originally,

34 The central
hall of the
Osireion after
clearance.

trees were planted around the perimeter of the pit. In the first century BC it was visited by the classical geographer Strabo: 'And there is a well there, situated at a depth, and thus one descends to it through a vault of monoliths, of exceeding size and workmanship. There is a channel leading to this place from the Great River. Round the channel there is a grove of Egyptian acanthus, sacred to Apollo.' (*Geography* xvii, 1). In his day one apparently had to enter via a gap in the roof.

The purpose of this strange place can be found in the tradition of building cenotaphs at Abydos: it was a home for the king's spirit at the place where the resurrective powers of Osiris could be experienced at their fullest. The building thus seems to combine the form of a contemporary royal tomb with a piece of architectural symbolism, that of the mound rising from the primeval waters on which, in religious texts, creation had first taken place.

Our knowledge of the Osireion comes to us, however, only from a long drawn-out programme of work. It was begun with a single season in 1902 funded through the Egyptian Research Account and under the direction of Margaret Murray and Mrs. Petrie. The Society took on the work in 1912 and put in two more seasons, initially under the direction of Naville. It resumed in 1925, and clearance was completed after a season of six months, under H. Frankfort. Study of the texts was carried out over three further seasons. The physical difficulties were considerable, and demanded the presence of an engineer on the team. Frankfort describes some of the ingenious solutions adopted in his report (*The Cenotaph of Seti I at Abydos* (1933), pp. 2–3):

> From 400 to 600 men and boys were employed to shift the huge masses of sand, though the railway made possible a considerable saving of labour. Mr. Gibson arranged a sloping track, so that most of the basket-boys were merely kept filling the trucks at the bottom of the excavation, but did not need to carry the sand up the slopes; supplementary chains of boys worked, of course, at other spots in the usual way. After various trials a *gravity-railway* was installed . . . It worked on the following lines: An old wooden water-wheel was bought and put upright on a mound between two artificial slopes; one of these led down to the centre of the work, the other sloped down in the opposite direction away from the wheel. An empty truck running on this latter slope, and connected by a rope with a full truck which was hauled up out of the excavation, counterbalanced the weight of that truck itself. The problem was to obtain the requisite power which should pull the extra weight of sand in the full truck. A horse proved powerless; two cows, and next two camels were tried, without success. At last a pair of water-buffaloes performed the deed; but then the villagers refused to hire them. In the light of later experience it seems doubtful whether buffaloes would have been as successful as the means ultimately adopted. Lateral bars for fourteen sturdy men were fixed on to the counterbalancing truck. These men (when a signal was given from below that a truck was full) fell forward against the weight and, with the inevitable shouting, pushed the counterbalancing truck down its slope, thus pulling up the full one.

For the lower parts pumping was necessary. This was done using a pump worked by a massive 16 hp steam-engine, such as would now find a place in a museum of industrial archaeology. It offered, however, only a temporary solution. Today the Osireion can be viewed only from above. The ground water now stands permanently above the level of the floor, and reeds grow in the channel. The island of creation awaits its own resurrection.

In the reign of Sethos I artists and craftsmen of wall sculptures attained a supreme mastery of their medium. On the fine white limestone chosen for important buildings they drew and carved with a sure accuracy of line and proportion, and brought depth and life to their images through a delicate modelling of surfaces in low relief. Some of the finest of this work is to be found in the king's temple at Abydos. Although the front part of the building has been much destroyed, the same drifting sand that preserved so much brickwork in the cemeteries also buried much of the rear, and so protected large areas of the sculptured wall scenes, some with much of their original bright colouring. The sand was cleared out in the nineteenth century, and a token publication of the reliefs attempted. The Society's work at the nearby Osireion led to thoughts of attempting a full publication of the temple in a manner which would do justice to the superb quality of the originals, and provide a lasting record for scholarship. The genesis and development of the project are described in Chapter 8 below. The skill and artistry of Amice Calverley and Myrtle Broome resulted in four volumes which are the most sumptuous published by the Society. They cover the rear part of the temple, but not the front part, from the first hypostyle hall outwards, or the annexe on the south-eastern side of the rear. For these several more volumes are required. But here the volumes already published set a standard of excellence which, in the absence of special funding and of the artistic skills of the two ladies involved, may be difficult, if not impossible, to match in present circumstances.

Archaeologists add their own debris and chapter of history to a site. By 1914 the Society had constructed or made use of five separate expedition houses at Abydos. Petrie's first house was on the side of the shallow wadi which runs out to the Umm el-Qaʻab. The Rawnsleys' romantic description does not disguise its essential austerity (*Resurrection*, pp. 8, 14–15):

It consists of a row of little huts, facing east and constructed of grey mud bricks and the roughest thatch. At the top, on a levelled terrace, is the common room with narrow open slits for windows, and the extreme distinction of having two wooden doors and a short flight of plank steps before it. Then follow, side by side, a set of tiny rooms, each like a little cubicle and having an opening to act as door and window. Such are the bed sitting rooms of the party . . . Outside, rough red clay pots are spread in rows, all shapes and sizes, valuable to us, but holding little merit in the eyes of Arabs. There too, is a queer collection of sun bleached skulls and bones . . . At night, rolled snug in bed, one felt the pleasures of being wild. To snuff deliciously the sun-burnt blankets, to dodge the twinkling stars which peered laughingly through a gap in the plank roof, to hear a wild dog lap, lapping at the water in the canvas bath a few feet off in the dead, still night, all such experiences thrill the mind . . . We sit on empty boxes to discuss our meals. The dining room is floored with sand. It is an oblong room and down its centre is a rough trestle table. The boards are somewhat warped and stained, and on them range the bowls of food or opened tins, covered with dishes or saucers to exclude the dust . . .

Visions of ham and eggs are lost in the reality of other food; and though the tea is somewhat strong and scarcely nice instead of milk with porridge, and though ship's biscuits ill replace the bread, or cold tinned tongue the contents of the sizzling frying pan, we manage well enough with these. Thoughts of digestion must be set aside and, as for cold – the sun will soon be strong.

Of this house, all that now remains is a concentration of sherds, easily mistaken for an ancient site itself.

On moving to the Osiris temple, Petrie took over another and more convenient house, apparently built by John Garstang for the Egyptian Research Account. It was used more as a storehouse than a dwelling, and contemporary photographs show it to have possessed an equally rudimentary character. This house has vanished without trace. For the later Society work, beginning in late 1909, use was made of a far more commodious house, which had been built in 1907 by Harold Jones for Garstang's Liverpool expedition to Abydos. This lay further along the valley from Petrie's first house. Its most prominent feature was a battlemented tower. In Garstang's day it had also been provided with a tennis court and miniature golf-course, but old photographs suggest that the Society's directors lacked the necessary enthusiasm, or perhaps just the time, to maintain them. This house remained the Society's headquarters throughout the work of the 1920s and 30s, becoming in the end the residence of Miss Calverley. She regarded it as a home, and planted a garden beside it of sweet peas and mignonette, and from it dispensed medicines to the villagers of the neighbourhood. Without a roof, its tower collapsed, the shell was still standing in 1967, when it was replaced by an even grander expedition house for the newly arrived Pennsylvania-Yale expedition to Abydos. During the time that both Peet and Naville were simultaneously working, a second and very isolated house was built for Naville and his wife in the desert to the south-east of the main house. This double residence served to keep apart the two temperamentally opposed directors. Naville's house, too, has vanished.

The fifth house was occasioned by the work at Abydos South. Here, in a lonely outpost beneath the cliffs, the work was superintended by C. T. Currelly. Again the Rawnsleys provide a contemporary description (*Resurrection*, pp. 33–4):

> His house, just ten feet square, of sun-dried brick, roofed with rough planks and thatched with stalks of Indian corn, looks in the distance but a tiny speck upon the shimmering sand . . . And inside what do we find? On one side of the room a palm-stick bed, which has not been made for many a week, and on the other two rough plank shelves. That is all the furniture, and the rest is chaos. For on the shelves 'anticas' and eatables, books and tools, and on the sandy floor tins of every description are piled in rough confusion. Tins of salmon and mincemeat jostle each other among pots of the First Dynasty; a shaving brush and a revolver, a ship's biscuit and a fine 'ushabti' find themselves quartered together; Huntley and Palmer and the plans of King Aahmes lie side by side with tomatoes and a hammer and nails.

Abydos has produced for the Society a great many volumes in the series of excavation memoirs. It remains an important archaeological concession. But, apart

35 Using a
steam-engine
to pump out
the water
from the
Osireion.

from further epigraphic work of uncertain scale in the Sethos temple, it appears also to represent a chapter of the Society's history that is now closed. It seems fitting to end with a valedictory passage written by the Rawnsleys, participants of those busy, early seasons (*Resurrection*, p. 34):

> Have you ever watched the lights appear along the Thames Embankment when London is all smoky blue after an autumn sunset? Have you ever felt a thrill of pleasure on seeing town lights from a distant height or from a ship at sea?
>
> If so you will know what it means to stand high up upon the desert under the shadow of those great cliffs; to see far out across the Nile valley hundreds of camp fires, twinkling in the dark; to catch a glimpse, not far below you, of ruddy faces in the firelight of the huts, and hear the buzz of a reed flute and the sound of happy human voices in the stillness of the night.

5 El-Amarna

CYRIL ALDRED

Opposite Mallawi in Middle Egypt the eastern bank of the Nile presents the appearance of a gorge with sheer limestone cliffs plunging into the river and affording no space for a continuous highway or cultivation at the water's edge. This rocky escarpment extends further south for some sixty-five kilometres with a notable interruption immediately south of El-Sheikh Said where the cliffs recede in an abrupt curve from the bank for a distance of some twelve kilometres and to a maximum depth of five, forming the sandy plain of El-Amarna. This name is derived from the Beni Amram, a tribe with an evil reputation for feuding and violence, who settled in the region on both sides of the river in the early eighteenth century. Their villages on the east bank, Et-Til, El-Hagg Qandil, El-Amiriya and El-Hawata, are spaced at intervals from north to south along the sparse cultivation. The full description of the northernmost village, Et-Til el-Amarna, was misheard by early European visitors as Tell el-Amarna; and although this name persists, it is a complete misnomer since there is no single *tell* or great mound marking the ancient site which extends far beyond Et-Til.

It was in the vast amphitheatre of El-Amarna that one of the great dramas of ancient Egypt was played out when for scarcely more than a decade in the fourteenth century BC it became, in the words of Norman de Garis Davies, 'a chance bivouac in the march of history, filled for a moment with all the movement and colour of intense life, and then abandoned to a deeper silence, when the camp was hurriedly struck and the course of Egyptian history relapsed again into more wonted highways'. For this was the site to which King Akhenaten, mystic and religious reformer, was directed by divine inspiration in his fifth regnal year as the place where his sole god, Re-Harakhty, immanent in the sunlight that streamed from the Aten, or disk of the sun, had manifested himself at the Creation of the World. Here it was that the king founded a great capital city on virgin ground, Akhetaten, the Horizon or Seat of the Aten, which was built, occupied and extended during the remaining twelve years of his reign.

Here the palaces, temples and official buildings, the mansions of the wealthy and the hovels of the poor were hastily constructed of mud brick and stone, only to be abandoned by his successor, Tutankhamun. Half a century later, when Akhenaten and all his works had become anathema to the kings of the next dynasty, iconoclasts were sent to the desolate site to smash statues of the king and his family, and to obliterate his features and names, and sometimes the names of his god, on the temple and tomb reliefs. In the reign of Ramesses II demolition gangs squatted in the ruins while they removed the stonework right down to its foundations for utilisation in buildings elsewhere in Egypt, and particularly for new constructions at Hermopolis across the river.

36 One of Akhenaten's boundary stelae surrounding his city.

All such information has had to be retrieved by the spade during the past century, since the records of the reign were expunged in Ramesside times, and if it was necessary to mention events in the reign of Akhenaten, he was referred to obliquely as 'the Criminal of Akhetaten'.

The sandy expanse that lies in front of the hills to the east of the site of Akhetaten, and slopes gently to the thin strip of cultivation on the river bank is scored by a number of dried water-courses which occasionally become charged with raging torrents from storms over the desert hinterland. A recent flood, scouring the Royal Wadi, for instance, is reported to have washed away part of the village of El-Hagg Qandil and exposed some ancient ruins. Excavation, however, tends to show that the northern part of the site has largely escaped such natural calamities.

A prominent wadi lying a little to the north of Et-Til, and another to the north of El-Hagg Qandil, mark the limits of the central portion of Akhetaten which skirted the edge of the cultivation for a distance of three kilometres; to its south lay the southern portion of the city, extending for about another kilometre. Other isolated buildings, to be mentioned later, have been uncovered to the north and south of this nucleus. Akhetaten can thus be described as a township that straggled with varying density for a distance of some eight kilometres along the chord of a vast arc following the flow of the Nile. It has proved an archaeologist's paradise with its simple stratigraphy. Despite systematic destruction in antiquity and woeful vandalism in recent times, much of it has survived, even to the chariot roads, and the paths trodden into the desert by ancient feet in their daily walk between residence and place of work.

The prime witnesses to the importance of the site are not, however, such frail vestiges, but the substantial monuments that still remain above ground. These are firstly fourteen great stelae, most of them with attendant groups of statuary showing Akhenaten, his chief queen Nefertiti, and two of their daughters, hewn at different points into the cliffs flanking the east and west boundaries of Akhetaten and defining its limits. On them are carved texts, now much damaged and weathered, recounting how the king came to choose and demarcate the bounds of his city, and listing the various buildings he proposed to erect there, including palaces, temples, a family tomb in the eastern hills and tombs nearby for his followers. Except for an earlier proclamation on three greatly ruined stelae, all these texts are dated to his sixth and eighth regnal years. A codicil on two stelae on the western bank dedicates the entire area enclosed by these tablets to the Aten, including all its people, animals and produce, 'and his rays are joyous when they receive them'.

The other monuments that have induced travellers to stop at El-Amarna on their way up and down the Nile, and which are indeed its main attraction, are those private tombs which Akhenaten promised his followers on the Boundary Stelae. They lie in two different locations, the Northern Group hewn in the cliffs of the Gebel et-Til to the north of the Royal Wadi, and the Southern Group in the foothills of the Gebel Abu Hasah. The first visitors were mystified by the epicene form in which Akhenaten chose to have himself represented in the tomb reliefs, with heavy breasts, swelling hips and ample thighs. They believed that two queens were in question here, instead of a Pharaoh and his consort, but this did not lessen the appeal of the place; on the contrary, it heightened its mystery.

Sir John Gardner Wilkinson was evidently the first of these visitors to explore El-Amarna. He went there in 1824 and again two years later with James Burton, the antiquary, geologist and draughtsman. The Northern Tombs, cut in a terrace halfway up a cliff, were still standing open at the time of Wilkinson's visits, and he copied sculptured scenes on the walls of the large tomb of the High Priest, Mery-re I. He was followed in 1833 by Robert Hay, the prince of copyists, who with his surveyor G. Laver was the first to uncover some of the Southern Tombs from enveloping sand drifts. The copies made by Hay and Laver remain mostly unpublished in the British Library, and a similar fate has attended the work of the French draughtsman Nestor L'Hôte, who had accompanied the great Champollion on his mission to Egypt in 1828–9; his copies, notes and squeezes rest largely unpublished in the Bibliothèque Nationale in Paris.

The great Prussian Expedition to Egypt under Richard Lepsius paid two visits to El-Amarna in 1843 and 1845, where a total of twelve prodigiously industrious days were spent in making drawings and paper squeezes. It was upon the engraved interpretations of these drawings in the massive volumes of the *Denkmäler* that most scholars for the rest of the century were dependent for their knowledge and interpretations of many of the scenes and inscriptions in the private tombs and on some of the Boundary Stelae at El-Amarna. But it became clear as time elapsed that the accuracy of the *Denkmäler* plates was of a limited kind; furthermore, the published record was far from being complete.

In the early years of the Archaeological Survey of the Egypt Exploration Fund the attention of its first Surveyor, Percy Newberry, was directed to El-Amarna. In 1892–3 an attempt was made to obtain permission to copy the monuments there, and some details of its failure are given in Chapter 8 (p. 148). Ten years later the Fund again applied for permission to copy the private tombs, and this was readily given by Gaston Maspero who had resumed the position of Director-General of the Antiquities Service in 1899. The Fund's Surveyor now was Norman de Garis Davies, one of those persons, small in stature, but possessed of a superabundant energy, who do not hesitate to tackle formidable tasks that would daunt larger men.

From 1901 to 1907 Davies worked at El-Amarna for a yearly stint of between six to eight weeks, usually in the winter, but sometimes in the heat of summer, during which time he succeeded in copying all the decorated and inscribed private tombs and the Boundary Stelae. At the start of his enterprise Ludwig Borchardt placed scaffolding at his disposal. The artist Harold Jones assisted him for two weeks in 1906 and was responsible for the fine copy of the relatively undamaged relief of the royal family worshipping the Aten at the entrance to the tomb of Apy. Herr Schliepback, the expert photographer of the Neue Photographische Gesellschaft, took photographs of scenes in the dark interiors of such tombs as those of Tutu, Ay and Parennefer, as well as of the Boundary Stelae. These photographs, reproduced in *Rock Tombs of El-Amarna*, Parts v and vi (1908), are still the only readily available means of forming an impression of the present state and quality of these damaged monuments. Herr Schliepback is also responsible for the photograph of Davies, snatching some ease outside his quarters in the tomb of May. The portrait succeeds in bringing out the serious driving force that was so often concealed behind Davies's impish high spirits

37 Norman de
Garis Davies
at the
rock-tombs
of El-Amarna.

38 Limestone relief showing Akhenaten and Nefertiti worshipping the Aten (Cairo Museum, no. 30/10/26/12).

and drolleries.

Apart from such assistance, and the general editorship of Griffith, the six volumes of *Rock Tombs* were produced virtually single-handed by Davies. The record was rapidly and economically published and is among the Fund's major achievements. The volumes contain accurate copies of drawings, paintings, reliefs and texts painfully extracted from walls that were unfinished, decaying, damaged and often filthy from infestation by generations of bats and human squatters. The scenes which Davies recovered in line and photogravure, with their vivid pictures of the daily life of the royal family at Akhetaten, and the modest part played in them by the tomb-owner, are almost our only means of learning of events that happened at this critical and exciting moment in Egyptian history.

The private and state functions in the palace, the entertainments by night and day, the reception of foreign embassies bearing gifts, the investiture of faithful officials with orders, decorations and other honours, the daily visit to the temple, and the ecstatic worship of the Aten at an altar heaped with offerings under the open sky – all these subjects, new to Egyptian art in design and content, are represented in these private tomb chapels with a wealth of engaging detail and an entire absence of funerary ambience. In retrieving them from their decay and gloom, Davies succeeded in rekindling a light that failed.

While the work of publishing accurate copies of what the standing monuments had to reveal was being prosecuted, the evidence below ground at El-Amarna was not neglected. In 1887 a local peasant woman digging for *sebakh*, the nitrous compost into which ancient brickwork so often decays, unearthed a cache of over 300 clay tablets impressed with cuneiform signs in what we now know were the ruins of the 'House of Correspondence of Pharaoh', or Records Office. By the time these tablets had been accepted as genuine historical documents, they had mostly been dispersed among the museums of Cairo, Berlin, London and Paris. But when it was realised that they were part of the diplomatic archives of the reign of Akhenaten, El-Amarna awoke to a wider fame among the informed public, and to a more intense interest among archaeologists anxious to repeat the success of the peasant woman, though not her methods of retrieval.

The first upon the scene was Flinders Petrie who in one momentous season in 1891–2, working independently of the Egypt Exploration Fund, made some remarkable discoveries with his usual flair. Although his explorations would now rank as little more than a sondage, he succeeded in investigating the remains of the Great Temple of the Aten, the Great Official Palace, the King's House, the Records Office and several private houses in the Central and Southern parts of the City. He also unearthed more cuneiform tablets, the remains of glass factories and the plaster cast of a sculptor's study which he believed was a death mask of Akhenaten. With his customary attention to unconsidered trifles, he sifted the palace rubbish heaps and recovered many fragments of discarded faience, glass and pottery, including hundreds of contemporary Mycenaean sherds. From such materials he attempted a reconstruction of the main course of the history of El-Amarna. With commendable speed Petrie published his results and so directed a general interest in the archaeological potential of the site.

But it was another fifteen years before his promising beginning was continued by others. In 1907 the Deutsche Orient-Gesellschaft under the direction of Ludwig Borchardt began excavations which were not to cease until the end of the season of 1913–14 when the outbreak of the Great War closed the site to any subsequent operations on their part. Their most striking discovery was of a painted limestone bust of Queen Nefertiti, a timeless masterpiece, which has since become the most publicised portrait from the ancient world. When it became generally known after the War, the new and startling aspect that it gave of the sculptor's achievement in ancient Egypt created the liveliest stir, even outside the arcane world of the scholar. A little later still, the sensational discovery of the tomb of Tutankhamun, who as a child had lived at Akhetaten, increased popular enthusiasm for things Egyptian, which was reflected in a surge in the membership of the Society and the funds it could devote to exploration and publication.

Even before this, however, the society had obtained in 1920 the concession to excavate at El-Amarna. From 1921 until 1936 they were active on the site, their operations hampered only by shortage of funds, particularly in the years of economic depression after 1930, when work had to be suspended for a season.

Petrie had demonstrated that the important historical results were often to be derived from unprepossessing fragments, dockets written on scraps of pottery, broken faience ring-bezels, stamped impressions on crumbling mud, and the like. But as the Society was almost entirely dependent upon private subscriptions, chiefly from sympathetic American sources, it was important that public support should be stimulated and maintained by producing finds with popular appeal and of museum quality. Such spectacular results could not be expected every season, but areas were selected for investigation as much for the likelihood of yielding exhibitable antiquities as for their intrinsic importance. Nevertheless, other explorations of a less promising kind were also made, and this dual system worked reasonably well until new regulations for the division of finds, introduced by the Antiquities Service in 1936, made excavation by foreign missions so little worth while that most of them ceased their operations.

During the decade and a half during which the Society dug at El-Amarna important evidence was skilfully uncovered, and some attractive pieces were added to the museum collections of Cairo, New York and London. Moreover, the discoveries, and deductions to which they gave rise, were published each season in the pages of the *Journal of Egyptian Archaeology* and more fully in the excavation memoirs *City of Akhenaten* I-III (1921–51). At the end of every season a display of the share of finds allocated to the Society was arranged in London to arouse and sustain public interest. The writer has a nostalgic recollection of attending these exhibitions as a schoolboy in the 1930s. They were usually held in the Wellcome Historical Medical Museum, then located in Wigmore Street, where it was possible, if one was sufficiently bold, to buttonhole some of the excavators in attendance and hear from their own lips how a particular item had been found.

The main aims of the first expedition were stated by its Director, T. E. Peet, with characteristic logic and clarity as follows:

39 Interior of the Society's house at El-Amarna in the 1920s. The hieroglyphs were painted by Battiscombe Gunn.

1. The systematic clearing of the town-site begun by the Germans, so as to gather details of the architecture and arrangement of the houses, to learn more of the daily life, and to secure objects for museums.

2. The throwing of fresh light on the numerous difficult problems raised by the so-called religious revolution of Akhenaten.

3. The investigation of the question of dating, and in particular to determine whether the site had been occupied before the reign of Akhenaten, and whether it was ever re-occupied, either partially or wholly, after the great abandonment.

These objectives were not fully achieved in the first season, but subsequent excavations did produce satisfactory answers to the first and third items on Peet's list. Unfortunately, however, more shadow than light was thrown on the difficult problems of the religious revolution, and a new theory emerged of religious and political schism between adherents of Akhenaten on the one side, and of Nefertiti on the other towards the end of the reign, to account for certain ambiguous evidence that was exposed by the excavations. These problems still vex students of the subject and are not likely to be resolved without the recovery of further clues.

A striking feature of the Society's excavations at El-Amarna was the high professional competence of the field directors, most of whom were soon enticed away to more lucrative prospects elsewhere. The pattern was set by Leonard Woolley, the experienced excavator with T. E. Lawrence of Carchemish, who was in charge during the fruitful season of 1921–2, after which he left for even greater triumphs at Ur of the Chaldees. He was eventually succeeded by the architect Francis Newton whose sudden and premature death on camp in 1924 interrupted the routine of direction. During this period all the diggers, Qufti, local basket-boys and the specialists had become familiar with the peculiar features of the terrain. The work, begun by the Germans, of uncovering the great private houses in the southern quarter, built of mud brick with stone and wood fittings, was vigorously prosecuted. The notable discovery of the large mansion of the vizier Nakht, containing its reception halls, bedrooms, bathrooms and lavatory, yielded valuable data on the architecture of such domestic buildings and their interior decoration. An unexpected bonus was the opportunity of studying town planning and construction in the ancient world for virtually the first time.

But the Society made investigations on other parts of the vast straggling site. Excavations in an industrial quarter, adjacent to the official part of the central city, revealed cottage industries in glass and faience similar to those examined by Petrie in 1892. The village occupied by the workmen employed on the hewing and decoration of the royal and private rock tombs was also identified and partially excavated, and its correspondence recognised with the similar site at Deir el-Medina in Western Thebes just then being uncovered by the French. The associated chapels built on the adjacent *gebel* were examined and planned. These latter constructions were distinct from a small cluster of ruins discovered by Petrie in the desert about two kilometres west of the tomb of Panehesy in the Northern Group. These were skilfully re-excavated by the Society in 1931–2 and published under the name of the Desert Altars (in *City of Akhenaten*, II (1933)), although their exact function has never been convincingly explained.

In the southern area, between the modern villages of El-Hawata and El-Amiriya, what had been described as 'palace-ruins' proved to be something quite different. A. Barsanti, of the Egyptian Antiquities Department, had removed parts of a painted pavement from here in 1896, and the Germans had reidentified the site in the space of one rainy day in 1907. When Woolley came to excavate it, he was able to expose the remains of an unusual *maru* or viewing-temple with its quay, pools, gardens, temple and 'sunshades' (or kiosks for the daily rejuvenation of members of the royal family by the sun's rays), despite the almost total demolition of the stonework in Ramesside times and the destruction of the mud brick by modern seekers after *sebakh*.

Perhaps the most notable discovery made during this phase of the Society's explorations was the ruins of a palace in the northern area beyond the village of Et-Til. Nearly all its stonework had been robbed in antiquity, but some of the mud-brick walls survived up to a height of 2 m in places. It had a throne-room, pool, hypostyle halls, administrative offices, courts and quarters for cattle and antelope. Its novel feature, however, was a courtyard flanking the palace section, with a garden in the centre enclosed by a colonnade on three sides, behind which lay a series of small rooms. From the remains of their decoration, these chambers appear to have been fowl-houses or aviaries. One of them on the north side, built with staggered rows of niches acting as nesting-boxes, and with a large window-like opening giving access to the garden, was painted with a continuous decoration showing bird-life in the marshes.

The surface of the painted mud plaster was in an extremely fragile state, rain, fire and tunnelling by white ants having reduced it to a mere film that would collapse at an incautious touch. The death of Newton, who was in the process of copying these scenes, imperilled the record of this unique painting; but happily the Metropolitan Museum of Art generously stepped into the breach and lent the Society the services of Charles Wilkinson who succeeded in the delicate and onerous task of tracing the paintings on the west wall in 1925. He was succeeded in the following year by Norman Davies, making a return to the El-Amarna scene, this time with his wife Nina. They traced the east wall, and copied the west wall from end to end and parts of the east wall in colour. Their facsimiles were sumptuously published in 1929 in a special memorial volume of the Society, *The Mural Painting of El-Amarneh*, as a tribute to Francis Newton. Davies added a perceptive essay on the nature and composition of the paintings, during which he remarks, 'The innovations by which the era of Akhenaten is peculiarly marked attain something like a culmination here. No essential element is new, but almost every element has received such novel handling that it is no wonder if the whole produces an effect of untrammelled creativeness'.

Apart from the paintings little else has been published from this important site, a loss which owes much to Newton's untimely death. It was not in fact until 1926 that excavations were resumed for a short season on the northern part of the site, under the direction of Henri Frankfort. A start was now made on investigating the huge and extensively devastated area of the Great Temple of the Aten that had been plumbed in some parts by Petrie in 1892. Frankfort excavated a curious structure based on four platforms which had been introduced into the boundary wall of the temple on its north side, and which he identified as the 'Hall of Foreign Tribute' represented in the

40 Painted
limestone stela
showing the
dead King
Amenophis III
and Queen Tiy
(British Museum,
EA no. 57399).

41 Trial carving of two royal heads from the Great Temple (Cairo Museum, no. 59294).

42 (*Top*) Polychrome glass vessel in the shape of a fish (British Museum, EA no. 55193).

43 (*Bottom*) Excavation of the Central Palace at El-Amarna, 1934–5.

44 Unfinished quartzite head of Queen Nefertiti (Cairo Museum, no. 59286).

tomb of Huya. According to Frankfort this building had been raised for the ceremony of the reception of the gifts presented by foreign embassies to the Pharaoh in his twelfth regnal year. Some doubts have recently been thrown on this interpretation of the purpose of the structure, though no convincing alternative explanation has yet been offered.

Whenever operations on the primary sites were held up for any reason, the excavators switched their forces to the uncovering of more of the private houses, particularly the larger residences. Though these had usually been swept clean by their owners before abandoning the town on the death of Akhenaten, a great deal was discovered about their interior decoration. In particular, it became evident that such mansions incorporated small shrines in which the worship of the royal family was observed, either within the central hall or in a special kiosk built in the garden. The focal point of the cult was a group of statuary or a stela showing the king and queen, often accompanied by one or more of their daughters, worshipping the Aten. The Society had the good fortune to find an exceptional specimen, albeit somewhat damaged, in the chapel attached to the private residence of Panehesy, the Chief Servitor of the Aten, whose tomb was well known as the southernmost of the Northern Group. This particular example took the form of a limestone stela carved and painted with a relief, not of Akhenaten and his family but of his parents, Amenophis III and Queen Tiye, seated before an altar under the rayed disk of the Aten. This object, which is now in the British Museum, immediately aroused the suspicion that Amenophis III had lived at El-Amarna until well into the reign of Akhenaten.

In 1931 a second phase in the Society's excavations was inaugurated with the appointment of John Pendlebury, the Curator of Cnossus, as Field Director, a position which he held until 1936 when operations were closed down at El-Amarna, and he returned to his beloved Crete where he was to meet a heroic death in the fighting of 1941. For six years he gave a continuous and systematic direction to the work of uncovering and elucidating the ruins of the town.

The personality of John Pendlebury, athlete and Minoan scholar, is better known to us from the memoirs of such friends as Mary Chubb (*Nefertiti lived here* (1954)) and Dilys Powell (*The Villa Ariadne* (1973)), though it also transpires through his own writings. Describing the excavations in 1935, he says, 'one of the most fascinating points about the work is that we are concerned with the private lives of the whole population, slave and noble, workman and official and the royal family itself. So strong is this homely atmosphere that we feel we really know as individuals the people whose houses we are excavating. Alike as these houses are in plan, each one shows little variations indicating the tastes as well as the profession of the owner' (*Tell el-Amarna* (1935), p. xiv).

This enthusiasm informed his actions and those of the team he gathered around him, the remarkable quality of which was that its members were all still in their twenties at the time of his appointment. In retrospect this period seems a golden climax to the explorations of the Society at El-Amarna. The energy and virtuosity of the various members of the expedition, working with the slenderest resources, managed to achieve nearly all their objectives and to publish them worthily, though Pendlebury's tragic death prevented as complete a report as had been promised.

Between 1930 and 1936 the main effort was concentrated upon the central part of the city, with its difficult site of the brutally ravaged Great Temple, flanked by its magazines and storehouses. In this area of the city also lay the Great Official Palace, the King's House and the Castle or Mansion of the Aten (the smaller temple), with their gardens and magazines. To its east were the Records Office, the House of Life, or Scriptorium, and the police barracks. Most of these ruins, some like the Great Temple and the Palace of enormous extent, were cleared, planned and recorded. Often the work entailed removing the spoil-heaps of earlier investigators, and re-excavating their digs. All the buildings had been extensively destroyed, and the excavators had to try to recover the ground plan from what evidence remained in markings on the initial plaster sealing that covered the entire area, well below the vanished floor level. Sometimes even these vestiges had been obliterated, and the only clues surviving were depressions in the virgin sand where the heavy masonry supports of walls, columns and bases had been removed.

Although the material rewards from such devastated sites were meagre and fragmentary, notable finds came to light while a resurvey was being made of an area in the southern city which had been uncovered earlier. In seeking to tie this into an adjacent site dug over by the Germans, two or three houses left unexamined were excavated and yielded several pieces of sculpture. These included a life-sized quartzite head of a queen, from a composite statue in process of being finished, and a small steatite group, characteristic of the period, showing a scribe writing under the inspiration of the ape of Thoth squatting upon a podium. Both these finds are now among the treasures of the Cairo Museum.

In 1931 the Antiquities Service commissioned the Expedition to re-examine the area around the Royal Tomb in the central Wadi Abu Hasah, awarding a Government grant for the purpose.

The Royal Tomb had been found by native rummagers in the early 1880s, and was officially cleared and examined by A. Barsanti for the Antiquities Service in 1891, not before much damage had been inflicted upon the reliefs that decorated some of its walls. The reliefs and inscriptions, however, were recorded two years later by the expedition of the Mission archéologique française which had been operating at the Southern Tombs since 1883. In 1935, in view of further depredations in the Royal Tomb, the Antiquities Service arranged for the Society's expedition to fit a more massive door at the entrance. They also granted permission to make a complete record of the wall reliefs which had hitherto been published in a very perfunctory and inaccurate fashion. Herbert Fairman, Ralph Lavers and Stephen Sherman spent over a fortnight at the tomb making tracings and photographs of all the reliefs, while Pendlebury and his wife scoured both sides of the valley for other tombs, and turned over various soil-heaps. Pendlebury produced a brief report of their work in the *Journal of Egyptian Archaeology* (vol. 21 (1935), pp. 129–30), and expressed the hope that in the near future the results of the Society's operations in the Royal Wadi would be published as a separate memoir.

Unfortunately, he did not live to realise this ambition, and it has been left to Geoffrey Martin to bring the project to fruition thirty-five years later. This he is in process of accomplishing, and has already produced as the thirty-fifth memoir of the

45 Houses in
the Eastern
Village at
El-Amarna.

Society's Archaeological Survey *The Rock Tombs of El-'Amarna*, VII, *The Royal Tomb at El-'Amarna*, I, *The Objects* (1974), in which he gives an account of the operations, official and illicit, of which some report has been made, and catalogues all the objects that have been recovered and which he is able to trace. A second volume will contain the facsimile record in line-drawing of the surviving scenes and texts which are now for the most part in very poor condition.

Leaders of the Society's field expeditions to El-Amarna had long deplored the lack of a large-scale plan showing in detail all the sites that had been uncovered at various times by the British and Germans. In 1977, when the Society renewed its concession at El-Amarna, a complete, accurate and co-ordinated survey was projected as a preliminary to assessing what results any further excavations may promise.

This exacting task was entrusted to Barry Kemp who undertook the preparation of a 1:5,000 scale map of the entire area, and a 1:2,500 scale map of the main city site from El-Hagg Qandil northwards. The project was completed in two seasons, during which time small but significant discoveries have been made incidentally, including a stone village, probably for the overnight accommodation of workmen engaged on the cutting and decoration of the private tombs. Investigations were also made at a site marked as 'Roman Camp' on the maps made by Petrie in 1892 and Timme in 1911. Kemp's survey leaves him in little doubt that the site is essentially of Akhenaten's reign. Another find was the discovery of a palace bakery among the magazines south of the Great Temple. A map was also prepared on a 1:1,000 scale of the structures incorporating the North Riverside Palace and the houses lying to the east of it, which have not been fully published. It is in the further investigation of these ruins that the best hope lies of finding data which will throw more light on the obscure and controversial events of Akhenaten's last years of rule.

The possibilities revealed by Kemp's survey are already being exploited. In the neighbourhood of the workmen's village a careful excavation based on a grid of 5 m squares has brought to exploration at El-Amarna a rigour and precision in techniques which should extract far more information from this devastated site than any previous excavation. Mr. Kemp's work has already shown that in some places at least the Amarna site possesses a stratigraphy, a fact not generally taken into account formerly. Work has also been reopened in the area of the North City to complete the Society's pre-war records, with the hope of publishing a fourth volume in the *City of Akhenaten* series. There is no doubt that the painstaking methods now being used at El-Amarna will produce results which will substantially supplement the discoveries of earlier expeditions. It is probably true to say that our knowledge of what happened at El-Amarna is more likely to expand from the recovery of objects in carefully recorded contexts than from more spectacular finds.

6 Saqqara

GEOFFREY T. MARTIN

The Egypt Exploration Society's connection with Saqqara, the necropolis of the ancient capital Memphis, began as long ago as 1898 when Norman de Garis Davies began the copying in facsimile of the scenes and inscriptions in the great *mastaba*-tomb of Ptahhotpe and Akhtihotpe, north-west of the Step Pyramid. His work set new standards for Egyptian epigraphy, and the results were subsequently published in two fine volumes. This expedition, and the more recent epigraphic work of the Society in the *mastaba* of Khentika and in a group of Old Kingdom tombs north of the pyramid of Teti are dealt with in more detail in Chapter 8. No excavation was undertaken by the Society at Saqqara until W. B. Emery was appointed its Field Director in 1952 to work in the Archaic Necropolis.

Emery was to dominate the Society's archaeological affairs for the next twenty years, both in Saqqara and in Nubia, until his death in Cairo in 1971. Previous to his studies in the Institute of Archaeology at Liverpool he was trained as a marine draughtsman, and the skills he acquired served him in good stead when he turned his attention to archaeological drawing. Indeed, his plans and isometric and axonometric projections of ancient tombs and other structures deservedly became famous for their skill, clarity and beauty of presentation.

Emery attributed his early interest in Egyptology to his reading of the novels of Rider Haggard. Like most archaeologists he affected to disdain the lure of treasure, but at heart was always something of a romantic who liked nothing better than 'to dig holes in the desert', to use his own words, and to find interesting and often wonderful things. He was never a man to vaunt his own achievements, but by any standards they were numerous and often spectacular.

In 1935 Emery came to Saqqara as an Antiquities Department official, to take over the work of C. M. Firth, who had for a number of years been uncovering a series of mud-brick *mastaba*-tombs of the Archaic Period and early Old Kingdom in the great necropolis north of the Step Pyramid. Until Emery published the results of his researches in the tombs of the First Dynasty there, almost all the information available on that remote epoch (about 3100–2890 BC) derived from the work of E. Amélineau and particularly of W. M. Flinders Petrie in the royal necropolis at Abydos. Emery's finds at Saqqara revolutionised our knowledge of Egyptian architecture, art and technology at the dawn of Egyptian history, and also threw light to some extent on administrative and social affairs. His work at Saqqara, before he became the Society's Field Director at that site, were published in three fundamental volumes, *The Tomb of Hemaka* (1938), *Hor-Aha* (1939), and *Great Tombs of the First Dynasty*, I (1949).

Early on in his work in the Archaic Necropolis Emery conceived the idea that the great *mastaba*-tombs he was excavating were those of the earliest Egyptian kings and of their families and entourages. He based his view on the size and elaborately recessed panelled decoration of the superstructures, and on the often sumptuous funerary furnishings found in the subterranean burial-chambers. The supposed royal tombs of the First and Second Dynasties at Abydos, regarded by Emery as cenotaphs, were by contrast small and their equipment, admittedly fragmentary, hardly comparable with the Saqqara material. Though Emery's viewpoint, reinforced by his subsequent work for the Society in the same necropolis from 1952–6, received powerful support from Jean-Philippe Lauer, renowned for his work on pyramid architecture, it was otherwise almost universally rejected by scholars. This did not worry Emery in the least; his excavations had provided fundamental new material for early Egyptian history, and in his estimation it was up to his fellow Egyptologists to make what they would of it. Single-minded to a fault, he was always too busy with his next piece of field-work to defend his views vigorously.

These great *mastaba*-tombs were built in an extended line along the eastern edge of the escarpment in the northern part of the Saqqara necropolis. Streets of tombs of the Second and Third Dynasties (about 2890–2613 BC) were constructed westwards beyond these, and a considerable number were cleared and recorded by Emery when he was working for the Egyptian Antiquities Department. Hardly any of this important material has been published. Most of it is perhaps more interesting from the point of view of tomb development than for the quantity of inscriptions and fine artefacts recovered.

Ultimately, Emery resigned his post with the Antiquities Department, took part as a combatant in the Western Desert in the Second World War, was an officer in the Intelligence Service, and subsequently entered the British diplomatic service in Cairo. To all appearances his fruitful career as an active field archaeologist was at an end. However, his archaeological achievements and especially his impressive work at Saqqara led in 1951 to the offer of the Edwards Chair of Egyptology at University College London, an honour totally unexpected by Emery, who was an academic neither by training nor by inclination. The position, at that time with minimal teaching responsibilities, offered ample opportunity for research in the field, and Emery accepted it with alacrity.

The following year Emery was appointed Field Director of the Egypt Exploration Society and resumed his work in the Archaic Necropolis. Four seasons' work resulted in the discovery of a further series of large mud-brick tombs of the First Dynasty, subsequently published under the Society's imprint as *Great Tombs of the First Dynasty*, II and III (1954, 1958). The results, presented in a characteristically clear and succinct (some would say sparse) manner, rounded out all previous work on the Archaic Period of Egyptian history. The plans, projections and reconstruction in the volumes were particularly fine and informative, and a clear typological development of tombs, whether royal or not, was discernible. This typology was firmly based on architectural forms and on inscriptional material, including royal seal-impressions found in the tomb chambers.

Reduced to its essentials a typical First Dynasty tomb consisted of a deep pit cut through the surface gravel into the bedrock beneath. In the more elaborate examples

46 The burial-chamber of tomb 3500, of the late First Dynasty.

the floor and walls of the pit were faced with wooden panels and even inlaid with strips of decoration in gold. Here was placed the simple wooden coffin, with the body of the tomb-owner in a crouched or so-called foetal position. Around him were his most precious grave-goods. Of necessity the burial pit had to remain unroofed until after the interment. In the meantime an elaborate rectangular superstructure of small mud bricks was constructed, with a panelled exterior of the 'palace façade' type. One or more boundary walls in the same material enclosed the entire structure. In the interior of the superstructure at ground level were magazines or rooms for storing further items of equipment needed by the owner in the next world. In one Emery found an extraordinary treasure of copper objects, in another two small rolls of papyri were unearthed, showing that this writing material was already in use at that remote epoch. The contents of such magazines testify to the wealth, taste and sophistication of the times, the very beginning of dynastic history.

In a later development around the middle of the dynasty (reign of King Udimu or Den) the entrance to the burial-chamber was made by way of a stairway leading from the centre of the east side of the exterior of the tomb. This improvement meant that the brickwork of the superstructure could be completed well in advance of the funeral. All that was necessary subsequently was to block the staircase and entrance doorway. Hefty portcullises of limestone, with holes bored through their upper parts for the insertion of ropes for lowering, were provided for the latter. These portcullis blocks were the prototypes of the granite examples which were to be a regular feature of pyramid architecture in the Old and Middle Kingdoms.

Of great interest was the discovery that one of the great *mastabas* had a stepped interior of mud brick retaining a 'primeval' mound of gravel. Emery thought that this feature was probably present in other great tombs of the First Dynasty at Saqqara, but that it had been destroyed when the tombs were robbed and the superstructures denuded by exposure to the weather. With disarming and refreshing candour he also remarked that the traces, if they still existed, might not have been observed during the course of the excavations.

Built on to the north side of one of the tombs, dated by seal-impressions to the very end of the dynasty, Emery found a chapel with the remains of wooden statues. The parallel with the Step Pyramid, the mortuary temple of which is against its northern face, was evident, and a pointer to the 'royal' character of one at least of the First Dynasty Saqqara *mastabas*. With a sole exception, royal mortuary temples thereafter were placed on the east façades of the pyramids.

This brief description may serve to show the paramount interest and importance of these Early Dynastic tombs, the wealth of new information they have provided, and the number of tantalising problems they still present to the researcher.

No doubt Emery's work for the Society at Saqqara would have been even more wide-ranging but for the Suez crisis of 1956 which led to the breaking of diplomatic relations between Egypt and Great Britain, and to the temporary abandonment of the rich site. The crisis coincided with the problem of salvaging the monuments of Nubia, which were soon to be under threat of total destruction due to the building of the projected new High Dam at Aswan and the creation of Lake Nasser. From 1957 to 1963 the Society's efforts were focused on Egyptian and Sudanese Nubia, with most

47 (*Right*) One of the
servant burials around
tomb 3504.

48 (*Below*) Tomb 3507
from the east. Middle
of the First Dynasty.

impressive and important results, outlined by H. S. Smith in Chapter 7.

When he fell heir to the work of Firth in the most ancient tombs of Saqqara, Emery also inherited Firth's dream of locating the long-sought tomb of Imhotep. This great official of the Third Dynasty King Djoser (Zoser), whose Step Pyramid dominates the Saqqara skyline, was deified in the Late Period of Egyptian history, and many achievements in the architectural, scientific and medical spheres were attributed to him. Actually almost nothing is known about his life save that he was a high-ranking courtier, and the whereabouts of his tomb is a matter of speculation. J. E. Quibell, who preceded Firth at Saqqara, Firth himself and Emery all believed it to be located in the Archaic Necropolis in North Saqqara.

Emery, before leaving the necropolis in 1956, had sunk trial trenches in a great mound of red pottery sherds of Ptolemaic date (fourth to third century BC) evident in the north-west part of the cemetery, and he immediately located a brick tomb datable to the Old Kingdom, and according to Emery to the Third Dynasty, the time of Djoser. The sherds were from smashed ibis-mummy jars, the ibis being sacred to the god Thoth, who in turn was associated with Imhotep, 'the great one of the Ibis', in the Late Period of Egyptian history. To Emery this meant only one thing: that the Third Dynasty tomb of Imhotep, or the shrine or cenotaph dedicated to his cult in the Late Period and Ptolemaic epoch, was in the vicinity. Thus was initiated 'the Search for Imhotep', which caught the imagination of the public and media alike.

In 1964 Emery returned to Saqqara to direct the Society's work in the area just described, and work continued until his death in 1971. The present writer was privileged to be a member of the team every year except 1969, and had first-hand experience of Emery's unflagging enthusiasm for the arduous work, despite ill-health and sundry setbacks. As the years went by it became clear that Emery had discovered not the site of Imhotep's tomb but a vast complex dedicated to the cult of sacred animals: ibises, falcons, baboons and the cow-mothers of the Apis bulls. He uncovered extensive catacombs for their burial, together with their associated shrines, chapels and administrative buildings on the surface above. Over the dismantled remains of these were found the settlement and church of a monastic community which had occupied the site in the fifth century AD after its abandonment by the pagan priesthood. The monks had doubtless assisted in the destruction of the earlier buildings dedicated to the ancient gods immanent in the sacred animals. Though realising the importance of the discovery, Emery to the last clung to the belief that Imhotep's tomb was close at hand, and in his very last days was sinking trenches in the hope of locating it.

Large areas of the northern part of the Saqqara plateau were taken over in the Late Period and especially in the Ptolemaic era for the cult of sacred animals, one of the most extraordinary phenomena in Egyptian history, and perhaps one of the manifestations of Egyptian nationalism at this period of foreign domination. Such cults are unique to Egypt. Animal cemeteries are not, however, unique to Saqqara, though here they are found at their most extensive and elaborate. At Bubastis, Tuna el-Gebel, Abydos, Thebes, Armant, Aswan and other places there were installations for the burial and worship of certain species of animals and birds, but the special interest of the Saqqara Animal Necropolis, so extensively worked by the Society, lies in the

49 (*Above*)
Limestone
relief of two
kings in the
dress of the
Sed-festival.
First Dynasty
(British
Museum, EA
no. 67153).

50 (*Right*)
Painted
wooden cow
image as
found (Cairo
Museum).

diversity of creatures that were worshipped: the Apis bull and Isis, his divine cow-mother, ibises, falcons, rams, cats, dogs, to mention the most important. A Greek text recently found near the Serapeum mentions a cult of lions, though catacombs of these ferocious animals have yet to be found.

The focus of the cult was the great Serapeum, the burial-place of Apis, and its associated temples and outbuildings. A magnificent paved way led due east from its entrance towards the escarpment overlooking ancient Memphis. Along the edge of this escarpment in antiquity were shrines as impressive in size as the Serapeum temple itself, but of the latter only a scattering of limestone chippings survives to show its extent, and of the former little remains except their gigantic *enceinte* walls of mud brick. These temples, located near the pyramid of Teti, have recently been the subject of a detailed investigation by the Society under the direction of H. S. Smith, and his work from 1974 to 1979 in the area is mentioned again below.

Another roadway now covered with a deep deposit of sand runs northwards from the Serapeum towards the village of Abusir, the name of which doubtless preserves an ancient toponym, *Pr-Wsir*, 'The House (temple) of Osiris'. There is little doubt that this ancient road was lined with shrines and other buildings for the animal cults, which attracted in antiquity not only Egyptian but also foreign worshippers to the site, partly in search of cures. The most extensive of these outposts of the Serapeum is that discovered by W. B. Emery for the Society in 1964. It is situated on the flank of the escarpment at the northern exit of the necropolis, adjacent to the dried-up bed of an ancient lake, a little before Abusir is reached.

To our way of thinking the ancient architects working in this necropolis site gave themselves an enormous amount of trouble by placing their buildings in such a location, but the truth probably is that they had little alternative: practically every part of the area was densely covered with ancient tombs, by the Late Period mostly denuded and masked by huge deposits of wind-blown sand. With regard to the temples they constructed here, initiated by Nectanebo ii, the last native Egyptian king (360–343 BC), their solution was to make a terraced platform of mud brick, buttressed to prevent it sliding down the escarpment, and filled with rubble and sand to provide a level surface for the building of the shrines and other structures. Small peripteral temples to the south of the main site were constructed on similar artificial bases. The galleries which had to be tunnelled in the rock behind the shrines presented another difficult problem, since the entire desert was honeycombed with Old King-dom tomb-shafts and burial-chambers, and very frequently the new galleries broke into them, with the consequent risk of the collapse of the fill of the shafts on to the workmen. The ancient architects overcame these hazards just as we did when re-excavating the galleries.

Most of the votive objects were found in the debris of the shrines or cached in groups around the terrace supporting the main temple. For the most part the galleries were used solely for the entombment of the mummified creatures, sometimes in unbelievable quantities running into hundreds of thousands, if not millions, in the case of the ibises and falcons. Dedicatory and other inscriptions were found in some of the galleries, and in the falcon hypogeum Emery found a wonderful cache of bronze temple furniture and cult implements which had doubtless been used for some time in

51 Professor Walter Bryan Emery at Saqqara.

the shrine of Horus the Falcon adjacent outside, and had outlived their purpose. Being sacred objects they could not be melted down for reuse, so they were buried in one of the side galleries amidst the stacked falcon-mummy jars.

The mention of millions of mummified birds in this site draws attention to one of the many unexplained elements of the animal cults at Saqqara and elsewhere. To provide such numbers these creatures must have bred in captivity for subsequent mummification and burial as votives; but how this problem was dealt with has yet to be explained satisfactorily. Suffice it to say that the animal cult must have engendered a major industry at Saqqara and in other centres in Egypt in the Late Period and after, particularly during the period of Greek rule, employing thousands of persons.

The quality and huge quantity of the objects found during the eight seasons' work in the Animal Necropolis were truly astounding. The categories of material are too numerous to mention in detail here, but there were, for instance, votive statues in bronze, stone, faience and other materials, great quantities of papyrus documents in various scripts (hieratic, demotic, Aramaic and Greek), hieroglyphic inscriptions and Greek and Coptic texts ranging in date from the Archaic Period to the fifth century AD, inscriptions in the enigmatic and as yet undeciphered Carian script, and ostraca (potsherds and limestone flakes) with dockets and texts in sundry scripts. Some of the papyrus documents survived intact, many others were torn and tattered, having been thrown away as 'waste paper'. If the entire archive had been complete and in good condition, it would have revolutionised our knowledge of Memphis in the Late Period and in Ptolemaic times. Even in their present state the papyri throw a flood of light on administrative, sacerdotal, legal and private affairs in these periods. A few literary texts have been identified as well. Objects of non-Egyptian type were also found in the excavations.

In and around the ceremonial entrance courtyard of the southernmost of the Ibis complexes were found a number of demotic ostraca which proved to be part of an archive of documents written or dictated by a certain Delta scribe called Hor, a soothsayer and interpreter of dreams active in the reign of Ptolemy VI (181–145 BC). Many other texts from the same archive were found during excavations in 1971–2 in the same area. Some of these documents are of great historical interest, since they mention the presence in Egypt of the Seleucid king of Syria, Antiochus IV Epiphanes, vilified in the Books of Maccabees, not least for his desecration of the Holy of Holies in the Temple of Jerusalem. The archive, published by J. D. Ray in *The Archive of Hor* (1976), is without doubt one of the most remarkable to have survived from this or from any other period of Egyptian history, and affords in addition an almost unique glimpse into the workings of the ancient Egyptian mind.

All in all the excavations in the Sacred Animal Necropolis have been among the most fruitful in Egypt in recent years, and a mass of information has accrued covering one of the most fascinating aspects of life in the Late Period and during the reigns of the Ptolemies. It has stimulated a new research into these periods, and the enormous amount of new demotic material found between 1964 and 1973 has encouraged a generation of young British Egyptologists to grapple with that difficult script.

Emery never lived to publish his finds, except in a series of preliminary reports in the *Journal of Egyptian Archaeology* and in other periodicals. Like Petrie, his great predecessor at University College London, Emery covered in his discoveries all the major periods of Egyptian history from the First Dynasty to the Graeco-Roman Period, though only part was carried out under the Society's auspices. His contribution to our knowledge of the Nile Valley has been truly fundamental. He loved Egypt, and it is fitting that his bones should have found their last resting-place in that remarkable and ancient land.

After Emery's death in 1971 his unfinished work at Saqqara was consolidated by the present writer as Site Director in two seasons' work under the general direction of H. S. Smith. Some remarkable finds were made in the areas left untouched in the previous campaigns, including a substantial proportion of the Archive of Hor, already alluded to, and many documents, including some of the earliest Greek papyri to have been discovered so far. One of the last, datable to the time of Alexander the Great (336–323 BC) and published in the Society's *Journal* (vol. 60, 1974), is a 'Keep Out' notice originally pinned to the door of one of the shrines in the Animal Necropolis, and doubtless addressed to the rough soldiery stationed in the garrison at nearby Memphis, and written by the order of their local commander.

H. S. Smith has concurrently been directing excavations, already mentioned, on the eastern edge of the Saqqara escarpment, in an area adjacent to the pyramid of Teti, where further ramifications of the Animal Necropolis are apparent. Indeed, it is clear that some of the largest and most important Memphite temple complexes, including the Anubieion and Bubastieion, were located there. Being so easily accessible to the local inhabitants these enormous structures have largely been dismantled over the centuries, and their cult and votive objects plundered and scattered. An archive of documents was, however, apparently found in the vicinity in the last century. Their huge mud-brick enclosure walls and foundation courses do, nevertheless, provide clues to their original splendour and importance. Like their counterparts on the western side of the necropolis, dealt with above, they were built on terraces approached from the valley below by way of impressive ramps. The recent excavations on the site were noteworthy, in that stratified occupation sequences were meticulously recorded perhaps for the first time at Saqqara, where excavation in the past has mostly been conducted as a matter of clearance.

One of the most neglected aspects of excavation for many years has been the lack of detailed study and analysis of the pottery which accrues, often in alarming quantities, on most Egyptian sites. This state of affairs is now rapidly being remedied, not least in the present excavations in the Anubieion and Bubastieion complexes, but also in the work in the New Kingdom necropolis at Saqqara, which will be described below. Petrie was amongst the earliest to recognise the importance of pottery, not only for the dating of sites and buildings but as pointers to the social and economic organisation of the people who produced, marketed, and used it. Inadequate recording methods, and neglect of the study of the techniques of manufacture and fabrics have until very recently meant that pottery vessels, the commonest Egyptian artefacts, have not yielded their full quota of information.

The last phase of the Society's work on the Saqqara plateau to be dealt with in this chapter concerns the excavations initiated by the present writer in 1975, in a part of the necropolis south of the causeway of the pyramid of Unas. This area, systematically

52 (*Right*)
Interior of the
Upper Baboon
Gallery in the
Sacred Animal
Necropolis.

53 (*Below*)
Demotic and
Aramaic papyri
as found in
1971.

examined by the writer on foot over a number of years, was clearly potentially rich
in archaeological material, and had to all intents and purposes remained undisturbed
since the days of rough and ready exploration in the first decades of the nineteenth
century. A number of clues indicated that here was the principal necropolis of the late
Eighteenth and Nineteenth Dynasties in Saqqara. Not the least interesting feature of
the terrain was a series of roughly rectangular depressions in the surface sand, indicating the presence beneath of open courts, indubitably of tombs of the characteristic
Memphite type of the New Kingdom. Such tombs, partially exposed, had been
visited in this area by the epigraphic mission of Karl Richard Lepsius, the great
Prussian Egyptologist, in the 1840s, but the monuments he saw have since been lost
to view under the ever-encroaching sand. Unlike most periods of Egyptian history,
the New Kingdom was represented by no standing monument at Saqqara, a puzzling
fact in view of the great importance of nearby Memphis as a major administrative
centre – some would say the actual capital city – during much of this very period.

A joint expedition of the Society was mounted in fruitful collaboration with the
National Museum of Antiquities, Leiden, in the winter of 1975. Dutch colleagues had
previously assisted at the Society's excavations in the Archaic Necropolis under
W. B. Emery and in the Sacred Animal Necropolis under the present writer.

Shortly after the excavation opened it became clear that we had been fortunate
enough to come down exactly on top of one of the most important tombs of the New
Kingdom in the Memphite necropolis, that of Horemheb, commander-in-chief of
Tutankhamun. Indeed, unwittingly we had positioned our *zirs*, the great water jars
used by our workmen, on the south wall of the First or Outer Courtyard of the tomb.
Relief blocks of outstanding workmanship from this monument had found their way
into many European and American collections in the early nineteenth and twentieth
centuries, but the location of the tomb itself was completely unknown, save that some
column fragments from it in the Cairo Museum, bearing the owner's name and titles,
were known to have come from Saqqara. But Saqqara is vast, and none of the early
explorers, who must have seen and partly cleared portions of the tomb, had bothered
to pinpoint its precise position.

The tomb itself, completely excavated between 1975 and 1978, must have been one
of the grandest of its type in the Memphite necropolis, not surprisingly so in view of
the fact that the owner was chief military adviser and later regent of the youthful
Tutankhamun. With little doubt he was the power behind the throne during the
king's brief reign of nine years or so. After his death without heirs Tutankhamun was
succeeded by Ay, a courtier of non-royal origin but of high military rank. He in turn
was succeeded after a reign of only four years by the great military chieftain Horemheb
(about 1348–1320 BC), who thus never occupied the splendid tomb he had been
preparing for years in the Saqqara necropolis. Nevertheless, his first wife, whose name
is still unknown, and more importantly his second wife, Queen Mutnodjmet, were
buried in it. The tomb itself became the *locus* of the cult of the deified King Horemheb
in the Memphite necropolis in the reign of Ramesses II, and one of the daughters of
that king was buried in it. Nearby is the tomb of a sister of Ramesses II: there is
therefore the possibility that the tomb was the focal point of a Ramesside royal burial
complex for some at least of the numerous offspring of Ramesses II. Only future

excavations will show if this supposition is correct. At any rate the Ramessides regarded Horemheb with veneration, perhaps as their putative ancestor.

The tomb itself, orientated east-west, consists of two colonnaded courtyards linked by a statue-room and storerooms. On the east side is a stone-flagged forecourt leading to a pylon entrance. On the west side of the inner court are three chapels, the central one designed to serve as the cult chamber, where offerings were doubtless subsequently placed for the two wives of Horemheb who were buried close by.

Mercifully, not all the reliefs were removed for reuse in antiquity, nor were the remainder taken away in the nineteenth century. Indeed, it is clear that no systematic excavation was undertaken in the tomb at that period: a minimum of clearance was carried out to reveal blocks just below the surface of the sand. Most of the reliefs removed in the last century can now be reassigned to their original positions on the walls. The wonderful series in the Leiden Museum, for example, came from the south and west walls of the Second or Inner Courtyard. Indeed, the reliefs in this court as a whole provide historical material of prime importance for the reign of Tutankhamun, since they deal in part with Horemheb's foreign exploits on behalf of that king in Western Asia and in the lands south of Egypt. A number of hostages or representatives of foreign nations are depicted: Libyans, Hittites, Syro-Palestinians, Nubians, and other southerners. So graphic is the physiological detail in the reliefs that it is possible to visualise exactly how these peoples looked in real life. Some highly unusual scenes are shown: in one a southern chieftain, very haughty of posture, is about to be thrown on his knees in the dust before the great military commander Horemheb. In another an Egyptian soldier punches a Nubian prisoner on the jaw.

The subterranean parts are no less interesting than the superstructure. The principal burial shaft, leading to a complex of chambers, is located in the inner courtyard. Two minor shafts flank the cult chapel on the west side of the tomb; a fourth is located in the north-west corner of the First or Outer Courtyard. It is apparent that all were originally shafts of Old Kingdom *mastabas* demolished to make way for the tomb of Horemheb, and in the case of the two larger shafts subsequently altered and extended. Evidently the cemetery of the Unas pyramid-complex extends much further to the south and east than had hitherto been suspected, and indeed probably reached to the edge of the escarpment.

Quantities of funerary objects were found in the two principal shafts in the Inner and Outer Courtyards. The one in the latter contained material of the Ramesside period, including two *shabti* figures of Ramesses II's daughter Bint-anat, who is known to have died in the reign of Merneptah. A magnificent gold earring with inlays, recovered from one of the rooms, was perhaps part of her parure. From the historical point of view one of the most interesting finds here comprised three imported Mycenaean vases of a type, usually dated, on the basis of similar material found by Petrie at El-Amarna, to about 1360 BC. The presence of such vases in a much later context has yet to be explained satisfactorily. But the existence of Aegean material in the tomb of Horemheb is encouraging, and gives rise to the hope that much other foreign material in closed contexts may await us in future work in the New Kingdom necropolis at Saqqara. Such pottery deposits, datable from the associated Egyptian material, are crucial for the chronology of the Aegean world.

54 Fragmentary wooden panel with a Greek painting of a goddess, c.300 BC (British Museum, G & R no. 1975. 7–28. 1).

55 Asiatic and negro prisoners depicted in the tomb of Horemheb.

The principal burial shaft was designed originally for the burial of the tomb-owner and his wife, but in the event was used for the latter and for Mutnodjmet, his royal consort and second wife. It is generally supposed that he married her to cement his claim to the crown, and that she was one of the last surviving members of the old Eighteenth Dynasty (Amoside) royal house. All the objects found in this burial complex were of late Eighteenth Dynasty date, and several royal names are inscribed on them: Amenophis III and his wife Tiy, King Ay, Horemheb as Royal Scribe and as King, and Queen Mutnodjmet. Some fragmentary bones found near the rim of the shaft leading to the burial-chamber are very probably those of the queen herself, and with them were the bones of a foetus or newborn child. Expert study of all this skeletal material has revealed the nature of the diseases and disabilities suffered by the queen, and how ultimately she succumbed to them in middle age after several pregnancies. She failed to give the king an heir, and the throne after his death passed to an elderly courtier and confrère of Horemheb named Paramessu, of a military family from the Delta, who ascended the throne in about 1320 BC as Ramesses I.

Apart from pottery wine and storage jars all the funerary equipment had been removed from the queen's burial-chamber. All the fine funerary objects had been seized by plunderers, broken up and scattered in other parts of the underground complex. Two of the jars *in situ* in the burial-chamber bore ink dockets, one giving the prenomen of Horemheb, Djeserkheperure, the other describing the contents as 'very good quality wine from the vineyard of the estate of Horemheb beloved of Amun, may he live, be prosperous and happy, in the house (temple) of Amun'. It is precisely dated to Year 13, third month of the Inundation, and the document is of great interest from the chronological point of view, providing a clue to the date of Queen Mutnodjmet's death and burial, and even more significantly giving the highest certain regnal date of King Horemheb.

In the spring of 1981 excavation was extended to the west of Horemheb's tomb. Two Nineteenth Dynasty tombs were uncovered, one belonging to Paser, Overseer of Builders, and his wife Pepuy, the other to Raia, Chief Singer of Ptah and his wife Mutemuia. This new discovery reinforces the view, substantially confirmed by the work already undertaken, that the area of the Society's concession will yield exceptionally rich information about the Eighteenth and Nineteenth Dynasties in the Memphite region. Old Kingdom material too will doubtless be forthcoming since, as has been indicated, the New Kingdom cemetery occupies the site of an Old Kingdom necropolis. Until now most of our information about Egypt in the fifteenth, fourteenth and thirteenth centuries BC, a crucial period of its history, has been derived from the Theban necropolis in the south, and to a certain extent from El-Amarna and the Delta. One of the primary objectives of the Society's present work in the New Kingdom necropolis at Saqqara has been to redress the balance by providing new material for study from the northern part of the country.

Memphis and its necropolis Saqqara still present many problems and challenges to the archaeologist and historian, and the Society is indeed fortunate in having a base for its activities, archaeological as well as epigraphic, in such a famous and beautiful part of Egypt.

7 Nubia

H. S. SMITH

Physically, Egypt is part of the continent of Africa. This fact has not much currency among modern Egyptians, who for good historical reasons of faith, language and history feel themselves to belong culturally and socially to the world of the Near East and of the Mediterranean littoral. Nor, one suspects, was it popular among the ancient Egyptians, who aspired to a leading political and cultural role in the civilised world of their day, which centred upon the Near East and eastern Mediterranean; Africa was regarded as an alien, hostile and uncultured hinterland, into which one did not venture without the prospect of good material return. Yet it was the rains upon the highlands of Ethiopia and Central Africa that caused the annual flood of the Nile and brought down the alluvium that has formed the fertile plain of Egypt. It was the Nile itself, despite its rocky cataracts, that served as a highway allowing access to rich and rare products from eastern and central Africa: incenses and spices, ebony and rare woods, ivory and pelts: strange fauna, pygmies and human slaves. It was the north-east African deserts cloven by the Nile which provided Egypt with its richest source of mineral wealth: fine building stone, semi-precious gems, copper, gold. Of the contrast between the valley and the hostile wilderness of the deserts, the Egyptians were sharply aware; it was enshrined in the myth of Osiris and Seth, and it dominated their thinking about life and death. But dangerous though the deserts and the hinterland might be, their wealth was from the earliest times a compelling lure. Hence came the historic role of the land of Nubia.

Nubia, properly the land of the Nubian people, who can be traced back perhaps as far as the third century AD, is a convenient term to describe the lands adjoining the Nile south from the First Cataract at Aswan to the Sixth Cataract north of Khartum. Lower Nubia, the ancient Wawat, is applied to the area between the First Cataract and the southern end of the Second Cataract at Semna; Upper Nubia to the area between the Second and Sixth Cataracts, the ancient Kush. The modern political boundary between Egypt and the Sudan crosses the Nile at Ballana, sixty-five kilometres north of Semna. Few contrasts could be starker than that between the Egyptian and the Nubian Nile since the raising of the First Aswan Dam in 1934. In Lower Nubia the dark sandstone cliffs rose direct from the river's edge, split by desert wadis, varied occasionally, as at Ballana, by towering isolated inselbergs. A capping of friable black ironstone scorched and pierced the feet, relieved only by long, golden dunes of soft sand, hard to climb. Isolated villages perched on the cliff-tops; the whitewashed façades of the large mud-brick courtyard houses, often decorated gaily with old plates or paintings of the Hajj (the pilgrimage to Mecca) gleamed in the unrelenting sun-light. Shade temperatures varied from 38°C. in winter to over 43°C. in summer – if one could find shade; only bat-infested caves and a few palms round villages provided it. At most, a narrow strip of vegetation along the river edge marked settlements; the villages, mainly of old men, women and children, with a couple of stalwarts to man the boats, conducted their lives between sunrise and 9 am, and after sundown. Still more desolate were the Cataract areas, where great granite boulders strewn across the landscape resembled a minefield or a lava flow; yet no sight could be more beautiful than the islands of the Second Cataract from the towering battlements of Mirgissa fort in early morning sunlight, or the colonnades of some ruined temple in the lurid light of the westering sun. This strange, silent, dry and empty land, and its noble people, have won the hearts of all its explorers.

In older times, before the dams, it was different, but only in degree. More cultivation graced the Nile banks; stands of palms were more widespread; the desert scrub more plentiful, and wild fauna more in evidence, though only in the damper clime of the earlier third millennium BC can game have been plentiful. Throughout that period, however, and the first half of the second millennium, large herds of cattle, sheep and goats were kept, and a wandering, pastoral life was possible in the oases and on the desert fringes. In Upper Nubia, especially in the relatively fertile Dongola Bend and the isle of Meroë, more cultivation was always and still is possible; in the fourteenth century BC at Soleb vines were grown, and there seems to have been a wine industry in Meroïtic times. The wide open plains south of the Fourth Cataract supported pastoral life amply, and large numbers of cattle were imported annually from Kush by the Egyptians. Nevertheless, the basic contrast between fertile Egypt and barren Nubia has always been present.

Ancient exploitation and modern exploration of Nubia have alike proceeded from north to south, the former governed by improving military technique, the latter by the construction and raising of the dams at the First Cataract. The Egypt Exploration Society, however, arrived rather late on the scene of Nubian exploration.

The flooding of temples caused by the building of the First Aswan Dam in 1898–1904 caused public protest. The Egyptian Ministry of Public Works responded by strengthening temple foundations, especially those of Philae. The raising of the dam was soon mooted. In 1904–5 Gaston Maspero, Director-General of the Egyptian Antiquities Service, visited the principal monuments of Nubia, and directed A. E. P. Weigall to make a complete tour of inspection as far south as Abu Simbel by boat and on foot. Weigall's *A Report on the Antiquities of Lower Nubia* was the first scientific record of Nubian archaeological sites, and made abundantly clear the interest of Nubian history. In consequence Maspero organised the recording of the temples of Lower Nubia and the first full archaeological survey of Nubia while the dam was being raised (1907–11). This survey was conducted by G. A. Reisner, who examined the whole terrain on both banks of the Nile on foot, plotting each site on his survey maps, and excavating each either in full or in part according to the new information it was yielding. Simple in concept, exacting in practice, this method became the model for subsequent surveys; by it Reisner laid the foundations of Nubian archaeology and history. From his results he evolved a chronological scheme of the native cultures of Lower Nubia which subsists in broad outline to this day.

In 1929 a second raising of the dam at Aswan threatened the sites from Wadi

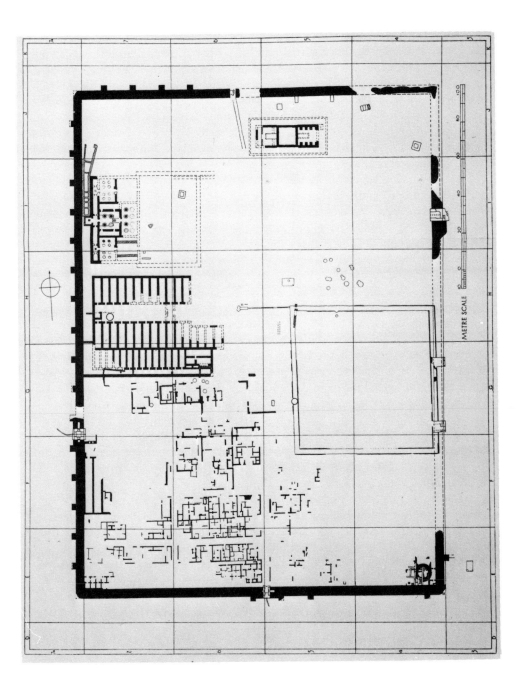

56 Plan of the New Kingdom town at Sesebi (Sudla).

es-Sebua to the Sudanese frontier, and a second archaeological survey was commissioned under W. B. Emery assisted by L. P. Kirwan, with a separate expedition under U. Monneret de Villard to record the Christian monuments. The great discovery of this survey was that of the tumulus-tombs of the X-Group kings of the third to sixth centuries AD at Ballana and Qustul, south of Abu Simbel. These extraordinary burials, with their human and equine sacrifices and rich funerary equipment showing a mixture of Meroïtic and Byzantine motifs, were the first revelation of the wealth and power of these opponents of Byzantine rule in Egypt, who considered themselves the successors to the kingdom of Meroë.

Though British scholars had taken a considerable part in pioneering Nubian archaeology, the Egypt Exploration Society had not, for historical and organisational reasons, participated. But in the aftermath of their excavations of the city of Akhenaten at El-Amarna in Middle Egypt, the Society was attracted in 1936-7 to the site of Sesebi (Sudla) opposite Delgo near the Third Cataract by the presence of three standing columns of a temple reported to bear erased reliefs of Akhenaten. The expedition was led by one of the early recorders of Nubian temples, A. M. Blackman, with H. W. Fairman as his deputy.

The excavation proved that the temple, comprising a small hypostyle hall and three columned sanctuaries, had been founded by Amenophis IV in his early years before he took the name of Akhenaten (about 1373 BC). In a crypt he and his wife Nefertiti are shown worshipping gods of the Heliopolitan Ennead and 'Nebmare Lord of Nubia', that is, his deified predecessor Amenophis III. A small sun-temple was erected outside the main temple, perhaps later in Akhenaten's reign. In the main temple the scenes of Akhenaten and Nefertiti were defaced and overcut by scenes of Sethos I, who extended the temple and rededicated it probably to the triad of Amun, Mut and Khonsu.

The town, excavated in the following season by H. W. Fairman, was surrounded by an enclosure wall which had also been founded by Amenophis IV. It protected an area of about 270 m by 200 m, which contained a large block of storerooms adjacent to the temple, and a domestic quarter in its south-west corner. This included a few medium-sized villas of the kind found at El-Amarna, and streets of small back-to-back houses for the working populace; cellars for food storage and shelter during the heat of summer were common. These houses had been built close in time to the foundation of the settlement; later they had been deserted, and subsequently reoccupied in the reign of Sethos I or of Ramesses II. Gradually they had been subdivided to provide more rooms, until their final abandonment in late Ramesside times (about 1100 BC). It was clear, however, that the original town as planned was never completed, for half the area was left empty. In this portion was a dry ditch enclosing a square, empty space, which may, as Fairman suggested, have been for the protection of workmen while constructing the town; but an early Eighteenth Dynasty royal head, a door-jamb of the Vizier Amenemope of the time of Amenophis II, and scarabs of Tuthmosis III from the pillaged cemetery may possibly indicate that there was an earlier Eighteenth Dynasty settlement at Sesebi.

From Sesebi, Fairman moved the Society's expedition to Amara West, site of another interesting New Kingdom town, 185 kilometres south of Wadi Halfa. Though smaller than Sesebi, it was better preserved. The town wall, enclosing an area of about 150 m by 100 m was built by Sethos I (about 1318–1304 BC). The temple, asymmetrical in plan, may have been begun in his reign, but was decorated under Ramesses II. Later in Ramesses' reign it was enlarged, and a gate to the temple was constructed through the town wall, flanked by copies of the Dream and Marriage Inscriptions of Ramesses II which appear at Abu Simbel. Inscriptions found in the temple show that it remained in use to the time of Ramesses XI; they have provided valuable clarifications of the history of the Viceroys of Nubia in the Ramesside period.

Owing to the war, the Society did not return to Amara West until 1947–8, when Fairman excavated the town. There he identified a large building comprising official quarters, private apartments, stores and offices as the residence of the 'Deputy of Kush', who governed Upper Nubia under the Viceroy. Initially the town contained large storage areas, to be expected in a depot on the Nile route, but these were gradually divided up for domestic occupation. There were three phases of New Kingdom occupation covering the period from Sethos I to near the end of the Ramesside period. The place was then completely abandoned, but there was a reoccupation later, probably in Napatan times (about 700 BC). Though no finds of the El-Amarna period were discovered at Amara, as had been the case at Sesebi, earlier monuments perhaps indicate some Egyptian activity from at least the time of Amenophis II. Thus the sites of Sesebi and Amara West may together represent the three phases of Egyptian colonisation of Upper Nubia in the New Kingdom: the original penetration to the Fourth Cataract under the early Tuthmosides and Amenophis II; the great building campaign of Amenophis III and IV which was intended to make the relatively fertile reach of the Dongola bend into a new Egypt; and the final attempt to colonise Nubia north of the Third Cataract by Sethos I and Ramesses II, which produced the great temples of Abu Simbel, Gerf Husein and Beit el-Wali.

Two separate, though linked, events caused the Society to return to Sudanese Nubia in 1957, the Suez crisis, and the threat posed to the sites and monuments of Nubia by the Soviet Russian undertaking to build a new High Dam for Egypt at the First Cataract. On the advice of its Field Director, W. B. Emery, the Society chose the great mud-brick fortress of Buhen opposite Wadi Halfa as the Society's first objective, and excavation began in the autumn of 1957. When the UNESCO rescue campaign for Nubia was launched in 1959–60, the Society took on four further commitments: the final archaeological survey of Egyptian Nubia; the epigraphic recording of the New Kingdom temples of Buhen, and of the rock-shrines at Qasr Ibrim (the temples of Semna and Kumma were added later); the removal of the temple of Hatshepsut at Buhen to Khartum; and the excavation of the fortress and cemeteries of Qasr Ibrim in Egyptian Nubia. Though these works were but a contribution to the great international effort to save the history and monuments of Nubia, they constituted a formidable scientific commitment for the Society.

The third archaeological survey of Egyptian Nubia was conducted by the present writer in the spring and autumn of 1961. The survey party, traversing both banks of the Nile from the Sudanese frontier to Shallal, recommended for full excavation two Christian sites (Qasr el-Wizz and Abdallah Nirqi), a rock-shelter with early paintings in the Khor Fum Atmur at Korosko, and an A-Group (Early Dynastic) settlement at Afya. The last two, together with cemeteries at Tunqala and elsewhere investigated by the survey, shed interesting light on the cultural connections of the A-Group Nubians.

The earliest site at Buhen, first observed by Mrs. Emery, presented itself as a scatter of copper ore and slag along the bank of the Nile north of the fortress. Excavation in 1962 revealed a settlement comprising rectangular mud-brick buildings laid out on a fairly symmetrical plan within a low, irregular defensive wall or breastwork built of rough-hewn local stone. Within the buildings, which were presumably open to the sky, were a series of simple updraft furnaces for the smelting of copper, constructed of mud brick and beaten clay. Copper ore, copper slag, crucibles, ladles and nozzles were found, with traces of copper adhering in one or two cases. Though no local source of copper ore was discovered, an ancient desert road leading out westwards from the gate of the later fortress may well have led to one; it was only traced for about ten kilometres. Mud sealings from jars found on the site bore impressions which included the names of Egyptian kings from Sneferu at the beginning of the Fourth Dynasty (about 2620 BC) to Nyuserre in the middle of the Fifth Dynasty (about 2420 BC). The pottery consisted of 95 per cent imported Egyptian wares and only of 5 per cent local Nubian, showing that the site was mainly populated by Egyptians. It also confirmed the date-range of the site, though the stratification showed that there was a lower level of occupation. Emery suggested, on the basis of the doubtful evidence of one or two sealings, that the settlement might have been founded rather earlier than the reign of Sneferu. This remarkable though denuded settlement, unique in Nubia both for its early date and its industrial character, provided important evidence for the practical, commercial character of the initial exploitation of Nubia by the Egyptians, and perhaps a clue to the reason for the decline of the Nubian A-Group as a settled valley people some time during the Archaic Period.

The great mud-brick fortress of Buhen had been partly excavated by Randall-MacIver and Woolley for the Philadelphia Museum before the First World War. Emery's new excavation, however, demonstrated that both its structure and its history were more complex than had been thought. The Inner Fortress (150 m by 138 m) was constructed by Sesostris I in the early Twelfth Dynasty (about 1965 BC). The fortifications consisted essentially of a great mud-brick wall, 5 m thick and over 11 m high, with square towers projecting from its outer face, probably surmounted by battlements with loopholes and cantilevered wooden machicolations. Along its outer face ran a brick-paved rampart, defended by a rampart wall overlooking a broad, dry ditch with a steep counterscarp and a sloping scarp, to prevent mining. The rampart wall was pierced by groups of three ranged in two tiers, each with a single internal embrasure, so that two echelons of archers could fire from the fire-step across and into the ditch. The same wall was punctuated by round bastions projecting into the ditch to ensure that cross-fire could be maintained. Above the counterscarp was a light breastwork and glacis, the open terrain beyond being covered from the great wall. On the landward side there was a single central gate, flanked by two large towers projecting beyond the ditch which was crossed by means of a timber drawbridge capable of being withdrawn on wooden rollers in the event of attack.

This Inner Fortress protected the main buildings of the town, but an Outer Forti-

57 (*Top*) Work in the New Kingdom temple of Amara West in 1939.

58 (*Bottom*) Dismantling the Eighteenth Dynasty temple of Buhen for transport to Khartum.

fication with a perimeter of 712 m was constructed to protect a much greater area, probably occupied by the cantonments of the Egyptian troops, and perhaps also by Nubian troops and by animal lines. This outwork in its original form consisted of a wall of brick and probably stone, punctuated by large round bastions, no doubt supplied with a parapet and loopholes. It was, however, reconstructed, probably when Sesostris III built the forts at the head of the Second Cataract (about 1860 BC), as a massive mud-brick fortification, 5.5 m thick and probably 12 m high, with large towers and spur walls on its outer face following the lie of the land. It was entered from the desert road by a huge twin-towered barbican gate with two internal baffles. Lesser gates stood on the north and south sides with narrow indirect entry systems. The whole was surrounded by a dry ditch. Between them these two fortifications, containing something over 13,000,000 mud bricks might seem to have been absolutely impregnable to the slings, arrows and spears of the contemporary Nubians. Yet there is clear evidence that the Inner West Gate was stormed and fired by Kerma Nubians, perhaps in about 1650 BC.

Within the Inner Fortifications the town was laid out on a grid pattern in strict military fashion. A baffle within the West Gate gave on to streets running under the western battlements to the two main streets of the town. These streets, running from west to east, and paved with baked-brick tiles, were provided with central stone drains for run-off in the event of an occasional violent storm. They led through towered river-gates on to long stone quays projecting into the Nile, where not only the great barges bearing reinforcements, food, wine and supplies for the garrison (probably over 1,000 men), but also the royal fleet bearing the precious products of Kush and beyond drew up. Inside these quays were constructed underground passages reached by stairways within the gates, allowing the camp water-supply to be drawn directly from the Nile without any danger from enemy action.

The Commandant's Palace, a spacious brick building, occupied the north-west corner of the fortress, protected from the wind. It comprised at ground level a colonnaded courtyard, a large painted audience-hall with columns, an inner hall, domestic offices, stores and guardroom; one stairway led to an upper storey, the other to the battlements. Adjoining it was the main storage magazine and scribal offices of the town, beyond which lay the temple treasury and the modest brick temple of Horus of Buhen. In the south-west corner of the town were the officers' quarters, medium-sized houses with about four rooms on the ground floors. The remainder of the town at ground level was occupied by large blocks containing small square and rectangular rooms, mostly without doors, with occasional courts or light-wells; probably these were used as cellars for storage and for escaping the heat of summer, the main accommodation being on an upper floor.

The results of the excavation allowed a fairly detailed history of the fortress to be built up. In the early Twelfth Dynasty the fortress probably marked the frontier against the Kushite enemy, later in the dynasty becoming the chief depot for traffic both with Egypt and with Upper Nubia, and a base for troop movements. The subsidiary walled garrison with a small harbour at Kor, three kilometres south of Buhen, which probably supplemented this function, was also excavated for the Society by the present writer. When the frontier was established at Semna by Sesostris

59 Clearing the Middle Kingdom fortress at Buhen.

III (about 1865 BC), the role of Buhen and Kor became less military and more administrative. Buhen became the centre of a signalling system for patrols watching the
desert routes, as is shown by a series of posts in the hills round the fortress, where the
names of Middle Kingdom soldiers on guard duty are preserved in hieratic graffiti,
copied by the Society. In the Governor's Palace scraps of papyrus letters were found,
sufficient to show that Buhen was in constant communication with the other Nubian
forts and with the administration in Egypt. After the reign of Ammenemes III, a
weakening of the garrison and the ever-increasing boldness and military skill of the
Kerma warriors probably led to the sack of the fortress about 1650 BC. During the
independent rule of the Nubian princes of Kush which followed, bands of Kerma
warriors appear to have camped in and about the partly ruined fortress while Egyptian
officials seem actually to have served the Kushite princes as local governors.

Early in the sixteenth century BC, however, King Kamose of the Seventeenth
Dynasty defeated the ruler of Kush and reannexed Lower Nubia as far as and including
Buhen. The Inner Fortifications of Buhen were hastily repaired, and when King
Amosis had expelled the Hyksos, the Commandant of Buhen, Turi, later to become
Viceroy of Kush, restored and rededicated the North Temple to Horus of Buhen.
During the early reigns of the Eighteenth Dynasty Buhen may have remained a
military base of some importance, as well as one of the residences of the Viceroy when
on tour. But by the time that Hatshepsut had built and decorated the splendid new
South Temple for Horus of Buhen, the place had probably become virtually an open
town. A wealth of inscribed material reveals its importance in the administration of
Nubia and as a station on the Nile route; sealings and jar-labels recording the import
of wine, meat, honey and other luxuries from Egypt attest the regularity of the
Viceroys' visits. From the time of Akhenaten onwards, however, there is a decline in
such evidence, with only a relative increase in the reigns of Sethos I and Ramesses II
during the Nineteenth Dynasty. Subsequently, the administration of Buhen became
progressively run by the priests, the civil population declined, and by 1090 BC it may
have been virtually deserted. A long history of destruction began, interrupted by a
brief restoration of the temple under the Napatan king Taharqa (about 680 BC). The
ruins of Buhen were reoccupied by the X-Group in about the fifth century AD.
After Christianity reached Nubia, a church was set up in the ancient South temple
precinct, and for a brief period a Christian community flourished there, before Buhen
was deserted for ever.

While excavation proceeded, the all-important task of copying and recording the
inscriptions of the temples was completed in 1960–1 by R. A. Caminos of Brown
University, whose work at Buhen, Qasr Ibrim, and Semna and Kumma is outlined
in Chapter 8 (p. 155).

In 1963 it became urgent to move the temple of Hatshepsut to Khartum. This was
effected by Emery using the ancient methods of sand-fills, sand-ramps, simple levers
and man-haulage; the only modern machine used was a lewis. The blocks were
conserved, gently lowered on to sand, packed on the spot, slid down the ramps into
barges, and transported direct to the railway terminal at Wadi Halfa by the Sudan
Antiquities Service. The whole operation was completed in four months at minimal
expense without mishap; it was a triumph of organisation and a most interesting

demonstration of the practicality and efficiency of ancient methods. The temple is now one of the chief attractions of the splendid new Museum of Antiquities at Khartum.

The Society's final task in the Nubian Rescue Campaign was the excavation of the citadel of Qasr Ibrim, perched on its high rock opposite Aniba, and its cemeteries below. Because they were immediately threatened by rising water Emery excavated the cemeteries first in 1961. The main body of tumulus-tombs belonged to the X-Group period from the third to the sixth centuries AD, and were small copies of the great royal mounds of Ballana and Qustul. Most were heavily plundered, yielding only disturbed burials, containing at best quantities of fine thin white pottery cups and large red-ware bottles, gaily painted with floral and other motifs. In two burials vaulted magazines built beside the burial-chambers under the tumulus were missed by the plunderers. These contained fine bronze dishes with decorated handles, bronze jugs and lamps (one in the form of a camel, another in that of a Greek hero), orna-mented faience vessels, iron spears, arrowheads and horse trappings. These objects vividly illustrated the bizarre mixed culture of the X-Group people, initially evidently a warlike, pagan race, who sacrificed and buried with them their wives, domestics, horses and camels, yet considered themselves heirs to the Meroïtic kingdom, and enjoyed something of the cultural heritage of both Meroë and Byzantine Egypt. In a few graves, however, were found Christian symbols which had not been noted at Ballana and Qustul. In one tomb-chamber, from which a normal X-Group assemblage was recovered including crudely carved ivory plaques with pagan Egyptianising and Hellenising designs, there was a Christian cross engraved on the end wall. This suggests that the X-Group must have accepted Christianity during their rule at Qasr Ibrim. Equally important historically was the discovery of Meroïtic burials, which had been surmounted by typical brick or stone pyramidions with a niche in the east side containing a statue of the deceased's soul (ba) in the form of a bird, one of which was found intact.

The excavation of the fortress of Qasr Ibrim, directed by J. M. Plumley until 1976, began in 1963 and still continues. For, fortunately, contrary to the original expectation, the waters of Lake Nasser, though they have destroyed the east gate of the citadel and damaged a Meroïtic temple at its north-eastern corner, have still not reached the 'Acropolis' of Qasr Ibrim, where the Cathedral proudly stands. Since 1972 W. Y. Adams of the University of Kentucky has been closely associated with the excavation.

The rock of Qasr Ibrim stands on the east bank of the Nile, opposite the ancient fortress and town of Miam (modern Aniba). Founded in the early Twelfth Dynasty as one of the great chain of Nubian forts, Miam became in the New Kingdom the centre of the administration of Lower Nubia, a residence of the Viceroy and the head-quarters of the Deputy of Wawat. Probably the great rock of Ibrim had always been a sacred place. It now seems likely from the excavations that in the Eighteenth Dynasty the Egyptians built a temple on its summit, founded by the time of Tuthmosis III (1504–1450 BC) and in use into the Twentieth Dynasty (after 1160 BC). A stela showing Amenophis I with his mother and wife worshipping Horus of Miam suggests the importance of the chief local god of Miam, the high cliff no doubt being a suitable sanctuary of the falcon god of the sky; but the stela is not necessarily contemporary with Amenophis I, of whom there was a posthumous cult. The shrines of Nubian

60 (*Right*) Objects in an
X-group grave at
Qasr Ibrim.

61 (*Below*) Bronze
lamp from an
X-group burial at
Qasr Ibrim (British
Museum, EA no.
66576).

Viceroys and other dignitaries in the river face of the rock of Qasr Ibrim, copied and published by R. A. Caminos, clearly reflect the sanctity of the site in the New Kingdom.

As at many sites in Upper and Lower Nubia, Taharqa, King of Napata, the penultimate king of the Twenty-fifth Dynasty (690–664 BC), built at Qasr Ibrim. His inscriptions confirm that the small temple he constructed was dedicated to Horus of Miam. After the defeat of Taharqa's successor Tanutamun by the Assyrians and his flight to Napata, Ibrim became deserted.

The site must have been resettled by the Meroïtes before Augustus' general, Caius Petronius, drove them off the rock and occupied it from 25–21 BC. West of the Taharqa temple have been found the much destroyed ruins of a later and larger stone temple, from the paving of which the excavations recovered Roman coins running from the early second century AD to the early fifth century AD. However, the temple pavement was incised by pilgrims with stylised footprints in which they carved their names, one of which reads 'For Ptolemy', suggesting perhaps a Ptolemaic date. A great stone balustraded platform in the south fortifications, known as 'the Podium', the temple-quay to this temple complex, is considered by its excavator to be possibly of Hellenistic workmanship. Further, a careful investigation of the fortifications in this sector has shown that there was with little doubt a rebuilding of the girdle wall during Petronius' occupation. The original girdle wall must therefore belong to a previous Meroïtic occupation, and the round tower and bastion in the same area to a still earlier period. There is thus good evidence for the Meroïtes having made Qasr Ibrim (the Primis of classical writers) a northern bastion of their empire during the last centuries BC. It was in rubbish from the fortifications mentioned above that one of the most remarkable textual finds of the whole excavation was made, Latin elegiacs on papyrus, written by Cornelius Gallus, the first Governor of Roman Egypt.

The Meroïtes reoccupied Qasr Ibrim soon after the Roman frontier had been withdrawn to Hierasykaminos (Maharraqa) by Augustus, and there are all the signs of a long and important occupation. There are extensive domestic structures below the X-Group town which must have been occupied in Meroïtic times. Three temples were in use by the Meroïtes: the old Taharqa temple, the large temple adjoining it, a temple on the north-eastern corner of the site, now partly submerged by Lake Nasser. Meroïtic grave-stelae in the cemeteries show clearly that people using the Meroïtic language were buried at Ibrim. Of two very large stelae which may be of secular content one bears the names of Queen Amanishakhete and Prince Akinidad, who ruled at the same time as Petronius' garrison. In addition, a large range of non-monumental texts written in cursive Meroïtic on sherds, wooden tablets, and, for the first time, on papyrus seem, in so far as they are understood, to include documents of day-to-day life. An indication of the length of the Meroïtic occupation is provided by a stone figure of a lion inscribed for the Meroïtic King Amani-Yeshbeke, whose reign is estimated to have been about 286–306 AD. It is likely, therefore, that when the Emperor Diocletian in 297 AD invited the Nobatai to occupy the territory of Lower Nubia to protect Egypt from the marauding of the Blemmyes (Beja), Qasr Ibrim was still under the suzerainty of the Meroïte king.

It is in the next phase of occupation, characterised by X-Group pottery, that we can see the development of Qasr Ibrim into a large and well-developed town. One major and central building was first interpreted as a 'Governor's Palace', but subsequently called 'The Tavern', because an amphora on a stand and a bunch of grapes were sculptured on its external masonry, and because over 85 per cent of the 15,000 sherds found there belonged to wine vessels, amphorae and goblets. This building was clearly an important centre. Streets were ranged in alinement with it, along which were important structures with large storage crypts, which seem not to have been dwellings. Indeed, it is possible that the inhabitants had their normal dwellings in light structures in the valley below. Among a number of most interesting discoveries were Meroïtic papyrus letters with their clay seals which were found just above the original floor of a house in which all the pottery was X-Group. In another building a Coptic liturgical papyrus was found in a storage crypt containing X-Group refuse, above which were three X-Group floor levels. These discoveries, taken with the evidence from the cemeteries (earlier X-Group burials with Meroïtic survivals in the funerary equipment and pagan sacrificial customs; later burials with Christian symbols), provide some evidence for the hypothesis that the Christianisation of Nubia occurred in the middle of the X-Group period, and not, as formerly thought, at the end of it.

This hypothesis has been somewhat strengthened by the discovery on the floor of a storeroom under an X-Group house of a number of documents, one of which, written in bad Greek, is a letter from a king of the Blemmyes (Beja), named Phonen, to Abourni, King of the Nobatai, asking him to give back territory so that in future they will keep peace with one another. A Silko mentioned in the letter should probably be identified with the 'Silko, chief king of the Nobatai and all the Ethiopians', author of a famous inscription, also in bad Greek, on the walls of Kalabsha temple, in which he claims to have been victorious over the Blemmyes three times and to have made war with them from Primis (Ibrim) to Telelis (Shallal?). What seems possible is that about 425 AD the king of the Blemmyes, perhaps resident in Talmis, was suzerain, but that by the middle of the century victories by Silko and Abourni had wrested the suzerainty for the Nobatai, who may have had their residence at Primis (Ibrim). Though it is not certain from the Greek texts that the Nobatai Silko and Abourni were Christians by this time, it is significant that three scrolls found in proximity to Phonen's letter contain letters in Saᶜidic Coptic written to the phylarch Tantani, who is described in one of them by a Byzantine official as 'the lord of those who belong to Nouba'. Thus a high official of the Nobatai was being written to in a specifically Christian language and being addressed in specifically Christian words. The probability seems to be that the Nobatai were Christian by the mid-fifth century, and that they are to be identified with the X-Group. Ibrim, perhaps, was the first Christian city of Nubia, and the Temple Church one of its earliest churches.

The Temple Church, however, was probably not the most important church of Qasr Ibrim (known as Phrim in Christian documents), for on the highest point of the site the remains of a large church have been traced under the Cathedral; this earlier church may have belonged to the sixth century AD. The Cathedral, probably of the seventh century, is exceptional among Nubian churches not only for its size but also for the fact that it is constructed of stone, mainly large sandstone blocks which were evidently taken from the earlier Napatan-Meroïtic temples. It is basilican in form with

62 The Meroïtic temple at Qasr Ibrim.

five aisles. The east end had a spacious apse flanked by a baptistry and vestry (?), while the entrance at the west end was through three doorways, flanked by a large square tower, presumably with belfry, another exceptional feature for Nubia. The reason for this magnificence was undoubtedly that the Eparch of Nubia, the deputy of the High King of Nubia, resided there, and it may prove that a large stone building nearby was the palace of the Eparch. Phrim was also a bishopric, and under the east end of the Cathedral were found crypts containing the burials of bishops.

Round the 'Acropolis' was a Christian city of considerable size, of which only part has been excavated so far. In the Early Christian Period the X-Group houses were still in use, though often extended and rebuilt. During the Classic Christian Period the city was extended along a north to south axis, but earlier buildings, including the 'Eparch's Palace', remained in use. In the Late Christian Period major changes in the character of the city appeared. Then the Meroïtic girdle wall, which had been allowed to crumble, was hurriedly renewed round the whole perimeter; on the 'Podium' a 'watch-tower' was built; the housing within the city, too, gives the impression of being reoccupied and partially or wholly reconstructed, mostly in a rather flimsy and unsystematic fashion. The impression is of a community under military threat, but nevertheless maintaining their churches in use and continuing their way of life.

The history of Qasr Ibrim can be illumined by the magnificent finds of documents in Greek, Coptic, Old Nubian and Arabic, most of which remain to be studied and published. Four scrolls found in the cellar of a house, one in Arabic and three in Saʿidic Coptic, are among the earliest and most significant. The Arabic scroll contains the text of a letter of complaint dated in the autumn of 758 AD from Musa Ibn Kaʿb, the Governor of Egypt, to the King of Nubia, whose name is unfortunately lost. Its burden is that the treaty (*baqt*) agreed a century earlier, though observed by the Governor of Egypt, has been breached by the King of Nubia, in as much as he has allowed merchants from Egypt to be oppressed and robbed contrary to his under-taking, that runaway slaves have not been returned, and that he has sent as his con-tribution of slaves under the terms of the *baqt* 'the one-eyed, or the lame, or the weak old man, or the young boy'. The Governor demands restitution on pain of penalities. The accompanying Coptic scrolls seem to be letters to the King of Nubia, perhaps from the Eparch, drafting replies to the Governor's letter, so the Nubian king was not necessarily resident at Phrim. The correspondence, apart from its intrinsic interest, proves finally that the Blemmyes are to be identified with the Beja.

Among the funerary stelae of the Christian bishops and clergy (the more important generally in Greek, the others in Coptic) one records the death of Marianos, Bishop of Pachoras (Faras) in 1037 AD, filling a gap in the list of the bishops of Pachoras found by the Polish expedition at Faras. Liturgical and biblical texts in Greek show that, at least in the Early Christian Period, Greek was used in the liturgy. Biblical and homiletic fragments in Saʿidic Coptic suggest that Coptic was later widely read, and Plumley has suggested that monks and priests from Egypt were present at Qasr Ibrim. Old Nubian fragments are also mainly biblical and homiletic, suggesting a gradual increase with time in the use of the vernacular in the liturgy, but there are also fragments of letters reflecting official correspondence in the native language. Arabic texts are mainly letters from Muslims to the Eparch of Ibrim, under his title 'Lord of

63 Remains of
the temple
and church
at Qasr
Ibrim.

the Horsemen'. The most interesting dates to 1169 AD, just before the date of the raid of Saladin's brother, Shams ed-Doulah, into Nubia in 1173 BC, when he laid siege to Phrim and captured it, despoiling the church and throwing the Bishop into prison. Probably the Late Christian reconstruction of the fortifications was in preparation for or in response to this attack.

But despite this blow the Christian community continued; the most spectacular proof of this was provided by the discovery of the intact burial of Bishop Timotheos in the north crypt of the Cathedral Church. Hidden in his robes were two paper scrolls, one written in Arabic, the other in Bohairic Coptic containing the Letters Testimonial from the Patriarch of Alexander, Gabriel IV, dated 1372 AD, informing the people of Nubia that he had consecrated Timotheos in succession to the deceased Athanasius as Bishop of Phrim. Further, nine leather scrolls in Old Nubian show that Christianity was still practised in the late fourteenth and probably the fifteenth centuries, when there was still, according to the latest in date, a Christian king reigning in Nubia at Dotawo (Gebel Adda).

In the early sixteenth century the Ottoman Sultan Suliman the Magnificent sent a company of 500 Bosnian mercenaries to Nubia to capture the fortress of Qasr Ibrim. Thus ended the Christian history of the site; the Cathedral, after pillage, was converted into a mosque, though the basic structure was not much altered. The Christian houses, however, were mostly levelled and replaced by stout stone-walled houses. The wages of the Bosnian garrison were paid by the Turkish treasury in Cairo over a number of years, while their number was reduced from 500 to 50. Eventually, however, those who remained lapsed from the pay-roll and intermarried with local people. An Aga ruled over the fortress, and many documents show that the official language was now Arabic, though a few Turkish fragments also survive.

This occupation continued for nearly 300 years, and the finds illustrate the type of life led. Rather crude pottery, pipes, gaming-pieces, stone querns, iron tools, glass beads, a mass of basketry, leather, and coarse cloth are relieved by the occasional fragment of Chinese porcelain, of Egyptian glazed ware, and even a bronze cannon. The final episode at Ibrim was macabre. In 1811 the Mamelukes, fleeing from Mehemet Ali, the Albanian conqueror of Egypt, ejected the Bosnians from the fortress with considerable slaughter. In 1812 the Mamelukes in turn were compelled by Mehemet's son, Ibrahim Pasha, to retreat south to Dongola. Before they left they murdered the reigning Aga, enslaved those of the native populace who had not escaped downstream to Derr, and devastated the fortress. From that date Qasr Ibrim remained deserted.

Thus, though the Egypt Exploration Society was late in the field in the exploration of Nubia, its works there have thrown much light on Nubian history from the fourth millennium BC to the nineteenth century AD. There is no doubt that the splendid site of Qasr Ibrim, if spared from the waters of Lake Nasser, has still more to tell.

8 The Archaeological Survey

T. G. H. JAMES

In *The Times* of 15 October 1890 this letter from Miss Amelia Edwards was published:

> May I ask your permission to say a few words with reference to the interesting letter by my friend, Mr. Villiers Stuart, which appeared in your issue of the 7th inst.? Mr. Villiers Stuart is a highly valued member of the Committee of the Egypt Exploration Fund, and if he could more frequently have given us the advantage of his presence at our Committee meetings, he would have known that the society has for several months had it in contemplation to make an archaeological survey of Egypt. We hope, with the sanction of the Egyptian Government, to be very shortly in a position to send out two gentlemen fully qualified as archaeologists, Egyptologists, and surveyors, whose duty it will be to map, plan, photograph, and copy all the most important sites, sculptures, paintings and inscriptions yet extant, so as to preserve at least a faithful record of these fast-perishing monuments.
>
> I note with pleasure Mr. Villiers Stuart's generous offer to contribute towards the expense of such a project, and I gladly embrace the present opportunity of inviting all lovers of ancient art and ancient history to assist our society in this new and important undertaking.

This eloquent announcement of the foundation of the Archaeological Survey of Egypt made known to the general public the successful outcome of a campaign to protect, preserve and record the monuments of Egypt which had led in 1888 to the foundation of the Society for the Preservation of the Monuments of Ancient Egypt, to a great deal of discussion within the Committee of the Egypt Exploration Fund and to much excited correspondence in the pages of *The Times*. Mr. Villiers Stuart's contribution to the correspondence, which stimulated Miss Edwards to write the letter quoted above, was distinguished by his offer to help financially with any positive scheme designed to save Egyptian antiquities so greatly threatened by neglect, carelessness, active vandalism and the mindless behaviour of tourists. He had himself visited Egypt in 1883–4 while he was a Member of Parliament for Waterford, and had first-hand experience of the circumstances which he so much deplored. His ignorance of what was planned by the Egypt Exploration Fund – inexcusable, it might be thought, for one who was a member of its Committee – exposed publicly by Miss Edwards's letter, could scarcely be other than acknowledged, and he subsequently wrote offering to make a generous donation to the proposed Archaeological Survey. He volunteered to give £50 towards the expenses of the Survey provided that forty-nine other well-wishers gave the same amount. In the records of the Fund this offer became known as the Villiers Stuart Challenge, but sadly it never achieved the success which its founder had, presumably, expected. From the careful records of donations published in the successive reports of the Fund, only two donors appear to have met the challenge, and it would seem that Villiers Stuart was never required to fulfil his pledge. He died in 1895, unchallenged, but scarcely unaware that the success of the Archaeological Survey was by then secured.

In the discussions which led to the foundation of the Archaeological Survey the officers and leading lights of the Egypt Exploration Fund were united in their desire to do something to improve the sad state of affairs which threatened the survival of the ancient monuments of Egypt, but their attempts to achieve anything positive scarcely amounted to more than the composition of well-intentioned motions and the writing of impassioned letters to the civil officials and officers of the Antiquities Service in Egypt. It remained for one of the youngest members of the Fund, but one who was to become probably the greatest British Egyptologist in the history of the discipline, to make the practical proposal which transformed intention into achievement. In this, as in so much else he did, Francis Llewellyn Griffith, displayed remarkable judgement.

Griffith, a true autodidact in Egyptology, had quite deliberately neglected his studies at Oxford in order to concentrate on his chosen subject for which there was in the early 1880s no tutorial provision in the University. By 1884, at the age of twenty-two, he had already attracted the attention of Flinders Petrie and of Amelia Edwards. At the second Annual Meeting of the Egypt Exploration Fund Miss Edwards identified among the outstanding 'discoveries' of the Fund during the year 'an object of the utmost rarity, quite new, and in admirable preservation . . . ; an object more curious than any antiquity in the British Museum – namely a young student of Egyptology, being the first specimen of that article which has turned up for a whole generation'. Griffith's arrival on the Egyptological scene was no less than providential. Although he was only twenty-two in 1884, his command of published sources and his grasp of the Egyptian language were quite exceptional. To his theoretical knowledge he was soon to add considerable practical field experience, working with Petrie and with Edouard Naville at Tanis, Naucratis and other Delta sites. He could provide the rigour derived from systematic scholarship which was so needed at a time when the Fund was largely in the hands of talented amateurs and of scholars trained in disciplines other than Egyptology. His earliest written contributions to the excavation memoirs of the Fund were stamped with the authority of a master, young though he was, and he fully earned his appointment as Student of the Fund.

In the winter of 1886–7 Griffith joined Petrie in a journey by boat from Minya in Middle Egypt to Aswan, in the course of which they tramped vast lengths of both banks of the Nile, seeking monuments and ancient sites, copying inscriptions and taking copious notes. This was Griffith's first visit to Upper Egypt and it provided him with impressions of vast, untapped, sources of material and of precious antiquities unguarded, threatened and in the course of active destruction. His own principal published result of the journey was *Inscriptions of Siut and Dêr Rîfeh* (1889), in which he provided copies of a series of most important tomb inscriptions dated in part to the First Intermediate Period. In preparing his copies for publication he made every

64 Francis Llewellyn Griffith, founder of the Archaeological Survey.

effort to consult the unpublished copies made by earlier visitors to these places. By so doing he established a tradition of comprehensive research which has subsequently been the hall-mark of good epigraphic publication. The examination of these early copies provided textual readings obtained when the inscriptions were in a less damaged state. Griffith's anguish at the constant destruction led him to add this epigraph to his work:

> If a small portion of the sums of money that, *in the name of scientific research*, have been spent in Egypt on treasure-hunting for antiquities, on uncovering monuments and exposing them to destruction, on *unwatched* excavations from which the limestone sculptures have gone straight to the kiln or the village stone-mason – if a small portion of this had been utilised in securing systematically throughout the country accurate and exhaustive copies of the inscriptions above ground and in danger, the most important part of all her evidence of her past that Egypt has handed down to our day would have been gathered intact, instead of mutilated beyond recovery.
>
> If the remainder of those sums had been devoted to watching, and taking proper measures to preserve, the monuments of Egypt, the present century would not have been destined above all other periods to the maledictions of posterity on account of the searching and unrelenting damage of every kind done to these records, that had weathered so many centuries with hardly an injury, and that should have delighted mankind for so many ages to come.

Over sixty years later when the Egypt Exploration Society's epigraphers at Saqqara were preparing the publication of a *mastaba*-chapel, which was to be the thirtieth memoir of the Archaeological Survey, one of the Egyptian guards unexpectedly voiced Griffith's lament precisely. Commenting on the destruction of standing monuments he blamed those excavators who unearthed inscribed monuments and failed to publish or protect them. His remedy was to rebury after discovery and publication. Sadly his lesson remains unlearnt, and today the destruction is perhaps greater than ever as even the smallest inscribed or decorated fragment torn from a temple or tomb can find a ready buyer in the antiquities market.

At the Ordinary General Meeting of the Egypt Exploration Fund in November 1889 Griffith contributed a paper on his work at Siut (it was read for him *in absentia* by Reginald Stuart Poole) in which he developed his views on the recording of monuments, making specific proposals for the establishment of an Archaeological Survey. 'Is it fanciful', he claimed, 'to suppose that such an undertaking is possible? . . . With the countenance and support of the Egyptian Government, we might in a few years sweep the whole surface of the country, and gather in the harvest which hastens to ruin with every day that passes . . . what is needed is a sifting of information, an index to the monuments, a description from a new point of view, taking each city, its tombs and temples, as a whole, and not merely extracting scenes, inscriptions, and architectural features.'

What Griffith appeared to be advocating in this paper was a true survey of the whole of Egypt, to be carried out in a matter of about two years by a pair of suitably trained paragons 'acquainted with the whole literature of Egyptian exploration', knowing Arabic and being able to photograph. They would scour the country from end to end, 'verifying the accounts of travellers, collecting place-names, searching out new monuments, and describing the order and condition of those already known'. Their preliminary reports would attract the criticisms of scholars and supplementary information. In this way a work of reference for the whole land of Egypt could be prepared, which would become a foundation for further research.

The eloquence of Griffith's recommendations carried the meeting, and a resolution proposing the establishment of a survey was passed enthusiastically, the President, Sir John Fowler, noting with approbation the 'very moderate estimate' of expense which Griffith had made. Here indeed was a triumph for imaginative vision and practical wisdom. Griffith, young though he still was, and an academic to the point almost of caricature, had a quite remarkably apt appreciation of what the infant science of Egyptology needed. His practicality, however, did not run to accurate estimations of time and expense, and the Archaeological Survey of the Egypt Exploration Fund, as it subsequently emerged, was rather different from what had at first been envisaged. And if his original two years have been quite forgotten in the long history of the Survey – which indeed still flourishes – his intention should incur no depreciation. His insistence on knowing the monuments, on scouring the published sources, and on seeking out the manuscript sources represented a revolutionary approach to the study of ancient remains. The Survey, as it exists, is only one vast and continuing result of his vision; the other is the *Topographical Bibliography of Ancient Egyptian Hieroglyphic Texts, Reliefs and Paintings*, which he initiated privately, and which still continues in the Griffith Institute in Oxford.

After the crucial meeting in November 1889 plans were prepared for the launching of the Survey, and Miss Edwards's letter to *The Times*, with which this chapter began, represented the first public announcement of the enterprise. The team of two re-cruited by Griffith had been undergoing a crash course to prepare themselves for the work, the scope and nature of which remained of very uncertain measure. First to have been recruited was George Willoughby Fraser, a trained civil engineer, with some experience of working in the field with Petrie. He had on his own initiative made copies of inscriptions in the neighbourhood of Minya which had revealed a promising talent in Griffith's opinion. Fraser readily agreed to work for the Survey, and he was joined by Percy Newberry, a young enthusiast who had, since leaving school, passed most of his time in the Egyptological atmosphere of the Egypt Exploration Fund, teaching himself the rudiments of Egyptology and acquiring a knowledge of botany which had already been exploited to purpose by Flinders Petrie.

It was Newberry who proposed the modification to the original intention of the Archaeological Survey which in effect determined its nature for the future. In a preliminary report included in the publication of the proceedings of the General Meeting for 1889–90 Griffith explained the change: 'We first planned a sketch-survey from Minieh to Siût (Assyût). Our endeavour to prepare for this survey showed the impossibility of attaining any satisfactory result. Mr. Newberry then proposed to take up a small district and treat it exhaustively.' A stretch of the Nile Valley twenty-five kilometres long, including the well-known, but inadequately published, Middle Kingdom tombs of Beni Hasan was chosen. By careful study of manuscript sources in the British Museum Griffith and his assistants concluded that there were no less than 1,115 sq. m of painted scenes to be recorded at Beni Hasan. The magnitude of the task was emphasised by Griffith: 'All these twelve thousand square feet have to be puzzled out and the colours identified, while a faithful transcript, of which every detail is of as much importance as the *ensemble*, must be made by means of tracing paper.'

Newberry and Fraser began work at Beni Hasan in late November 1890, and worked continuously until early summer 1891, helped by M. W. Blackden, a trained artist, who made coloured facsimiles of many of the more interesting scenes. This long season saw the completion of most of the copying, and the balance was dispatched in the autumn of 1891 by Newberry who was assisted by a new young artist, Howard Carter, whom he had found by happy chance in Norfolk in the summer of that year. Carter was probably the most talented artist ever employed by the Society, and although his services were not long retained by the Archaeological Survey, he continued working for the Egypt Exploration Fund until 1899, spending six years drawing the exceptional scenes in Hatshepsut's temple at Deir el-Bahri. The care and skill he used to reproduce these wonderful reliefs, many of which were deliberately defaced, were inspired by the standards Carter had acquired working with Newberry. The six great volumes of *The Temple of Deir el Bahari* (1895–1908), may very properly be credited to the tradition of the Archaeological Survey, even though they were published as excavation memoirs.

The preparation for publication of the mass of tracings and notes resulting from the two seasons' work at Beni Hasan took rather longer than either Newberry or the Committee of the Fund had foreseen. The somewhat peremptory expectations of the home-based controllers of the field-worker's destinies were by present-day standards quite unreasonable. A volume a year was what was required by the Committee and expected by the supporters of the Archaeological Survey, the subscriptions for which were for many years kept distinct from those intended for the excavations of the Fund. *Beni Hasan* I, the first fruit of the Survey's harvest, did not appear until 1893, followed by *Beni Hasan* II and *El Bersheh* I in 1894, and *El Bersheh* II in 1895. Inadequate though the earliest volumes might be thought by the epigraphers of today, they nevertheless were revolutionary in their method and content. Here was attempted the comprehensive publication of all the monuments at a site, taking into account as much earlier work as could be consulted. Here were maps, plans and above all facsimile drawings of the ancient reliefs, paintings and texts reduced from full-scale tracings. In the Beni Hasan volumes for seemingly practical and economical reasons the reductions were to one-twentieth of the originals – far too great for reproducing the minute detail of tomb paintings quite exceptional in their interest. Reductions to one-fifth were employed in the El-Bersha volumes much to the advantage of clarity and legibility. Yet the two first volumes of the Archaeological Survey, *Beni Hasan* I and II, are so crammed with good and unusual things that they remain even today probably the most consulted of all the Pharaonic publications of the Egypt Exploration Society.

In the course of his second winter in Egypt Newberry undertook, in addition to copying the monuments at Beni Hasan and El-Bersha, a survey of sixty-five kilo-

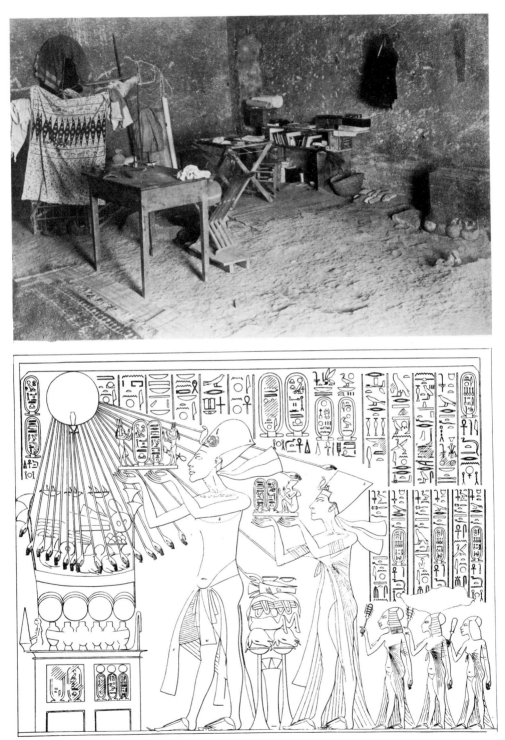

65 (*Top*) The tomb-dwelling of Percy Newberry at Beni Hasan, 1892.

66 (*Bottom*) Line-drawing of a relief in the tomb of Apy, showing Akhenaten and family.

metres of the Nile Valley from Minya southwards to El-Amarna. His journeys revealed many promising sites – groups of tombs, mounds which probably marked ancient settlements, cemeteries and quarries, including the important alabaster quarry at Hatnub. Among the tombs were those at Meir which were to form the subject of six volumes in later years. The important graffiti in the Hatnub quarries were, however, denied to the Archaeological Survey by the independent activities of Newberry's assistants, Willoughby Fraser and M. W. Blackden, who copied them and published them privately. An unfortunate element of competition had divided the field-workers of the Survey into two groups. Newberry, the official Surveyor of the Egypt Exploration Fund, with Howard Carter, considered his activities to be those agreed with Griffith and therefore officially authorised. Fraser and Blackden went their own way; they disputed Newberry's authority and ignored his wishes. There was, however, an element of farce in the way the two groups ranged Middle Egypt, claiming priority for discoveries, and attempting to secure the approval of the Committee of the Fund. Petrie, who had taken a great interest in the activities of the Archaeological Survey from its outset, gave Newberry much help and advice. In early 1892 he was working independently of the Fund at El-Amarna and was visited by Newberry and Carter in the course of their general survey. He noted their activities in his private journal while a search was being made for the tomb of Akhenaten (at that time called Khuenaten by many scholars):

> I sighted a print of a *boot* in the sand, and a boot in an out-of-the-way desert is as usual as the footprint to Robinson Crusoe. There was a wild hope that it was some official going to look after the tomb of Khuenaten; for that and Tutankh-amen's, have been known to all museums for two years past, and are now being kept in reserve by Grébaut [Director of the Antiquities Service] to float his repu-tation at the last gasp. We anxiously tracked 'Boot' who was accompanied by a native 'Barefoot', up and down little ravines. Boot went in the most headlong way, and after a couple of miles or so came some confusion, and Boot struck away from the mountain . . . Carter has come over, and the mystery of 'Boot and Barefoot' is out. It was Fraser and Blackden, intent on forestalling Newberry . . . The affair does not leave a pleasant taste in the mouth.

Clashes of temperament are not unusual in archaeological expeditions, but in this case the differences between Newberry and Fraser led to injudicious behaviour on both sides and ultimately to a suspension of field activities by the Survey. Plans to record the tombs at a number of sites in Middle Egypt were only partially fulfilled, and the intention to include the tombs of Akhenaten's officials at El-Amarna was frustrated by official opposition from the Antiquities Service. When operations were resumed in 1898, Griffith could look forward to a series of campaigns less encumbered with troubles arising from personal antipathies. The new Surveyor was Norman de Garis Davies, 'who', in the words with which he was introduced to the members of the Fund, 'is not only a skilled draughtsman, but has also had some training in Egyptology under Mr. Griffith, and was one of Prof. Petrie's party at Dendereh last year'. Trained as a Congregational clergyman, Davies became fascinated with Egyptology while exercising his ministry at Ashton-under-Lyme. His mentor was

Miss Kate Bradbury who married Francis Llewellyn Griffith in 1896. She it was who brought Davies back from Australia to join Petrie in Egypt, and no doubt recommended him to her husband for the vacant position of Surveyor to the Fund. In so doing she made a contribution to Egyptology of an importance which none could have foreseen at the time. Davies saw himself essentially as a draughtsman, and his ready pencil and accurate eye were to capture for posterity the damaged and deteriorating reliefs, inscriptions and painting in a vast number of monuments. He was much more, as Alan Gardiner pointed out in his obituary notice in the Society's *Journal* in 1942: 'But in course of time he acquired a profound knowledge of Egyptian archaeology, to which was added a competent familiarity with the language of the hieroglyphs.'

In 1898 Davies was a mere beginner, but his ability, determination and energy were very evident, and ripe to be exploited by Griffith, who never spared himself in teaching in advance, and in helping with inspired guidance in the aftermath, of a campaign. A further distinct advantage could be found in employing Davies; he was a one-man-band capable in all aspects of the work, and happiest when working by himself. With him in the field the Archaeological Survey might expect a calm course and a prosperous voyage. And so it was. Between 1898 and 1907 very few years passed without Davies's spending a long season at a lonely site – often more than six months in duration – with no companions apart from his small band of Egyptian workmen. In his first campaign at Saqqara he unexpectedly discovered a part of the tomb-complex of Ptahhotpe and Akhtihotpe previously unknown, and collected material for two fine memoirs, when one had been expected. In the winter of 1899–1900 he tidied up some of the residue of Newberry's earlier surveys – work which yielded a volume on the tombs of El-Sheikh Said and two volumes on those of Deir el-Gabrawi. And then in 1902 Davies took up the copying of the tombs at El-Amarna, the undertaking planned for Newberry ten years earlier, but obstructed by the Antiquities Service. Gaston Maspero, one of the original foreign supporters of the Egypt Exploration Fund and a friend of Amelia Edwards, had returned to Egypt in 1899 to become once again the Director of the Antiquities Service. Under his administration the affairs of the Fund were sympathetically treated, and its field-workers spared the harassment of the previous regime.

The work at El-Amarna was particularly difficult. Most of the scenes and inscriptions were in sunk relief, carved in poor limestone, and badly damaged both in antiquity and in modern times. Davies's results, published in six volumes between 1903 and 1908, covered comprehensively all the private tombs and the boundary inscriptions which marked the limits of Akhenaten's city. In many ways these volumes represent his most impressive and, probably, his most important achievement. Fully did he deserve the Leibnitz medal of the Prussian Academy of Science, which was awarded to him in 1912 specifically for his work at El-Amarna. But more particularly he had earned the gratitude of Egyptologists for having recorded not a moment too soon the surviving records at that site. Davies himself remarked in his report in the Fund's *Archaeological Report* for 1906–7:

I must add that since last year violence has been done to the fine tomb of Ay, the

67 (*Top*) The rock-tombs at Meir.

68 (*Bottom*) Professor Blackman at Meir in 1950.

most exquisite relief and the invaluable Hymn to the Aten only escaping demolition by the caprice of the malefactor. This is the second injury to *locked* tombs in
this group during my stay . . .

When Davies left the Egypt Exploration Fund in 1907, he joined the Theban
Expedition of the Metropolitan Museum of Art, New York, accompanied by his wife
Nina whom he had married in the same year. Together they formed the most
accomplished pair of epigraphers in the history of Egyptology. Nina, trained at the
Slade School of Art and the Royal College of Art, became an outstanding copyist of
Theban paintings, working in tempera. The Davieses remained at Thebes for thirty
years employed by the Metropolitan Museum, but they retained a close association
with the Egypt Exploration Fund and Society, the results of which are described in
Chapter 3 (p. 70).

By 1913 the Archaeological Survey had issued twenty-one volumes and had fully
justified the confidence of its instigator, Francis Llewellyn Griffith, and the enthusiasm
of Amelia Edwards, who sadly died shortly before the publication of Newberry's first
memoir. Griffith had edited the series from the start, and had contributed untiringly
to the success and continuation of the project. In the fallow years after the departure
of Davies he had himself produced *Meroitic Inscriptions* I and II (1911–12), containing a
substantial assemblage of texts from the Sudan and Egyptian Nubia written in the
Meroïtic script, the decipherment of which owes most to his brilliant scholarship. The
future of the Survey, however, depended on the recruiting of a new Surveyor – not an
easy task while the memory of Davies's outstanding services remained so fresh.

In 1911 Griffith was able to recommend to the Committee of the Fund the appointment of Aylward Manley Blackman to the vacant position of Surveyor. Blackman
was already an accomplished field-worker with a distinguished academic career and
the beginnings of a substantial published *oeuvre* to his credit. He had almost single-
handed recorded the scenes and inscriptions in a number of temples in Egyptian Nubia
threatened by the lake created behind the Aswan Dam. His method of recording for
the Archaeological Survey of Nubia was less rigorous and painstaking than that which
had commonly been employed for the memoirs of the Fund's Archaeological Survey,
but the urgency attendant upon the work in Nubia had demanded exceptional speed.
He may have lacked the outstanding graphic skills of Norman de Garis Davies, but his
knowledge of Egyptology, and of the Egyptian language in particular, was far
superior to that of his distinguished predecessor. Indeed, Blackman's copying,
controlled by an informed eye, was more than adequate for the full-scale tracings he
was required to make in the tombs of Meir, to which attention had first been directed
by Percy Newberry in 1892. The provincial nobles of Meir prepared these tombs for
themselves during the Old and Middle Kingdoms. They contained many scenes of
unusual character which had sadly been greatly damaged in the years since their
discovery. Of two of them especially Blackman reported after his first season in 1912:

> The chapels of Ukhuhotep II. and III. are in a terribly injured condition. They
> have lain open to the assaults of man and of the tearing desert wind, which is
> laden with sand, since they were opened more than fifteen years ago. The con-
> tinual friction of the driven sand has worn away much of the colouring and

utterly ruined the appearance of the frescoes in the latter, while the exquisite moulded plaster work in the former is dropping off in every direction . . . We hope therefore that the 'Survey' will receive plenty of support in order that these valuable monuments may be recorded before it is too late. Even a year's delay may prove fatal!

For three seasons Blackman laboured to rescue the surviving decorations of the Meir tombs, but the First World War brought his activities in the field to an end. He was able, however, to prepare what he had already gathered for three volumes of *The Rock Tombs of Meir* which were published in 1914 and 1915. He returned to Meir for one post-war season in 1920–1, and the fourth volume of his series appeared in 1924. His obligation (in the best tradition of the Egypt Exploration Society) to complete an exhaustive publication of all the Meir tombs then looked as if it would never be fulfilled. But more than twenty years later, after he had retired from the Chair of Egyptology at Liverpool, he returned to Meir with M. R. Apted in the season 1949–50. Blackman's scholarly, and – as he would have insisted – moral, debt to Meir was finally discharged in 1953 with the publication of *The Rock Tombs of Meir*, v and vi.

An era came to an end in the history of the Archaeological Survey with the appearance of *The Rock Tombs of Meir*, IV, in 1924. This volume, the twenty-fifth memoir of the Survey, was the last to be edited by Griffith. It also marked to a great extent the completion of the survey of monuments in the region between Asyut and Minya which had seemed to present the most necessary target for effort when the Survey was first set up. Much had been achieved in the comprehensive recording of monuments, many of which were already in a wretched state. Of almost equal importance was the establishment of principles and techniques in recording; new standards were set for other epigraphic enterprises to follow.

A glance at the list of publications issued in the Survey series shows that no volumes appeared between Blackman's fourth Meir memoir in 1924 and his fifth and sixth in 1953, apart from the two volumes of H. A. Winkler's *Rock Drawings of Southern Upper Egypt* in 1938 and 1939 which were opportunist publications of material offered by the author. It would seem that the Survey had lost its driving force with Griffith's concentration on other areas of Egyptological enterprise. It is perhaps true that the pioneering spirit of the early years had gone, but the appreciation of what still needed to be done remained strong. And there remained the *Theban Tomb Series*, described in Chapter 3 (p. 68), the somewhat independent undertaking, inspired by Alan Gardiner, but differing little in its purpose from the Archaeological Survey. It was to be a suggestion of Gardiner's which led to the next and most ambitious enterprise of the Society.

For various reasons the focus of the Society's field-work was transferred in the winter of 1925–6 from El-Amarna to Abydos. Among the team recruited for work on the strange subterranean monument known as the Osireion was Herbert Felton, an engineer who was also a very skilled photographer. Gardiner proposed that Felton should also undertake a photographic survey of the two great temples of Sethos I and Ramesses II, and this proceeded with considerable success for two seasons. Felton concentrated on the Sethos temple, but his results, excellent though they were, were

69 Amice Calverley and Myrtle Broome at Abydos, 1932.

thought not to provide an adequate record of the very fine reliefs which make this temple one of the most beautiful in the whole of Egypt. A decision therefore was taken to produce a publication in line-drawing based on Felton's photographs, with the inscriptions rendered in schematic hieroglyphs. A. M. Blackman, who had recently completed his fourth Meir volume, but was unable to undertake further work in Egypt, agreed to help in finding someone to take up the enterprise. He was successful beyond belief; he recruited for Abydos Amice M. Calverley, a trained artist of very varied talents. Her ability to master accepted epigraphic techniques and to devise new ones convinced Griffith and Gardiner – now known as the Director and Editor of the Archaeological Survey – that a publication of finer quality should be attempted. How this might be achieved remained in doubt until Professor J. H. Breasted of the Oriental Institute of the University of Chicago brought John D. Rockefeller Jr. to visit Abydos during the winter of 1928–9. Here they saw the excellent results achieved already by Miss Calverley and admired in particular the coloured reproductions she had made of some of the best-preserved painted reliefs. It needed little advocacy on the part of Breasted, with encouragement from Gardiner, to persuade Rockefeller to promise to finance the publication in a suitably grand style, for which he put up £21,000, a vast sum in those days. The published volumes, which could now be of a format greater than any previously used by the Society – the chosen size was known as 'small royal broadside' – would be considered as the joint work of the Egypt Exploration Society and the Oriental Institute of the University of Chicago.

Miss Calverley was joined in 1930 by Miss Myrtle Broome, an equally talented artist who had already obtained a little field experience in Egypt. Thus began a partnership of the greatest harmony and achievement. They established at Abydos not just a working camp, but a comfortable and hospitable home where all were welcome, especially if they could spend a few days checking the drawings and helping with the hieroglyphs. From the letters written to her parents by Miss Broome, it appears that the Abydos house was rarely without visitors, many of them being the most distinguished Egyptologists. The happy atmosphere helped the work forward. It was not all comfortable and easy. Soon after her arrival in 1929 Miss Broome wrote:

> We are now settling down to work. I have started near the roof and have to climb up a huge erection which feels very wobbly but has a good wide platform, room enough for a trestle, a chair, and wooden box. Sardic [Sadiq?] our head man carries my drawing board and materials aloft for me and sharpens my pencils. This is our daily programme. We get up 5.30, breakfast 6 o'clock. We are at the temple by 7 and work till 12, then our donkeys are brought round and we mount and scamper back to the house for lunch. After lunch we have an hour's rest. At present it is still too hot to do much work in the afternoons. The heat makes the pencils smudgy.

So they took to working by night:

> We did a couple of hours' tracing by electric light. We have a projector which throws the image from the negative on the drawing board. We trace the outline and so get the whole picture correctly spaced very quickly. Abdallah brought our

supper down to the temple and we sat among the mighty columns and eat [*sic*]
omelets, bread and butter, and chocolate mould, our white robed servants waiting
on us like attendant priests. It was a weird scene.

The field-work made possible by the Rockefeller gift came to an end in 1937.
Thereafter Miss Calverley concentrated her work on the preparation of the publication. Some further work was undertaken after the Second World War, but ill-
health in particular forced Miss Calverley to abandon her visits to Egypt by 1950. The
first great volume of *The Temples of King Sethos I at Abydos* had appeared in 1933, and
the fourth was published in 1958. After Miss Calverley's death in 1959 efforts were
made to produce a fifth volume, and at present some work continues with this end in
view. But sadly, the splendid format of the first four volumes can not now be con-
templated for future volumes, and the inclusion of colour plates, which formed such
an important element in the publication, will no longer be possible.

The Sethos volumes, quite the most magnificent produced by the Society, were not,
strictly speaking, published as part of the Archaeological Survey, but they were,
nevertheless, the outcome of work begun under the auspices of the Survey. The Survey
itself did not resume activities until after the Second World War, when other field-
work in Egypt was not possible. Blackman returned to Meir, and the author of this
chapter spent a season at Saqqara with M. R. Apted, recording the *mastaba* of Khentika.
It was Sir Alan Gardiner who then proposed the recording of the monuments at
Gebel es-Silsila in Upper Egypt – a place of great beauty and interest, but much
neglected. There were private cenotaphs of the Eighteenth Dynasty, royal stelae, a
host of graffiti in the sandstone quarries which had first brought people to the place,
and above all the speos or rock-temple of Horemheb, crammed with religious and
historical records of the greatest importance. R. A. Caminos of Brown University,
Providence, Rhode Island, an epigrapher of considerable experience, enthusiastically
agreed to undertake the work, and one season's work in 1955 with the present writer
resulted in a volume devoted to the cenotaphs or shrines (1963). Work thereafter at
Silsila was carried on when possible, but with long interruptions. It was seriously
resumed in 1976, and is now in sight of completion.

The association, through Ricardo Caminos, of the Egypt Exploration Society with
Brown University was to develop quite unexpectedly during the years of the great
Nubian Rescue Campaign which preceded the construction of the High Dam south of
Aswan. As part of its participation in the campaign the Society offered to undertake
the copying of the scenes and inscriptions at a number of sites, particularly those at
which the Society's excavators were at work. Happily Caminos was ready and willing
to shoulder the burden of this work and the authorities of Brown University prepared
to give him leave of absence. In the winter of 1960–1 he completed single-handed the
recording of the whole of the two temples in the fortress of Buhen, at the Second
Cataract in the Sudan. In the autumn of 1961 he copied the surviving records at Qasr
Ibrim in Egyptian Nubia – rock inscriptions, and shrines not unlike those at Gebel
es-Silsila. Next on the list were the Eighteenth Dynasty temples at Semna and
Kumma, about 100 kilometres upstream from Buhen. Here Caminos spent two long
seasons, in 1962–3 and 1963–4, making a permanent record of all that could still be

70 Religious scenes in the temple of Sethos I at Abydos.

71 Professor Caminos copying in the temple of Buhen, 1960.

seen in these two monuments before they were dismantled and moved to Khartum, like the southern of the two temples of Buhen.

All this concentrated copying, carried out in remote places and under difficult conditions, was completed to the highest standards of the Archaeological Survey, to which Caminos added his own special qualities of determination and an eye of quite exceptional accuracy. So much time in the field, however, left little opportunity for the preparation of memoirs. *The Shrines and Rock-Inscriptions of Ibrîm* was eventually published in 1968, and the two-volume *New-Kingdom Temples of Buhen* in 1974. When the temples of Semna and Kumma are published, a quite remarkable chapter in the Nubian Rescue Campaign will be completed.

When Griffith first advocated the setting up of the Archaeological Survey, he saw its activites as wide-ranging and essentially of a preliminary kind, at least in the early years. In practice the work of the Survey became from the first concentrated on particular monuments and groups of monuments. Much of what Griffith first advocated remains to be done; many of the monuments in need of copying then remain neglected, partially recorded, or even destroyed. There is still great scope for the work of the Survey, and happily there are Egyptologists prepared to work in this field which generally lacks the glamour of excavation. One project near completion will add two volumes to the series *Rock Tombs of El Amarna*, the outstanding achievement of Norman de Garis Davies in the early years of the century. The new memoirs, one of which has already been published, deal with the royal tomb of Akhenaten, the clearance of which was effected by the Society's excavators in the 1930s. A further enterprise concerns a group of Old Kingdom *mastabas* at Saqqara; the work of copying, carried out in conjunction with the Egyptian Antiquities Organisation, has been completed, and the publications are in an advanced stage of preparation. We can also look forward to epigraphic work at Memphis, the site of the northern capital of Egypt for the greater part of the Pharaonic Period. And the Egypt Exploration Society is not alone in this salvaging of rapidly disappearing scenes and inscriptions. Many other organisations now produce careful, comprehensive records of Egyptian monuments long neglected. The resulting publications are of permanent value, increasing in importance as time passes and destruction continues. Griffith's clarion call was not sounded in vain.

.72 Grenfell and Hunt at Oxyrhynchus.

9 *The Graeco-Roman Branch*

Sir Eric Turner

Greeks found their way to all parts of the ancient world, including Egypt. Under the later Pharaohs they figured as mercenaries, travellers, merchants and settlers; with Alexander the Great in 332 BC they entered Egypt as 'liberating' conquerors. They formed the ruling class under the Ptolemaic kings, provided middle-level administrative talent for the Romans and Byzantines until the time of Mahomet: a millennium, more or less. Literate men and women, proud of their artistic heritage and the resources of their language, like their forefathers they read and copied their literature on papyrus manuscripts; they had already adopted it for their private and administrative papers. They continued to use it in Egypt, and the papyrus codex (a manuscript in book, not roll, form) was in all likelihood the invention of the early Greek Christians of Egypt. Greek papyri written in the ancient world are preserved principally in Egypt, where it does not rain very much. They are an archaeological deposit of the written word.

It was in the 1880s that scholars first awoke to their importance, their abundance and the profligacy with which they were being destroyed. *Cognoscenti* of an earlier date had prided themselves on the possession of an occasional papyrus roll or book. But in the 1880s such were generally little valued. Egyptians, becoming aware of the potential of their agriculture and eager to improve it, treated ancient town sites as a source of ready-made fertiliser. Of Europeans, Austrian scholars were the first to undertake papyrus salvage (mainly by organised collection) at Kiman Faris, the ancient Crocodilopolis. In 1888 Flinders Petrie (at a time when he was at loggerheads with the Egypt Exploration Fund) uncovered a beautifully written roll of Homer at Hawara. In 1889 he discovered the unplundered Ptolemaic cemetery at Gurob and, to his great surprise, found that the mummy cases of its burials were built up of written papyrus, treated as waste in antiquity. In 1888 and 1889 Wallis Budge tracked down Greek literary rolls found at Meir, and brought them to the British Museum. They included the lost monologues of Herodas, the *Constitution of Athens* by Aristotle, the choral poetry of Bacchylides; of these F. G. Kenyon was to give the first edition (of the Aristotle in January 1891).

Petrie's Homeric roll of 1888 (together with a lock of its owner's hair, for she was a literary lady) was presented by Petrie's backer, Jesse Haworth, a Manchester manufacturer, to the Bodleian Library. It is not fanciful to suppose that two young Oxford men, Bernard Pyne Grenfell and Arthur Surridge Hunt, would have seen it there. Both were undergraduates at The Queen's College, to which the former went up in 1888, the latter in 1889. They were friends (they walked together in the Tyrol in summer 1889). Both had distinguished records as students of Greek; after taking

Greats, both were appointed to the Craven Fellowship. Grenfell set himself to study economics, but A. C. Clark diverted him to Greek papyri. In the winter of 1893 he worked in Egypt under Petrie at Coptos, and began to purchase papyri on his own account. Petrie himself in the spring of 1894 bought the first roll of what was published under the title *The Revenue Laws of Ptolemy Philadelphus*, and Grenfell was entrusted with the edition. He sent the manuscript to the printer in summer 1895. This speed he achieved in spite of working for another season at Coptos, discovering a second roll of the *Revenue Laws* finding additional mummies at Gurob, and preparing a separate volume of purchased papyri for press. This miscellaneous volume of seventy texts, *An Alexandrian Erotic Fragment and other Papyri chiefly Ptolemaic* (*P. Grenf.* i to scholars) was published in spring 1896 at almost the same moment as *The Revenue Laws*. A second volume of miscellaneous texts (*P. Grenf.* ii) appeared in spring 1897, containing 146 items.

These 220-odd papyri (one of first-rate interest) acquired by desultory purchase during two winters were, no doubt, typical of the collection an individual traveller might form at this date. Grenfell used them as tangible proof of the need for a more positive approach. The great advances in knowledge of Pharaonic Egypt were clear to all; Greek and Roman settlements, so Grenfell argued, should equally be investigated before they disappeared. In the summer of 1895 the Committee of the Egypt Exploration Fund was persuaded to give financial backing to an exploratory tour of sites in the Faiyum. So in the winter of 1895 Grenfell and D. G. Hogarth made a trial excavation at Kom Aushim and Umm el-Atl (or Kom el-Asl), ancient Karanis and Bacchias. In December the results were sufficiently promising for Grenfell to telegraph A. S. Hunt to join him. Hunt had chosen the palaeography of the Latin manuscripts of Spain as his field of study. He responded almost instantly, and in January 1896 began a partnership more lasting and at least as productive as that of Gilbert and Sullivan.

The Committee of the Egypt Exploration Fund agreed to continue its financial support, but the locale of the next winter's exploration was changed to Bahnasa, Oxyrhynchus. The Committee's decision was endorsed at the Fund's Annual General Meeting on 13 November 1896, of which the minutes record: 'Mr. Hogarth pressed upon the Society the necessity for consistently devoting some fixed share of their energies and income to the recovery of classical papyri and the prosecution of Greek archaeology in Egypt . . . Professor Petrie described the destruction of history continually going on in Egypt and urged that every effort should be made by extended scientific excavation to rescue what still remained. He cordially agreed with Mr. Hogarth's proposal and pointed out that the work of the English-speaking races for Egyptology in Egypt could no longer be reported in a single annual volume, but that at least four separate branches with separate subscription lists and separate publications were imperatively needed.'

The excavation begun shortly afterwards at Bahnasa by Grenfell and Hunt did not disappoint expectations. After an initial uncertainty (the excavators were looking for cemeteries and could not believe that the object of their search was to be found in the ancient rubbish mounds), Greek papyri were harvested by the basketful. One of the earliest finds was a leaf of a papyrus book containing hitherto unknown *Logia Iesu*:

The Sayings of Our Lord. In the 1950s it was shown that they were a part of the uncanonical *Gospel of Thomas*. At the end of the season Grenfell and Hunt estimated their finds at 300 literary items, 3,000 Greek documents, together with a sprinkling of Latin, Coptic and Arabic texts. 'After handing over to the Egyptian Government 150 of the most complete rolls (the publication of which is reserved to the Fund) the explorers brought to England upwards of 280 boxes of papyri' (Prospectus, autumn 1897).

The excavation had been run on a shoe-string budget. 'Mr. Grenfell received in all the sum of £50 towards his personal expenses, during an absence from this country of more than five months; Mr. Hunt received nothing whatever' (Honorary Treasurer's report to the Annual General Meeting of the Fund, November 1897). Tribute must be paid now, as it was then, to the generosity as well as farsightedness of the Egypt Exploration Fund in supporting work which was only marginal to its main aims. However, it was realised in 1897 that it was unfair to expect the indefinite continuation of such support. Besides, printing costs had to be faced. The *Logia* were published as a separate pamphlet within six weeks of the arrival of the papyrus in England at the beginning of June 1897. More than 30,000 copies were sold (price two shillings with collotype plates, sixpence in a cheap edition with reproduction from blocks). Less sensational texts could not expect to find the ready sale of the *Logia*. *Revenue Laws, P. Grenfell* i and ii had been published at the charges of the Clarendon Press. A University Press, generous to scholarship as it was, was not unreasonable in being reluctant to guarantee the costs of what might prove a series of volumes somewhat limited in market appeal. The solution was found in the adoption in part of Petrie's suggestion of the previous autumn.

The minute of a Special Meeting of the Committee of the Fund on Thursday, 1 July 1897 records:

> Sir E. Maunde Thompson in the chair, Mr. Cotton Hon. Sec., Mr. H. A. Grueber Hon. Treas., Professor Sayce, Mr. Crum, Mr. Farmer Hall and Mrs. Tirard:
> The Publication Sub-Committee submitted a report on the measures they had taken for the publication of the *Logia*.
> The publication Sub-Committee also submitted a draft prospectus, inviting subscriptions for a new department of the Fund, to be called the Graeco-Roman Research Account, for the discovery and publication of the remains of classical antiquity and early Christianity in Egypt. The draft prospectus was approved.

1 July 1897 was the birthday of what is now known as the Graeco-Roman branch of the Egypt Exploration Society. It was the first association in the world formed with the specific object of excavating for papyri and publishing them.

No doubt the special meeting was needed quickly so that the prospectus could be printed at once on the back cover of the *Logia*. It was, and on 13 July Petrie wrote to Cotton pointing out that the title 'Graeco-Roman Research Account' was already in use for a fund in favour of students at University College London. By October the new name 'Graeco-Roman Branch' was appearing on a separately issued prospectus. A guinea a year entitled the subscriber to a volume of the new Graeco-Roman memoirs as well as the Archaeological Report of the Egypt Exploration Fund, and

73 (*Right*) Fragment of 'The Sayings of Jesus' found at Oxyrhynchus in 1897. (Bodleian Library, Ms. Gr. Th. e 7(P)).

74 (*Below*) View of the site of Oxyrhynchus.

subscriptions came in satisfactorily. At the Fund's Annual General Meeting on 10 November 1897 it was announced that subscribers included the Prime Minister, the Lord Chancellor, the Speaker of the House of Commons, seven bishops, three deans, seventy members of the ancient universities (including twelve college libraries), Trinity College, Dublin, and the four Scottish universities.

The winter of 1897/8 was the only one between 1893 and 1908 that Grenfell did not pass in Egypt. He and Hunt spent it in the preparation of the first Graeco-Roman memoir, *The Oxyrhynchus Papyri*, Part I. Its preface is dated April 1898, eleven months after the first papyri reached Oxford. It is of 284 pages, has eight superb collotype plates, and 158 texts published in full (six 'theological', twenty-three of Greek literature new and old, three Latin). Forty-nine additional documents were described briefly. The selection was made to illustrate the range in both subject and time of the finds; and the transcriptions are careful and thoughtful. The increase of knowledge has faulted them occasionally: it is instructive to note how often it is the editors themselves who later corrected their own readings.

In lay-out *P. Oxy.* I was at once recognised as setting a pattern for the publication of papyri, which has now been almost universally adopted as model. A concise introduction summarises the content and interest of the text transcribed; the transcription (in the documents articulated into words, given accents and punctuation) retains the spelling of the scribe, faulty orthography or syntax being mended in a succinct critical appartatus. 'I have not thought it worth while to disfigure the pages by the constant insertion of *sic*', wrote Grenfell in *Revenue Laws*, p. vi. There follows a translation, and a brief commentary on the content, 'evading no difficulty but free from superfluity', as H. I. Bell wrote (*Dictionary of National Biography 1922–30*, s.v., Grenfell, p. 362).

The progress of excavation and publication over the next ten years is most easily comprehended in the tabulation, shown on pp. 177–8, which has the additional advantage of freeing my narrative from the need constantly to catalogue and calendar, and allowing me space to give a short account of excavation practice and methods. Since in *Greek Papyri* I have given long extracts from reports on the first thrilling season at Bahnasa, I shall not repeat them here, but quote from accounts of the work of later seasons at that site. I have taken the liberty of quoting at some length passages from an unpublished lecture by Grenfell.

Activity on the site seems to have gone on until sunset – a long day of work began at first light. Normally there were only Grenfell and Hunt to take charge. Both would have exchanged shifts, but Grenfell writes as though he directed operations out of doors on the dig, and Hunt took responsibility for registering finds in the expedition house, undertook preliminary cleaning and relaxing of the crumpled papyri, and supervised the packing. Under an experienced nucleus of thirty foremen, up to an additional 150–80 men and boys could work in the trenches. When finds were coming in steadily but not in a rush, 100 men would be employed and the wages bill ran to £30 a week. Grenfell's letters speak highly of the skill of his foremen, and of the honesty and quickness to learn of the men from Bahnasa. By contrast those at El-Hiba were idle and careless. Grenfell believed that on the whole he lost very little. Of course, some texts would have been held back or cut for private gain. Those of us who edit the papyri long after the discovery and identify a piece in another collection as part of one of ours can be sure of theft only if there is a knife-cut edge between joining pieces. Supervision of 200 men was difficult. On 17 January 1906 Grenfell wrote to H. A. Grueber, Honorary Treasurer of the Fund, at a time when large extra numbers had been taken on: 'Most of the men are by this time equally expert and untrustworthy and ceaseless vigilance is necessary. Various dealers have been hanging about recently, and last Sunday we decoyed and arrested 3, confiscating the anticas upon them, which were not from this site. It is fairly clear that the leakage has not been serious at any rate.'

It has already been remarked that the finds made at Bahnasa were obtained, not from Graeco-Roman cemeteries or from buildings, but from ancient rubbish mounds. Let Grenfell tell the story in his own words:

> The papyri which one finds in the mounds have all been thrown away as rubbish. In this respect Oxyrhynchus offers a marked contrast to the town sites in the Fayum, like Dimeh, from which so many Greek papyri have come. There owing to the contraction of the margin of cultivation in the fourth century many towns were abandoned by their inhabitants, and in the ruins of the houses one may find on the floor numerous papyri, often tied together in bundles, just as they were when the houses were deserted. But at Oxyrhynchus there are hardly any remains of buildings; the bricks and still more the stones have been carried away to be used as building material for succeeding generations. Of the massive Ptolemaic temple dedicated to Isis, Sarapis and Osiris, which once rivalled in splendour the shrines of Dendera and Edfou, the walls can only be discerned by the lines of limestone chips where the stone-masons have removed the blocks.

This passage is repeated in full to counter the calumny (which I have heard uttered in 1980 by Egyptologists who should know better) that Grenfell and Hunt destroyed the sites at which they worked in their mad scramble to win papyri for their collections. True, they published few or no site plans: it was a question of priorities in the use of scarce time. Grenfell's statement about Bahnasa is corroborated by Flinders Petrie, who spent two months there in spring 1922, and found a railway laid down to the mounds: 'Every day a train of 100 to 150 tons of earth leaves this area.' Petrie found only one inscription (of Byzantine date); Grenfell records none. Yet Graeco-Roman Oxyrhynchus must have been filled with inscriptions. They, like the walls on which they were placed, have been robbed for stone, and the marble will have found its way to the lime kiln.

Grenfell continues:

> The method of digging a mound on a large scale is extremely simple. The workmen are divided into groups of 4 or 6, half men, half boys, and in the beginning are arranged in a line along the bottom of one side of a mound, each group having a space two metres broad and about 3 metres long assigned to it. At Oxyrhynchus the level at which damp has destroyed all papyrus is in the flat ground within a few inches of the surface, and in a mound this damp level tends to rise somewhat, though of course not nearly so quickly as the mound rises itself. When one trench has been dug down to the damp level, one proceeds to excavate another

75 (*Top*) Picking out the papyrus fragments.
76 (*Bottom*) The Sheikh's tomb on the rubbish mounds of Oxyrhynchus.

immediately above it, and throw the earth into the trench which has been finished, and so on right through the mound until one reaches the crest, when one begins again from the other side. The particular mixture of earth mixed with straw and bits of wood in which papyrus is found, and which is to the papyrus digger what quartz is to the gold-seeker, sometimes runs in clearly marked strata between other layers of cinders, bricks or all kinds of debris containing no papyrus, but in many of the mounds at Oxyrhynchus papyri are found continuously down to a depth of five or even eight metres. As a rule the well preserved documents are discovered within 3 metres of the surface; in the lower strata the papyri tend to be more fragmentary, though our trenches in a few mounds have reached 9 metres at the highest parts before coming to the damp level . . .

Most of the larger pieces are found by the men working in the trench, who of course have to use their hands entirely, not the hoes, when it is a question of extricating so delicate a material; but it is inevitable that small pieces should be sometimes passed over by the man who is actually digging, and each basketful has to be examined carefully when it is emptied.

The clouds of dust and sand, which are quite inevitable when one is digging in very loose dry soil on the edge of the desert, give you an idea of the difficulties under which the excavator for papyri has to work. It is really marvellous how the men manage to keep their eyes open through it all. The brick building on the top of the mound [Grenfell comments on a lantern slide] is a much venerated shekh's tomb. The large mediaeval and modern Necropolis of Behnesa extends over part of the ancient mounds, and in this mound in particular the presence of the tombs on the summit presented considerable obstacles to our work, which however we were, fortunately for science, able to overcome. On completing our excavations in it, we restored and repainted the shekh's tomb, and this circumstance coupled with the fact that on one very windy day I was obliged owing to the dust to tie a handkerchief over one eye, has given rise to a curious legend. They will tell you if you go to Behnesa, how when we were digging that mound the spirit of the shekh appeared to me in a dream, and after vainly trying to persuade me to desist from our excavations threatened me with blindness, which duly fell upon me (there the handkerchief comes in). Afterwards however the shekh reflected that the poor people of the village had been earning very high wages by the work (one gives a bakhshish for each papyrus found in addition to the daily wage, and the luckier workmen were receiving what were for them considerable sums), and that after all we had no intention of disturbing his own tomb; so he repented and appeared again to me and consented to restore my sight on condition that I repainted his tomb and made it the finest of all the shekh's tombs in the cemetery, as indeed it now unquestionably is.

The winter of 1905 provided some sensational finds, and I quote from Grenfell's letters and reports:

[On 28 December 1905] we moved to a group of mounds, in which the papyri ranged from the 1st to the 5th century. This has been extremely rich not only in documents but also in literary fragments, principally of the 2nd and 3rd centuries. The climax in point of quantity was reached on Jan. 10, when we found more papyri than we have ever done, except on two days in 1897 and one day in 1900; while on Jan. 13 and 14 we were fortunate enough to make incomparably the largest and most important find of classical pieces that we have ever made (letter to Grueber).

Some picturesque details are added in reports in *The Times* for 14 May 1906 (where the date of this find is confused with a later one and wrongly given as 28 January), and the Egypt Exploration Fund *Archaeological Report* for 1905/6, p. 8 f.:

> . . . shortly before sunset [on 13 January] we reached, at about 6 feet from the surface, a place where in the third century A.D. a basketful of broken literary papyrus rolls had been thrown away. In the fading light it was impossible to extricate the whole find that evening; but a strong guard was posted on the spot during the night, and the remainder was safely removed in the following forenoon. Before being condemned to the rubbish heap, the papyri had as usual been torn up.

Four of these rolls were published in 1908 in *Oxyrhynchus Papyri*, v; by 1919 and the appearance of *Oxyrhynchus Papyri*, XIII, the whole find had been edited. It comprised a number of lost works: an extensive MS of Pindar, *Paeans*, another containing a history of the fourth century BC whose author we now call 'The Oxyrhynchus Historian', Euripides, *Hypsipyle*, Antiphon, *On Truth*, Aeschines Socraticus, some speeches of Lysias and of Hypereides, a commentary on Thucydides, a treatise on literature, and an oration on the cult of Caesar. Of known works there was an extensive MS of Plato's *Symposium* and two of his *Phaedrus*, one each of Thucydides and Isocrates.

The letter previously quoted notes: 'We are employing 210 men and boys, a number which represents the absolute limit, since Hunt cannot deal with more than 30 different lots of papyri a day.' Shortly afterwards Grenfell wrote again: 'On Jan. 16 work on a new mound was begun. It proves to be not only extraordinarily rich but very deep, and since many of the best papyri are in the very lowest levels, the progress of our trenches through it is extremely slow' (letter to Grueber, 25 January 1906). Then on 27–9 January a third find was made: 'Though it cannot be compared in importance to its predecessors, it was quite exceptionally good. It consists of a very large quantity of documents (chiefly 2nd–3rd cent.) interspersed with numerous literary fragments . . . The papyri were found at the bottom of the deepest part of the trench, over 25 feet down . . . From the upper levels we have continued to find nearly every day as I anticipated scattered pieces belonging to the second large literary find, occasionally in handfuls.'

The idea that excavation could be finished in 1906 had to be abandoned. More 'scattered pieces belonging to the second large literary find' were recovered in the winter of 1906/7, and Grenfell and Hunt did not even then finish the digging of this mound.

From time to time in his letters Grenfell refers to financial anxieties. Will the money hold out? In spring 1906, with finds abundant and money short, the excavators offered to forego their expenses. An intensive lecture campaign was planned for the following autumn to finance a campaign in the next season (no doubt it is from the text of that lecture that extracts have already been given). It may be suspected that the

77 (*Top*) Digging at Oxyrhynchus with Grenfell supervising.

78 (*Bottom*) Mummified crocodiles from Tebtunis, some of which had been wrapped in discarded papyrus documents.

reason why in 1900/1 the Egypt Exploration Fund was not a backer of the dig at Tebtunis was because the kitty was empty. Mrs. Phoebe Hearst and the University of California put up the money and paid for the publication. The texts from the mummified crocodiles went to Berkeley, where they are now in the Rare Book Room. *The Tebtunis Papyri*, I (1902), was a joint publication of the Fund and the University of California, *The Tebtunis Papyri*, II (1907), originally a publication of California only; it has now been reclaimed for the Graeco-Roman publications series of the Society's Graeco-Roman Branch.

The need to economise led Grenfell and Hunt to undertake personally all the ancillary tasks which would nowadays be performed by a technical staff. They themselves relaxed their finds and dismantled the mummy cases. The papyri were not mounted between glass but kept between sheets of the *Oxford University Gazette*. No photographs were made until wanted for publication, no cleaning or 'conservation' undertaken. As late as 1928 Hunt wrote that 'a comprehensive view of the material has not yet been obtainable. The editors have been obliged . . . to content themselves with a periodical opening of a few boxes' (letter to the *Daily Telegraph*, 13 October 1928).

The work was done cheerfully. Whether excavating, travelling or editing, Grenfell and Hunt remained firm friends. Their partnership constituted a 'single creative personality, *eine schöpferische Einheit*', in the phrase of Ulrich Wilcken. Such harmonious collaboration is rare among front-ranking scholars. Together they published far more in quantity and with a higher degree of accuracy and acumen than either of them could have achieved alone. Hunt has recorded the value of constant discussion and of two pairs of eyes for the solution of difficulties. 'In the winter at our Egyptian camp we seldom saw another European; in the summer months our editorial work was mostly done in the same room. Problems which arose in the field, difficulties of decipherment and interpretation were ventilated and discussed. Copies of papyri were exchanged for the purpose of collation, and whatever one wrote was revised by the other' (*Proceedings of the British Academy* 12 (1926), p. 362).

They were incomparable decipherers; and both had the power of grasping the bearing on old problems of new evidence and of penetrating quickly to the heart of a difficulty even in an unfamiliar field. 'Dynamic' is the favourite adjective used by his friends to describe Grenfell. When action was under discussion, his instinct was to find reasons for doing something, Hunt's reasons for not doing it. Grenfell was the faster worker. Analysis once completed, Grenfell would settle down to write and then move on to something else. Hunt was more cautious, steadier, readier to take a second look. In contrast to Grenfell's epistolary torrent, Hunt's letters are laconic, fussy about detail, almost prim. Grenfell especially enjoyed history, chronological complexities, economics, topography, textual criticism. Hunt understood the precisions of the law and the relevance of documents. It is likely that he was the more sensitive to literature of the pair; certainly his was the palaeographical brain. Mind and eye co-operated in palaeographical judgements that stand up amazingly to new discoveries. 'You had to get up early in the morning', E. Lobel once remarked to me, 'to catch Hunt out on a palaeographical question.' The level of Hunt's scholarship can be judged from the three volumes of *The Oxyrhynchus Papyri*, VII–IX, and two volumes of Rylands papyri on which his name only without his colleague's stands on the title-page. No failure of imagination or accuracy is to be observed in them.

The partnership was in fact interrupted in 1908, when Grenfell had a serious breakdown in health. An outside observer might reasonably infer that it was caused by over-exertion. Hunt denies the inference, and states that Grenfell had an inherited tendency to nervous depression. Illness had first struck him in Egypt in December 1906. During his absence from the dig for nearly two months Hunt had to manage alone at Bahnasa. He was helped by the young A. M. Blackman (on his first season of field-work). On leaving Egypt in March 1907 Grenfell and Hunt left their camping gear behind. A return was envisaged in spite of financial stringency and the prospect of infinite editorial work. In fact, neither man participated again in an excavation. A friendly Antiquities Service kept the concession at Bahnasa open for them. In 1908 a dig was planned, but abandoned on 15 October 1908 because of Grenfell's illness.

In July 1909 a new season of excavation was at the planning stage. In the event Hunt did not go, but put the expedition in the hands of J. de M. Johnson, later to be Oxford University's Printer. Sites were examined at Atfih and elsewhere, with no great success. In another season in 1913/14 Johnson made useful investigations at Antinoe, and brought back fragments of beautifully illustrated books, a welcome MS of Theocritus and the teaching material of a shorthand school. An exhibition of the finds was held at the Society of Antiquaries, Burlington House, on 13–28 July 1914. In the next week the First World War broke out and an era closed. John Johnson became Assistant Secretary to the Delegates of the Oxford University Press, and was lost to papyrological studies. The specified items of published papyri were sent back to Cairo, and the other published texts were distributed as gifts to libraries and institutions throughout the world.

Since 1914 the Graeco-Roman Branch has sponsored no excavation specifically to search for papyri. At its twenty-fifth anniversary exhibition organised in the British Museum in 1922 publication, not excavation, was declared to be its aim, and this has remained true. Of course, Greek and Roman papyri have come to the Egypt Exploration Society since that date and been published by its Graeco-Roman editors, but the Society's regular Egyptological expeditions have uncovered them. The Sacred Animal Necropolis at Saqqara has provided some texts, notably the oldest dateable papyrus document in Greek, discovered by Dr. Geoffrey Martin in 1972. Qasr Ibrim has supplied an unlooked-for wealth: in 1976 a letter of the king of the Blemmyes, in 1978 part of a roll containing verses of Cornelius Gallus. Both were published with a speed that would have earned the approval of Grenfell.

The editor who is confronted with a complete papyrus is a lucky man. The literary rolls torn up in antiquity which formed the bulk of the big literary finds of 1906 set a special problem. The fragments must be put together again. Grenfell and especially Hunt tackled the task courageously. Their editions of *Hypsipyle*, of Sophocles' *Searching Satyrs*, the *Iambi* of Callimachus ('the most difficult papyrus that I have yet had to deal with', as Hunt wrote to Grueber, 17 July 1909), Sappho and Alcaeus (*Oxyrhynchus Papyri*, x, 1231–4) yielded moving poetry as well as literary history. In 1914 acknowledgement is first made in print to Edgar Lobel (*Oxyrhynchus Papyri*, x, p. 45). Over the next sixty years his skill and scholarship were to reconstitute

79 Fragments of Satyrus' treatise on the Demes of Alexandria, second century AD (British Library, Dept. of MSS, Inv. 3048).

substantial portions of this lost literature. On Hunt's death in 1934 the Society entrusted the care of the collection to him. Between 1941 and 1972 his is the only name to appear as editor of nine volumes of the Oxyrhynchus series, to six others his is the major contribution. During these years his austere volumes were purchased by libraries throughout the world, and their sale maintained the Society's publication fund in the black.

The principles of this kind of work are worth a short characterisation. The first step is to assemble scraps which are judged to be in the same handwriting, then, if possible, to separate them into their original rolls and identify the authors involved. One and the same scribe frequently copied more than one MS (one, for instance, is known to have copied at least Bacchylides, Erinna, Herodotus and Aeschines): it is likely therefore that there will be some near misses in the process. Identification by content (recognition of a topic or a known fragment, metre, dialect) is only one of the means utilised. Sometimes more than 250 fragments have been combined according to rules worked out for each example. One set of rules derives from the physical properties of papyrus and the ancient mode of manufacturing a roll, a second set is furnished by what can be inferred about a scribe's habits and his methods of laying out his book. Normally the writing will be in columns, to reconstruct which it will be necessary to discover the number of lines in each and the number of letters per line. Titles, margins, line-ends or beginnings are aids to the establishment of a physical framework. The papyrologist is therefore not only a good reader of difficult hand-writing but a mender, comparable to the pot mender on an archaeological site. He must know a lot of Greek as well as have a good eye and quick mind – and, of course, perseverance. Working by such methods Mr. Lobel has recreated for the modern world considerable portions of lost poetry – Hesiod, Callimachus, Aeschylus, Sappho, Alcaeus, Anacreon, Alcmen, Stesichorus, Simonides, Pindar among others.

I hope Mr. Lobel will forgive me for writing these words which record his enormous contribution to modern Greek scholarship. He has always shunned publicity and acknowledgement: in scholarly achievement and temperament he resembles his own much-loved Callimachus. And he enjoys a reputation for pungency of comment on others, if not of polemic against them, reminiscent of the author of the famous preface to the *Aitia*. The remarks his colleagues treasure are barbed hyperbole, but they have a sting justified by knowledge: 'Euripides, like Wilamowitz, knew no Greek.' I must personally admit to trepidation on my first visit to him because of his reputation for severity. Severe he is. But his wit, courtesy and wide range of interest make a visit to him an occasion of intense pleasure.

Mr. Lobel has set a standard for papyrologists: they are expected to be impeccable, infallible and omnicompetent. As a member of the post-Lobel generation I recognise an ideal and a handicap. Exacting original work cannot be done in a hurry, nor can the preparation for publication of other people's labours. If work is to be speeded up, scholars must turn themselves into papyrologists. There is no short cut: a 'provisional transcription', often thoughtlessly demanded, is in effect an edition. The Oxyrhynchus team has resolved to adhere to the tradition that texts must be published before they are made generally available, on the ground that faulty transcriptions do harm that cannot be undone. *Nescit vox missa reverti.*

80 Graeco-Roman mummy masks of cartonnage from Tebtunis. The cartonnage often contained old papyri.

'The Oxyrhynchus Team': a committee has in effect replaced one man. There was a major effort of reorganisation in the 1960s, tried out with pilot grants from the Gulbenkian Foundation and the British Academy. Since 1966 the British Academy has shared the responsibility with the Egypt Exploration Society. The preface to Part XXXIII of the *Oxyrhynchus Papyri* sets out the details:

> In 1966 the British Academy accepted as one of its major research projects the task of cataloguing and preparing for publication the unedited Greek and Latin papyri in the Oxyrhynchus collection. Its generous support, and the prospect of continuation of that support over a period of years, has made it possible to set additional technicians and staff to work on the physical preparation of the material, on the compilation of an inventory of the damped-out papyri, and the formation of a corpus of photographs of them. This work is being done under the supervision of a committee of the British Academy, which has made it its business to combine effectively the resources of the Academy and the very considerable technical help and facilities offered in London by University College and in Oxford by the Ashmolean Museum (through the Grenfell and Hunt library) and the Faculty Board of Literae Humaniores. The Egypt Exploration Society will continue to bear the cost of and take scholarly responsibility for publication. Its general editors hope to be able to recruit additional scholars for the exacting task of editing papyri, a burden which Mr. Lobel has borne too long alone.

There is reason to be pleased with what has been accomplished since this arrangement was made. Fifteen volumes of the *Oxyrhynchus Papyri*, one of *Tebtunis Papyri* and a location list have been printed. The resources of photography have been utilised, indeed, developed, and conservation techniques pioneered. New methods of dismounting mummy cases are being tested: in the first trials at University College London the scientific methods have proved spectacularly successful, even if the Greek contents have so far appeared humdrum. In publication special attention has been paid to non-literary papyri, since Mr. Lobel confined himself to literature. Part XL contained a closely knit archive on the public corn ration at Oxyrhynchus in the third century of our era: its implications for the social and economic history of the Roman Empire are still being worked out. Documents are being marshalled by type and archives are being isolated. And there will still be a good harvest of Greek literature: work on some five or six collections of torn-up lyric poetry is making progress, as is the preparation of texts of prose authors. At present Part XLVIII of the *Oxyrhynchus Papyri* has appeared, and the general editors have more than enough material in hand in typescript to reach Part L. The Oxyrhynchus Committee is in good heart, confident that the illumination of Graeco-Roman antiquity will continue through the efforts of the Graeco-Roman Branch of the Egypt Exploration Society.

Grenfell and Hunt's first ten years

Excavation or Travelling	Publication (for E.E.F.)		Volume to sub-scribers	Editorial work; and other publications of Grenfell and Hunt[2]
1895 Grenfell with Petrie; Gurob	*Revenue Laws*	a. Oct. '95[1] b. 1896		
1896 Grenfell, Hogarth, Hunt in Faiyum (E. E. F. Season 1)	*P. Grenf.* I	a. Dec. '95 b. 1896		
1897 Bahnasa I (E. E. F. Season 2)	*P. Grenf.* II	a. Oct. '96 b. 1897		
	Logia Iesu	b. July '97		
Graeco-Roman Branch founded				
1898 (Not in Egypt)	*P. Oxy.* I	a. April 27 b. 1898	√	Revised text of Menander, *Georgos*
1899 Faiyum (G.–R. Branch Season 1)	*P. Oxy.* II	a. Sept. '99 b. 1899	√	
1900 (Tebtunis: Univ. of California)	*Fayum Towns*	a. n.d. b. 1900	√	*P. Amherst* I
1901 Faiyum (G.–R. Branch Season 2) (cartonnage unpublished)			√ See 1902	*P. Amherst* II
1902 El-Hiba (Faiyum) I (G.–R. Branch Season 3)	*P. Teb.* I	a. May '02 b. 1902	√ Double vol. 1901 and 1902	

[1]a. . date of Preface
 b. . date of imprint

[2]A selection

177

1903	El-Hiba 2				
	Bahnasa 2				
	(G.-R. Branch Season 4)	*P. Oxy.* III	a. June '03	✓	*P. Cairo*
			b. 1903		(Cat. gén . . .
					Musée du
					Caire, Nos.
					10001–10869)
1904	Bahnasa 3				
	(G.-R. Branch Season 5)	*P. Oxy.* IV	a. April '04	✓	
			b. 1904		
1905	Bahnasa 4				
	(G.-R. Branch Season 6)			✓	
				See 1906	
1906	Bahnasa 5				
	(G.-R. Branch Season 7)	*P. Hib.* I	a. May '06	Double	
			b. 1906	vol. 1905	
				and 1906	
1907	Bahnasa 6			✓	*P. Teb.* II
	(G.-R. Branch Season 8)			(late)	a. June '07
	(Grenfell ill)				b. 1907
1908	No excavation	*P. Oxy.* V	a. Oct. '07		
	(Excavation planned		b. 1908		
	but abandoned)	*P. Oxy.* VI	a. Sept. '08		
			b. 1908		

Postscript

In the preceding chapters of this book a very large part of the achievement of the Egypt Exploration Society has been outlined. But the story as told is far from complete. Among the excavations of Sir Flinders Petrie, uncommemorated here, are those at Dishasha, Dendera and Ehnasiya; and particularly his work at Diospolis Parva which resulted in the system of sequence-dates. His expedition to Sinai in 1904–5 was only partly a Society venture, but one of its results, *The Inscriptions of Sinai*, can certainly be claimed by the Society as being among its most important publications. G. A. Wainwright's excavations at Balabish for the American Branch and Sir Robert Mond's work at Armant have also escaped the net of this survey. The Armant excavations were not wholly a Society activity, but their publications are included in the Society's list, and proudly so, for they incorporate an entirely new approach to the reporting of excavations in the field of Egyptology.

The collaboration of many scholars, especially scientific and technical experts, in the preparation of the Armant excavation report pointed the way towards the modern scientific approach to archaeological field-work. Many of the early expeditions of the Society were conducted almost as one-man bands, the emphasis resting on the discovery of textual material and fine objects. In the context of their times they were not badly run, even though little regard was paid to the techniques already being developed by Flinders Petrie. And their purposes and procedures should not be gratuitously dismissed in the light of present-day standards. Petrie undoubtedly stood as an excavator head and shoulders above his contemporaries working in Egypt; but he was not the easiest of persons to work with. Nevertheless, both the Society and Petrie derived considerable advantage from their association; sites of the utmost importance were dug, results of lasting significance achieved, and publications produced with exceptional promptitude.

Many lessons can be learned from the consideration of the attitudes and practices of the Society's early field-workers; devotion to the task in hand, assiduity in the field and in the study, open-mindedness to new developments in scholarship and in archaeological techniques, confidence and strength in the prosecution of ideas and projects; but all should be tempered with a moderation and a spirit of co-operation not always evident in the past. Field-work in Egypt has lost none of its fascination, but it can no longer be carried out without extensive preparation in advance and protracted study subsequently. Determination to see a project through to the publication of the final report is one of the most difficult of the scholarly virtues for the field-worker to maintain. In consequence, the Society lays very special emphasis on the publication of results. An unpublished excavation is a wasted excavation. In the consideration, therefore, of what the Society plans to do in the future, publication occupies a major position. The highly successful excavations in recent years at Saqqara and Qasr Ibrim have yielded materials of such quantity and diversity that many volumes will be needed to expound the results of study. Some of the current field-work is aimed at completing for publication projects which had to be terminated in the past for various reasons. Excavation in the North City at El-Amarna and epigraphic work in the Temple of Sethos I at Abydos resume the pre-war activities of John Pendlebury and Amice Calverley. The continuing study of the papyrus treasures unearthed by Grenfell and Hunt at Oxyrhynchus is equally a labour of completion.

Continuity is built into the activities of the Society. The results achieved in the most recent seasons of work at North Saqqara draw the Saqqara team naturally to investigate the nearby site of Memphis, a city of metropolitan importance throughout antiquity. Like many ancient sites within the cultivated area of Egypt, the mounds of Memphis are increasingly threatened by the encroachment of agriculture, industry and housing. Under the general intention of recording ancient Memphis, the Society plans to survey standing monuments, to prepare copies of all inscriptions not yet properly published, to map the whole area, and to undertake excavations in carefully chosen places in order to illuminate the history of the site.

The investigation of town- and settlement-sites rarely yields the spectacular results sometimes achieved by the excavation of tombs and cemeteries. But it is from the painstaking examination of the former that a wide range of information concerning the history, culture and daily life of the ancient Egyptians will be retrieved. Apart from the threats mentioned above, changes in the water-table since the construction of the High Dam south of Aswan, and developments in irrigation have greatly increased the likelihood of the destruction of ancient settlements in many parts of Egypt. One of the primary aims of excavation for the Society in the future must necessarily be the investigation of such sites. Memphis is such a site. Another is Qasr Ibrim where the waters of Lake Nasser nibble away inexorably at the remains of a town which once stood high above the Nile. Both places will provide the Society with opportunities of work for many years. So too will the city of Akhenaten at El-Amarna with its dependent villages, although water does not represent the same hazard there.

As the expenses of mounting expeditions in the field, and of publishing their results, rise with frightening rapidity and regularity, the activities of the Society inevitably suffer some constraint. Already, however, ways have been found of co-operating with other organisations and institutions so as to spread the financial burdens. Co-sponsorship of the Qasr Ibrim excavations with the American Research Center in Egypt, with funds from the Smithsonian Institution's Foreign Currency Program, has enabled considerably more work to be carried out on that remote place than could otherwise have been afforded. The investigation of the New Kingdom Cemetery at Saqqara is similarly a joint project between the Society and the National Museum of Antiquities, Leiden. Some of the recent epigraphic work at Saqqara has been carried out in conjunction with the British Museum.

Plans for the future seem to be well laid. There is much to be done in Egypt and in the Sudan, and the Egypt Exploration Society has every intention of being fully engaged in the work, in accordance with the declared purposes of its founders. In 1882 the Egypt Exploration Fund embarked on a voyage of thrilling possibilities. Then it was alone in its endeavours. Now Egyptian archaeology is the concern of many similar organisations. The Society, after one hundred years, can justly be proud of what it started and of what it has achieved. It will surely continue to be inspired by the passions of Amelia Edwards, of Flinders Petrie and of Francis Llewellyn Griffith.

T. G. H. JAMES

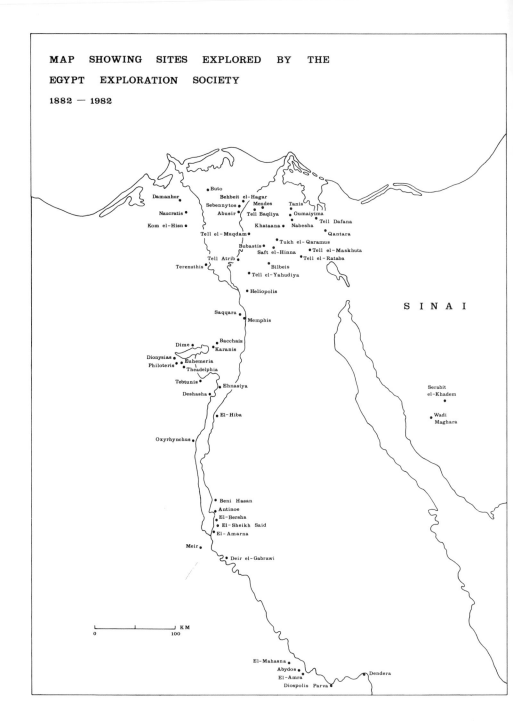

MAP SHOWING SITES EXPLORED BY THE EGYPT EXPLORATION SOCIETY 1882 — 1982

SINAI

Buto
Damanhur
Behbeit el-Hagar
Sebennytos • Mendes
Naucratis • Abusir • Tell Baqliya
Kom el-Hisn •
Tanis
Gumaiyima
Tell Dafana
Khataana • Nabesha
Qantara
Tell el-Muqdam •
Tukh el-Qaramus
Bubastis •
Saft el-Hinna • Tell el-Maskhuta
Tell Atrib • Tell el-Rataba
Terenuthis • Bilbeis
Tell el-Yahudiya
Heliopolis
Saqqara • Memphis
Bacchais
Dime • Karanis
Dionysias • Euhemeria
Philoteris • Theadelphia
Tebtunis • Ehnasiya
Deshasha •
Serabit el-Khadem •
El-Hiba
Wadi Maghara •
Oxyrhynchus •
Beni Hasan
Antinoe
El-Bersha
El-Sheikh Said
El-Amarna
Meir •
Deir el-Gabrawi

KM
0   100

El-Mahasna
Abydos • Dendera
El-Amra
Diospolis Parva

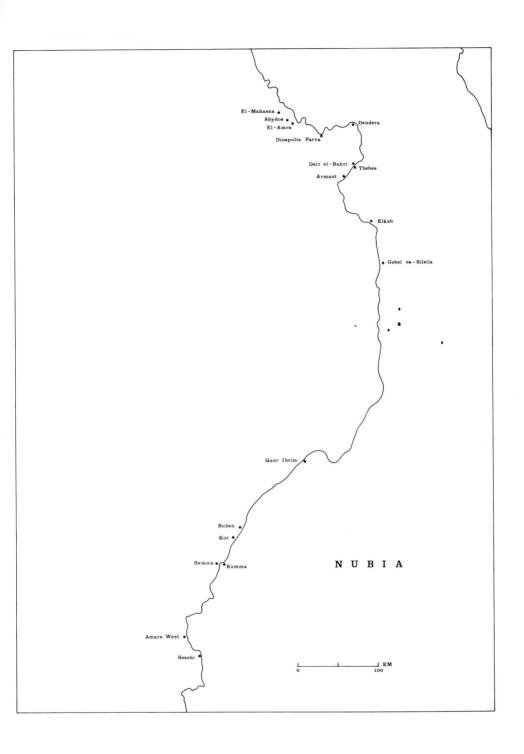

El-Mahasna •
Abydos •
El-Amra •
Dendera •
Diospolis Parva •

Deir el-Bahri •
Thebes •
Armant •

Elkab •

Gebel es-Silsila •

Qasr Ibrim •

Buhen •
Kor •

Semna • Kumma

N U B I A

Amara West •

Sesebi •

KM
0   100

Notes on Sources

All volumes mentioned in these notes are publications of the Egypt Exploration Society, unless otherwise described. A complete list of Society publications can be obtained on application to the Secretary at 3 Doughty Mews, London WC1N 2PG.

1 The Early Years

Most of the information on the formation of the Fund, on the development of policies on the choice of sites for working in Egypt, and on the relationships between the founders and the early fieldworkers is drawn from unpublished material in the archives of the Egypt Exploration Society. Much additional information is to be found in the published accounts of the General Meetings of the Fund, and in correspondence and reports in the daily and weekly press, particularly *The Times*, the *Morning Post*, the *Athenaeum*, and above all the *Academy*.

2 The Delta

The publications of the various excavations provide most of the information used in the compilation of this chapter. Naville's volumes include *The Store-City of Pithom and the Route of the Exodus* (1885), *The Shrine of Saft el Henneh and the Land of Goshen* (1887), *The City of Onias and the Mound of the Jew* (1890), *Bubastis* (1891), *The Festival Hall of Osorkon II* (1892); Petrie's reports are *Tanis* I (1885), II (1888), *Naukratis* I (1886), II (1888). For Naville's last season in the Delta, see the Fund's *Archaeological Report* for 1892–3. The recent excavations at Buto are reported in the *Journal of Egyptian Archaeology*, vols. 51 (1965), 52 (1966), 53 (1967), 55 (1969), 56 (1970).

3 Thebes

The excavations at Deir el-Bahri are published in Naville's volumes *Deir el Bahari*, Introductory volume (1894) and vols. I–VI (1895–1908), and *The Eleventh Dynasty Temple at Deir el Bahari*, I–III (1907–13). Communications from Petrie and others concerning the conduct of the work under Naville are to be found in the Society's archives. General accounts of the excavations, year by year, are contained in the Fund's *Archaeological Reports*, 1893–4 to 1906–7. The account of the discovery of the Hathor-shrine is taken from J. Lindon Smith, *Tombs, Temples and Ancient Art* (University of Oklahoma Press, 1956). Background to the epigraphic publications of Norman and Nina de Garis Davies is provided by the *Annual Reports* for 1912–13 (*Five Theban Tombs*) and 1913–14 (for the initiation of the *Theban Tomb Series*), Sir Alan Gardiner's *My Working Years* (privately published 1962), the obituary of Sir Robert Mond in the *Journal of Egyptian Archaeology*, vol. 24, and the introduction to *The Tomb of the Vizier Ramose* (1941) and *Seven Private Tombs at Kurnah* (1948).

4 Abydos

Sir W.M.F. Petrie's own publications provide the best source material for his excavations at Abydos: *Royal Tombs of the First Dynasty* (1900), *Royal Tombs of the Earliest Dynasties* (1901), *Abydos* I and II (1902, 1903); *Seventy Years in Archaeology* (Sampson Low [1931]). The quality of life on a Petrie excavation and the particular magic of Abydos are both well conveyed in Canon H. D. Rawnsley and N. Rawnsley's *The Resurrection of Oldest Egypt* (The Beaver Press, Laleham, Middlesex, 1904). Useful accounts are also contained in the *Archaeological Reports* for the appropriate years. Subsequent work is described in a series of volumes: *El Amrah and Abydos* (1902), *Abydos* III (1904), *Cemeteries of Abydos*, I–III (1914, 1914, 1913), *The Cenotaph of Seti I at Abydos*, I and II (1933); and in reports in the *Journal of Egyptian Archaeology*, vols. 9 (1923), 12 (1926), 14 (1928), 16 (1930).

5 El-Amarna

Material for the early history of the involvement of the Egypt Exploration Fund in El-Amarna can be found in the archival records of the Society and in the *Archaeological Report* for 1892–3. The volumes *The Rock Tombs of El Amarna*, I–VI (1903–8), contain the record of N. de Garis Davies's work for the Archaeological Survey. The three volumes, so far published, of *City of Akhenaten* (1923, 1933, 1951) provide final reports on much of the Society's excavations in the city area. Further information is included in the preliminary reports in the *Journal of Egyptian Archaeology*, vols. 7 (1921), 8 (1922), 10 (1924), 12 (1926), 13 (1927), 15 (1929), 17–22 (1930–6). A convenient general account of the place can be found in J.D.S. Pendlebury's *Tell el-Amarna* (Lovat Dickson & Thompson [1935]), and a lively picture of life in the Pendlebury camp is presented in Mary Chubb's *Nefertiti lived here* (Geoffrey Blas, 1954). Recent excavations at El-Amarna are reported in the *Journal*, vol. 64 (1978) and subsequently.

6 Saqqara

Great Tombs of the First Dynasty, II and III (1954, 1958) contain the most important results of Emery's excavations for the Egypt Exploration Society in the Early Dynastic cemetery at Saqqara. Further results are incorporated in his *Archaic Egypt* (Penguin Books, 1961). His subsequent excavations and those of his successors in the Sacred Animal Necropolis receive preliminary reports in the *Journal of Egyptian Archaeology*, vols. 51–3 (1965–7), 55 (1969), 57–60 (1971–4), 62, 63 (1976, 1977). One volume of the final excavation report has so far appeared, G.T. Martin's *The Sacred Animal Necropolis at North Saqqara* (1981). H.S. Smith's subsequent work in the temple-town is reported in the *Journal*, vols. 64–7 (1978–81), and G.T. Martin's excavation of the Tomb of Horemheb in vols. 62–5 (1976–9). The following volumes on documents discovered at North Saqqara have so far appeared: J.D. Ray, *The Archive of Hor* (1976), O. Masson, *Carian Inscriptions* (1978), G.T. Martin, *The Tomb of Hetepka* (1979), B. Segal, *Aramaic Texts* (1982). The essays by H.S. Smith in *A Visit to Egypt* (Aris and Phillips, 1974) draw on results from the recent Saqqara excavations and present a lively picture of life in the Memphite area in the Late Period.

7 Nubia

For general background to the history of Nubia and of the work of the Egypt Exploration Society, see W.B. Emery, *Egypt in Nubia* (Hutchinson, 1965), W.Y. Adams, *Nubia, Corridor to Africa* (Allen Lane, 1977). Preliminary reports on the excavations at Sesebi and Amara are published in the *Journal of Egyptian Archaeology*, vols. 23–5 (1937–9), 34 (1948). Final reports on the principal excavations at Buhen are contained in *The Fortress of Buhen*, I, II (1979, 1976). Preliminary reports on all the work in the Buhen area are published in *Kush* (the journal of the Sudan Antiquities Service), vols. 7–12 (1959–64), 14 (1966). Emery's work at Qasr Ibrim is published by A.J. Mills in *The Cemeteries of Qasr Ibrim* (1982). The later excavations in the fortress are reported in the *Journal*, vols. 50 (1964), 52 (1966), 53 (1967), 56 (1970), 60 (1974), 61 (1975), 63 (1977), 65 (1979). J.M. Plumley's *Scrolls of Bishop Timotheos* (1975) contains two of the most important documents found at Qasr Ibrim. The verses of Cornelius Gallus are published in the *Journal of Roman Studies*, vol. 69 (1979). A charming account of life in the camp at Qasr Ibrim is given by Gwendolen Plumley in *A Nubian Diary* (privately published, 1977). H.S.

Smith's *Preliminary Reports of the Egypt Exploration Society's Nubian Survey* was published by the Egyptian Antiquities Service in Cairo in 1962.

8 The Archaeological Survey

Information on the inception and early years of the Archaeological Survey is drawn from letters and other documents in the archives of the Egypt Exploration Fund, from the reports of the early General Meetings and the *Archaeological Reports* from 1890 to 1899 onwards, particularly the first of these which deals with the initial season at Beni Hasan. The record of the Survey is contained in the thirty-five volumes so far published, and in the associated five volumes of the *Theban Tomb Series*, the four volumes of *The Temple of Sethos I at Abydos*, and the two volumes of the Mond Excavation at Thebes – all Society publications. Miss Calverley describes her methods of work at Abydos in the introductions to vols. I–III of *The Temple of Sethos I*. Life at Abydos is vividly described in a series of letters written by Myrtle Broome, now in private ownership. Much of Sir Alan Gardiner's involvement with the Theban and Abydos projects is described in his *My Working Years* (privately published, 1962). Accounts of his methods of work and general life at Gebel es-Silsila, Semna and Kumma, are given by R.A. Caminos in *Journal of Egyptian Archaeology* vol. 41 (1955), *Kush*, vols. 12, 13 (1964, 1965).

9 The Graeco-Roman Branch

Much information on the formation and progress of the Graeco-Roman Branch has been drawn from the archives of the Egypt Exploration Society and from the private correspondence of Grenfell for 1903–7 and of Hunt for 1907–9, from a draft notebook of Grenfell containing jottings on the mounds of Bahnasa, and from the unpublished text of a lecture by Grenfell. The story of the sheikh's revenge was also told in *The Western Daily Press*, Bristol, for 3 March 1908. The *Archaeological Reports* and reports of General Meetings of the Fund provide published sources for the early years; also the prospectus issued in July 1897. Further detail comes from the prefaces to Grenfell and Hunt's early volumes of the *Oxyrhynchus Papyri* series; from Hunt's memoir on Grenfell in the *Proceedings of the British Academy*, vol. 12 (1926), and H.I. Bell's memoir on Hunt in the same *Proceedings*, vol. 20 (1934); from Bell's essays on Grenfell in *Dictionary of National Biography 1922–30*, and on Hunt in *Dictionary 1931–40*; and from *Guide to a Special Exhibition of Greek and Latin Papyri presented to the British Museum by the Egypt Exploration Fund London 1922*. The abbreviations used to refer to certain publications are those listed in E.G. Turner, *Greek Papyri* (Oxford and Princeton, 1968).

Participating Institutions

The principal Institutions contributing to the work of the Egypt Exploration Society, including those with major holdings of antiquities and papyri from the Society's excavations are as follows:

Antiquities

The British Isles

Aberdeen, Marischal College
Belfast, The Queen's University
Birmingham, City Museum and Art Gallery
Bolton, Museum and Art Gallery
Brighton, Museum and Art Gallery
Bristol, Museum and Art Gallery
Cambridge, The Fitzwilliam Museum
   Museum of Archaeology and Ethnology
Dublin, The National Museum of Ireland
Dundee, City Museum and Art Galleries
Durham, The Gulbenkian Museum
Edinburgh, The Royal Scottish Museum
Eton College
Glasgow, The Hunterian Museum
Godalming, Charterhouse School
Harrow School
Leeds, The City Museum
  The University
Liverpool, Merseyside County Museums
   School of Archaeology and Oriental Studies
London, The British Museum
  The British Museum (Natural History)
  The Horniman Museum
  University College London, The Petrie Museum
  The Victoria and Albert Museum
  Wellcome Historical Medical Museum
Macclesfield, West Park Museum

Manchester, The Manchester Museum
Oxford, The Ashmolean Museum
        The Pitt Rivers Museum
Reading, The University Museum

United States of America

Baltimore, Md., The Walters Art Gallery
Boston, Mass., Museum of Fine Arts
Chicago, Ill., The Art Institute
              Field Museum of Natural History
              The Oriental Institute
Cincinnati, The Art Museum
Cleveland, Ohio, Museum of Art
Corning, N.Y., The Corning Museum of Glass
Detroit, Mich., Institute of Arts
Louisville, Ky., The Jefferson Institute
New Haven, Conn., Yale University Art Museum
New York, The Brooklyn Museum
              Metropolitan Museum of Art
Pasadena, Calif., The Art Institute
Philadelphia, Pa., The University Museum
Princeton, N.J., University Art Museum
San Diego, Calif., Fine Arts Gallery
Washington, D.C., The Smithsonian Institution

Other Countries

Amsterdam, Allard Pierson Museum
Auckland, Institute and Museum
Berlin, Staatliche Museen
Brussels, Fondation Égyptologique Reine Élisabeth
              Musées Royaux d'Art et d'Histoire
Cairo, The Coptic Museum
        The Egyptian Museum
        The Islamic Museum
Copenhagen, Ny Carlsberg Glyptotek
Dunedin, Otago University Museum
Geneva, Musée d'Art et d'Histoire
Hildesheim, Pelizaeus Museum
Leiden, Rijksmuseum van Oudheden
Montreal, Museum of Fine Arts
Paris, Musée du Louvre
Sydney, The Australian Museum
        The Nicholson Museum
Toronto, Royal Ontario Museum
Wellington. The Dominion Museum

Greek and Latin Papyri

Allentown, Pa., Muhlenberg College
Baltimore, Md., The Milton S. Eisenhower Library
Berkeley, Calif., The Bancroft Library
Brussels, Musées Royaux d'Art et d'Histoire
Cairo, The Egyptian Museum
Cambridge, The University Library
Cambridge, Mass., Houghton Library
Chicago, Ill., The Oriental Institute
Dublin, Trinity College Library
Durham, The University Library
Edinburgh, The University Library
Ghent, The University Library
Glasgow, The University Library
Graz, The University Library
Ithaca, N.Y., Cornell University Library
Liverpool, The Harold Cohen Library
London, The British Library, Dept. of Manuscripts
Louvain, The University Library
Manchester, The Manchester Museum
New Haven, Conn., The Beinecke Rare Book and Manuscript Library
New York, The Butler Library, Columbia University
Oxford, The Ashmolean Museum
       The Bodleian Library
Philadelphia, Pa., The University Museum
Princeton, N.J., The University Library
Rochester, N.Y., Ambrose Swabey Library
Toledo, Ohio, Toldeo Museum of Art
Toronto, The Library, Victoria University
Urbana, Ill., Classical and European Culture Museum
Wellesley, Mass., The Library, Wellesley College

Index

Page numbers in italic refer to illustrations.

Abdallah Nirqi, 127
Abourni, 136
Abu Simbel, 10, 126, 127
Abu Sir, 44
Abydos, 71–88, *73, 75, 79, 81, 83,
  87*, 107, 108, 112, 152, *153,
  154*, 155, 180
Academy, 9, 10, 18, 20, 22, 34
Adams, W. Y., 133
Afya, 127
Ahmes, 56
Akhenaten, 70, 89, 91, *94*, 95, 98,
  99, 103, 126, 127, 132, *147*, 148,
  149, 159
Akhetaten, *see* El-Amarna
Akhtihotpe, tomb of, 107, 149
Akinidad, 135
Alexander the Great, 117, 161
Alexandria, 13, 16, 49
Alma-Tadema, Sir L., 29
Amanishakhete, 135
Amani-Yeshbeke, 135
Amara West, 126, 127, *128*
El-Amarna, 57, 89–106, *90, 93,
  97, 101, 105*, 120, 122, 126,
  127, 148, 149, 152, 180
Amasis, 40, 42, 49
Amélineau, É., 71, 72, 107
Amenemhet, tomb of, 68
Amenemope, 126
Amenophis I, 64, 133
Amenophis II, 126, 127
Amenophis III, 70, *100*, 120, 126,
  127
Amenophis IV, *see* Akhenaten
American Research Center in
  Egypt, 180
El-Amiriya, 89, 99
Ammenemes III, 47, *48*, 103, 132
Amosis, 80, 132
Amun, 54, 64, 126
Aniba, 133
Antefoker, tomb of, 68
Antiochus IV Epiphanes, 116
Anubis, 58
Aphrodite, 40
Apis, 112, 114
Apollo, 40, 84
Apophis, 46
Apted, M. R., 152, 155
Apy, tomb of, 92
Arabi Pasha, 14, 16
Archaeological Survey of Egypt,
  141–59

El-Arish, 44
Armant, 112, 179
Asha-Ikhet, 37, 39
Aswan, 32, 52, 110, 112, 123, 124,
  142, 151, 155, 180
Asyut, 29, 145, 152
Aten, 91, *94*, 95, 99, 103, 104
Athanasius, 140
Athenaeum, 9, 20, 23
Athens, 15
Augustus, 135
Ay, 92, 122
Ayrton, E. R., 29, 61, *65*

Bacchias, 162
Baden-Powell, Lord, 77
Bahnasa, *see* Oxyrhynchus
Bakakhuiu, *see* Asha-Ikhet
Balabish, 179
Ballana, 123, 126, 133
Baring, Sir Evelyn, 11, 32
Barsanti, A., 99, 104
Bastet, 39, 46, 47
Baylis, T. H., 33
Behbeit el-Hagar, 44
Beit el-Wali, 127
Beloe, H., *see* Tirard, Lady
Benha, *see* Tell Atrib
Beni Amram, 89
Beni Hasan, 36, 145, 146, *147*
El-Bersha, 30, 146
Bilbeis, 44
Bint-Anat, 120
Birch, S., 10, *12*, 13, 14, 24
Blackden, M.W., 146, 148
Blackman, A.M., 126, *150*, 151,
  152, 154, 155, 172
de Blignières, M., 11
Bonaparte, N., 16
Borchardt, L., 92, 96
Boston, Museum of Fine Arts,
  22, 34, 57
Bradbury, K., 22, 149
Breasted, J.H., 154
British Academy, 6, 176
British Library, 92
British Museum, 14, 16, 18, 20,
  24, 29, 34, 39, 42, 43, 44, 49,
  61, 64, 67, 103, 142, 146, 161,
  172
British School of Archaeology in
  Egypt, 78
Broome, M., 85, *153*, 154
Brown, P., 60

Brown University, 132, 155
Browning, R., 9
Brugsch, É., 33
Brunton, G., 29
Bubastis, 25, *35*, 46, 47, *48*, 112
Budge, Sir E.A.T.W., 13, 24,
  29, 161
Buhen, 127, 128–32, *129, 131*,
  155, *158*, 159
Bulaq Museum, *see* Cairo
  Museum
de Bunsen, E., 13
Burne-Jones, Sir E., 30
Burton, Sir F., 29
Burton, H., 70
Burton, J., 92
Busiris, 114
Buto, 49, 50

Cairo, 16, 19, 30, 32, 33, 47, 72,
  107, 108
— German Archaeological
  Institite, 72
Cairo Museum, 11, 14, 15, 16,
  18, 19, 30, 32, 33, 43, 54, 57,
  64, 66, 80, 104, 119
Calverley, A., 85, 86, *153*, 154,
  155, 180
Caminos, R.A., 132, 135, 155,
  158, 159
Carnarvon, Earl of, 9
Carter, H., 29, 52, 56, 58, 60, 68,
  146, 148
Carter, V., 58, 60
Champollion, J.-F., 54, 92
Charterhouse, 34
Cheops, 46, 76
Chephren, 46
Chester, G.J., 30
Chicago, Oriental Institute, 154
Chubb, M., 103
Clark, A.C., 162
Clarke, S., 29, 60
Cook, T. and Son, 7
Coptos, 162
Cotton, J.S., 14, 20, 163
Crawford, M., 36
Crete, 103
Crocodilopolis, 161
Cromer, Earl of, 33
Crum, W.E., 163
Currelly, C.T., 29, 49, 61, 66, 82,
  86

Daily Telegraph, 13
Damanhur, 40, 44
Davies, Nina de G., 67, 68, 99, 151
Davies, Norman de G., 67, 68, 89, 92, *93*, 95, 99, 106, 148, 149, 151, 159
Dega, tomb of, 24, 28, 32
Deir el-Bahri, 24, 28, *31*, 32, 50–68, *53*, *59*, *62*, *65*, 68, 146
Deir el-Gabrawi, 149
Deir el-Medina, 98
Delta, 9, 11, 16, 19, 28, 37–50, 116, 122, 142
Delta Exploration Fund, 14
Dendera, 11, 71, 148, 179
Derr, 140
Deutsche Orient-Gesellschaft, 96
Dioskouroi, 40
Diospolis Parva, 179
Dishasha, 179
Djer, 72
Djoser, 112
Dongola, 124, 127, 140
Dufferin, Lord, 16, 61, 67

Edfu, 11
Edwards, A.B., *8*, 9, 10, 11, 15, 20, 22–6, 28, 30, 33, 34, 36, 40, 141, 142, 145, 149
Egypt Exploration Fund, *see* Egypt Exploration Society
Egypt Exploration Society, *passim*
Egyptian Antiquities Service, 11, 32, 54, 61, 82, 92, 99, 104, 107, 108, 116, 142, 148, 149
Egyptian Research Account, 84, 86
Ehnasiya, 49, 179
Emery, Mrs. M., 128
Emery, W.B., 70, 78, 107, 108, 110, 112, 114, *115*, 116, 119, 126, 127, 128, 132, 133
Et-Til, 89, 91, 99
Evans, Sir J., 33

Fairman, H.W., 104, 126, 127
Faiyum, 23, 171, 177
Feras, 138
Firth, C.M., 107, 112
Fowler, Sir J., 33, 145
Frankfort, H., 29, 84, 99, 103
Fraser, G.W., 145, 146, 148
Fustat, 30

Gabriel IV, 140
Cornelius Gallus, 135, 172
Gardiner, Sir A.H., 68, 78, 149, 152, 154, 155
Gardner, E.A., 40
Gardner, P., 15
Garstang, J., 29, 86
Gebel Abu Hasah, 91
Gebel es-Silsila, 155
Gebel et-Til, 91
Gerf Husein, 127

Giza, 32, 40, 46
Goodwin, C.W., 13
Gordon, C.G., 22
Goshen, Land of, 9, 15, 16, 23, 43
Gosselin, H., 32
Grand Bey, 30
Grébaut, E., 33, 34, 148
Grenfell, B.P., 29, *160*, 161, 162, 163, 165, 166, 168, 169, *170*, 171, 172
Grenfell, Sir F.W., 30, 33
Griffith, F.Ll., 22, 25, 28, 40, 42, 43, 44, 47, 49, 95, 142, *143*, 144, 145, 146, 148, 149, 151, 152, 154, 159
Grueber, H.A., 163, 166, 169, 172
Gumaiyima, 43
Gurob, 161, 162

El-Hagg Qandil, 89, 91, 106
Haggard, Sir H.R., 107
Hall, H.R.H., 24, 61
Harkness, M., 20
Hathor, 54, 56, 58, 60, 61, 64, *65*, 66
Hatnub, 148
Hatshepsut, 32, 51, 56, 57, *59*, 60, 61, 63, 132, 146
Hawara, 161
El-Hawata, 89, 99
Haworth, J., 161
Hay, R., 92
Head, B., 15
Hearst, P., 171
Heliopolis, 44
Henhenet, 67
Hera, 40
Hermopolis, 89
Herodotus, 40, 42
El-Hiba, 165, 177
Hierasykaminos, 135
Hogarth, D.G., 58, 162, 177
Holman-Hunt, W., 30
Hor, Archive of, 116, 117
Horemheb, 119, 120, *121*, 122, 155
Horus, 39, 116, 130, 132, 133
L'Hôte, N., 92
D'Hulst, Count, 30, 52, 54
Hunt, A.S., *160*, 161, 162, 163, 165, 166, 169, 171, 172, 174, 177, 178
Huy, tomb of, 68
Huya, tomb of, 103

Ibrahim Pasha, 140
Illustrated London News, 22
Imhotep, 112
Ionides, C., 15
Isis, 39, 44, 114
Ismail, Khedive, 11

Jaillon, M., 23, 25
Johnson, J. de M., 172
Jonas, M., 34

Jones, H., 86, 92
Journal of Egyptian Archaeology, 96, 104, 116, 117, 148

Kamose, 132
Karanis, 162
Karnak, 11, 32
Karoma, 47
Kauit, 64
Keeves, W., 34
Kemp, B., 106
Kemsit, 64
Kenyon, F.G., 161
Kerma, 161, 162
El-Khadrah, 71
Khartum, 123, 132, 133, 159
— Museum of Antiquities, 133
Khataana, 44
Khentika, tomb of, 107, 155
Khenty-amentiu, 74
Khonsu, 126
Kiman Faras, *see* Crocodilopolis
Kirwan, L.P., 126
Kom Aushim, *see* Karanis
Kom es-Sultan, 76
Kom Ombo, 30
Kor, 130, 132
Korosko, 127
El-Kula, 14
Kumma, 132, 159
Kush, 123, 124, 130, 132

Laffan, W.F., 66
Lane, E., 9
Lane-Poole, S., 10
Langtry, L., 13
Lauer, J.-P., 108
Laver, G., 92
Lavers, R., 104
Lawrence, T.E., 98
Layard, Sir M., 9, 29
Leiden, 23
— Rijksmuseum van Oudheden, 120, 181
Leighton, Sir F., 29
Lepsius, K.R., 28, 54, 92, 119
Lisht, 29
Liverpool, University of, 70, 107
Lobel, E., 171, 172, 174, 176
Lowell, R., 22
Luxor, 14, 52, 56

Maidum, 11
Mallawi, 89
Manetho, 72
Marianos, 138
Mariette, F.A.F., 11, 13, 14, 51, 54, 56, 57, 60, 72, 77
Martin, G.T., 104, 172
Maspero, G.C.C., 10, 14, 15, 16, 18, 19, 33, 34, 54, 71, 92, 124, 149
Maxwell, Sir J., 33
Mehemet Ali, 140
Meir, *150*, 151, 152, 154, 155, 161
Memphis, 11, 23, 50, 107, 114, 116, 119, 122, 159, 180

Mendes, 49
Menkheperresoneb, tomb of, 68
Mentuherkhepshef, tomb of, 68
Mentuhotpe II, 61, *62*, 64, 66, 68
Merenptah, 42, 120
Meroë, 124, 126, 133
Mery-Re I, 92
Minya, 142, 145, 148, 152
Mission Archéologique
    Française, 104
Mond, Sir R., 6, 68, 179
Mond, Lady, 70
Monneret de Villard, U., 126
Montu, 39, 60, 64
de Morgan, J. J.-M., 52, 61
Morning Post, 13, 20
Murray, A.S., 15
Murray, M., 84
Musa Ibn Ka'b, 138
Mut, 126
Mutemuia, 122
Mutnodjmet, 119, 122

Nabesha, *27*, 33, 40, *41*, 42, 43,
    44, 46, 49
Nakht, 67
Napata, 135
Nasser, Lake, 110, 133, 140, 180
Naucratis, 9, 15, 22, 25, 39, 40,
    42, 43, 142
Naville, H.E., 14, 16, 18, 19, 22,
    25, 28, 30, 33, 34, *35*, 37, 43, 44,
    46, 47, 49, 51, 52, 54, *55*, 56,
    57, 58, 60, 61, 63, 64, 66, 72,
    78, 84, 86, 142
Naville, Mme. M., 57, 63, 67
Nebeira, *see* Naucratis
Nectanebo I, 43, 44
Nectanebo II, 114
Nefertem, 39, 47
Nefertiti, 91, *94*, 96, 98, *102*, 126,
    147
Nekhbet, 46
Newberry, J.E., 52, 56
Newberry, P.E., 52, 56, 145, 146,
    148, 149, 151
Newton, Sir C., 13, 15, 26, 29, 33
Newton, F., 98, 99
New York, Metropolitan
    Museum, 66, 67, 70, 99, 151
Nubia, 32, 68, 107, 110, 123–40,
    151, 155
Nyuserre, 128

Om el'Qa'ab, *see* Umm
    el-Qa'ab
Osiris, 44, 72, 74, 78, 84, 86, 114,
    123
Osorkon II, 47
Oxford, Ashmolean Museum,
    176
— Griffith Institute, 145
Oxyrhynchus, *160*, 162, *164*, 165,
    166, *167*, 168, *170*, 172, 174,
    177, 178, 180

Pachorus, *see* Faras
Paget, R.F.E., 60
Panehesy, tomb of, 98, 103
Parenefer, tomb of, 92
Paris, Bibliothèque Nationale, 92
— Louvre, 11
Paser, statue of, 64
Paser, tomb of, 122
Paterson, E., 33, 34
Patti, A., 13
Peet, T.E., 70, 78, 86, 96, 98
Pendlebury, J.D.S., 103, 104, 180
Pepi I, 46
Pepuy, 122
Petrie, H.M.I., *73*, 84
Petrie, W.M.F., 18, 19, *21*, 22,
    23, 25, 26, 28, 29, 33, 37, 39,
    40, 42, 43, 46, 49, 51, 52, 54,
    58, 60, 61, 71, 72, *73*, 74, 76,
    77, 78, 82, 86, 95, 96, 98, 99,
    106, 107, 116, 117, 120, 142,
    145, 148, 161, 163, 166, 179
Caius Petronius, 135
Philadelphia, University
    Museum, 128
Philae, 10, 30, 124
Philip Arrhidaeus, 44
Phonen, 136
Phrim, *see* Qasr Ibrim
Pithom, 9, 16, *17*, 18, 23, 25, 28,
    37
Plumley, J.M., 133, 138
Poole, E., 9
Poole, R.S., 9, 10, *12*, 13–16, 18,
    20, 23–6, 28, 30, 33, 34, 144
Powell, D., 103
Poynter, E., 29, 30, 32
Primis, *see* Qasr Ibrim
Psammetichus I, 40, 42
Ptahhotpe, 107, 149
Ptah-Sokar, 39
Ptolemy II Philadelphus, 40
Ptolemy VI Philometor, 116
Punt, 54, 57, 60

Qantara, 44
Qantir, 39, 44
Qasr Ibrim, *frontispiece*, 127, 132,
    133–40, *134*, *137*, *139*, 155,
    172, 180
Qasr el-Wizz, 127
The Queen's College, Oxford,
    161
Quft, 29
Quibell, J.E., 112
Qurna, 54, 67, 70
Qustul, 126, 133

Raia, 122
Ramesses, 9
Ramesses I, 122
Ramesses II, 10, *38*, 39, 42, 64, 71,
    74, 77, 89, 119, 120, 126, 127,
    132, 152
Ramesses III, 42
Ramesses XI, 127
Ramose, *69*, 70

Randall-MacIver, D., 128
Rawnsley, H.D., 82, 85, 86, 88
Rawnsley, N., 82, 85, 86, 88
Ray, J.D., 116
Re-Harakhty, 56, *59*, 89
Reisner, G.A., 124
Renouf, P. Le P., 13, 24, 29
Rockefeller, J.D. Jr., *154*, 155
Royal Archaeological Institute,
    19, 32

Saft El-Hinna, 43
Said Pasha, 11
Saladin, 140
Salisbury, Lord, 30
San, *see* Tanis
Saqqara, 11, 47, 78, 107–22, *109*,
    111, *118*, 144, 149, 159, 172,
    180
Sayce, A.H., 13, 14, 15, 30, 163
Schliemann, H., 15, 24
Scott-Moncrieff, Sir C., 30
Sebennytos, 44
Semna, 123, 130, 132, 159
Senenmut, 56
Senseneb, 56
Sesebi, *125*, 126, 127
Sesostris I, 68, 128
Sesostris III, 42, 49, 64, 80, 130
Seth, 123
Sethe, K.H., 63
Sethnakhte, 42
Sethos I, 71, 74, 82–5, 88, 126,
    127, 132, 152, 155, *156–7*, 180
Sethos II, 42, 71
Seton-Williams, M.V., 49
Shallal, 127
Shams ed-Doulah, 140
El-Sheikh Said, 89, 149
Shunet ez-Zebib, 78, 80
Sherman, S., 104
Sillem, 60
Sinai, 44, 179
Smith, H.S., 112, 114, 117
Smith, J.L., 66
Smithsonian Institution, 6, 180
Sneferu, 128
Society for the Preservation of
    the Monuments of Ancient
    Egypt, 29–32
Society for the Promotion of
    Biblical Studies, 24
Soleb, 124
Soped, 43
Strabo, 84
Stuart, Hon. V., 14, 15, 141, 142
Sudan Antiquities Service, 132
Suliman the Magnificent, 140

Taharqa, 132, 135
Tanis, 9, 18, 19, *21*, 23, 25, *31*,
    37, *38*, 39, 40, *41*, 46, 142
Tantani, 136
Tanutamun, 135
Tarrana, 44
Tebtunis, *170*, 171, 177
Tell Atrib, 39

Tell Baqliya, 49
Tell Dafana, *27*, 42, 44
Tell el-Kebir, 16
Tell el-Maskhuta, 16, 37, *38*
Tell el-Muqdam, 49
Tell Nebesheh, *see* Nabesha
Tell el-Rataba, 44
Tell Sueilin, 39
Tell el-Yahudiya, 28, 44, *45*
Terrien de la Couperie, A., 15
Thebes, 51, 54, 67, 68, 80, 98, 112, 151
Thompson, Sir E.M., 163
Thoth, 104, 112
The Times, 13, 20, 141, 169
Timotheos, 140
Tirard, Lady H.M., 20, 163
Tiye, *99*, 103, 122
Tomkins, H.G., 20
Troy, 15
Tukh el-Qaramus, 44
Tuna el-Gebel, 112.

Tunqala, 127
Tutankhamun, 68, 89, 96, 119
Tuthmosis I, 56, 57
Tuthmosis II, 57
Tuthmosis III, 54, 66, 68, 126, 133
Tutu, tomb of, 92

Udimu, 110
Umm el-Atl, *see* Bacchias
Umm el-Qa'ab, 71, 72, 78, 85
Unas, 117, 120
University College London, 29, 34, 108, 116, 176
Ur, 98

Valley of the Kings, 11, 51
Venus, 39
Vyse, R., 16

Wadi Abu Hasah, 104
Wadi Halfa, 126, 132
Wadi Tumilat, 16, 44

Wadjet, 40, *41*, 42
Wainwright, G.A., 29, 179
Wallis, H., 29
Watts, G.F., 30
Weigall, A.E.P.B., 68, 82, 124
Wellcome Historical Medical Museum, 96
Wharncliffe, Lord, 30
Whitehouse, C., 23
Wilcken, U., 171
Wilkinson, C., 99
Wilkinson, Sir J.G., 54, 92
Wilson, Sir E., 13–16, 20, 22
Winkler, H.A., 152
Winlock, H., 56, 64
Winslow, W.C., 22, 23, 24, 26
Wolseley, Sir G., 16
Woolley, Sir L., 98, 99, 128

Xois, 9

Zoan, *see* Tanis